Individual Differences

PERSPECTIVES IN PSYCHOLOGY

William Kessen

George Mandler

General Editors

George A. Miller

Mathematics and Psychology

Jean Matter Mandler and George Mandler

Thinking: From Association to Gestalt

William N. Dember

Visual Perception: The Nineteenth Century

William Kessen

The Child

Anne Anastasi

Individual Differences

Individual

Differences

Anne Anastasi, Fordham University

New York · London · Sydney   John Wiley & Sons, Inc.

Library of Congress Catalog Card Number: 65–25851
Printed in the United States of America

Foreword

Perspectives in Psychology is a series of original books written for psychologists and students who are concerned with the history of ideas in psychology.

It is our intention to present fresh and thoughtful assessments of the current psychological scene in the context of relevant historical changes. Many authors of the *Perspectives* books will examine a selected slice of the history of psychology by way of selected and annotated readings. This is not to say that *Perspectives* is a uniform or systematic encyclopedia of the history of psychology. Psychologists, by disposition and training, are reluctant to work their ideas into a standard weave—homespun or exotic—and *Perspectives* represents well the happy diversity of the discipline.

Some books in the series are scholarly disquisitions on the historical antecedents of a current problem in psychological analysis; some books move—after a brief glance at historical antecedents—directly toward a discussion of contemporary psychology and its future; some books deal with the past largely as a platform for polemical exposition. And, occasionally, *Perspectives* will present an original work in psychology that escapes the historical definition altogether.

Perspectives in Psychology, by using the avenues of documented history and informed discussions of current as well as classical issues, will emphasize that psychology has a history as well as a past and that it advances as it grows.

GEORGE MANDLER
WILLIAM KESSEN

9553

Preface

The purpose of this book is to place the psychological study of individual differences in historical perspective, rather than to survey the history of differential psychology. Even with this more modest goal, however, limitations of space require a high degree of selectivity. Other topics and other authors could have been chosen with good justification. The rationale underlying my selection of materials may be considered in two stages. First, topics were identified that represent foci of lively contemporary activity in the field. These include: the development and use of tests for the measurement of individual differences; quantitative research on the nature of intelligence through factor analysis and similar statistical techniques; behavior genetics and the heredity–environment problem; the role of cultural deprivation and other experiential factors in the development of individual and group differences; and studies of genius and creativity. Within each topic, I then chose individual publications to illustrate the origins and historical development of relevant psychological research. The period covered by the selected passages themselves spans a little less than a century—from the first edition of Galton's *Hereditary Genius* published in 1869 to an article in the 1962 *American Psychologist*. In addition, earlier antecedents of differential psychology are briefly outlined in the first chapter.

With regard to authors, there is of course no implication that those selected represent *the* most important contributors to the field. Many who have made contributions of equal or greater merit are undoubtedly absent. Although such leaders as Galton and Binet would be generally acknowledged as meriting inclusion in their own right, the works of other authors were chosen for a variety of reasons. One publication may have been included because it clearly illustrates a particular step in the development of differential psychology, another because it provides a concise summary of many relevant studies, and still another because it typifies a major approach to the problem under consideration. The selection of specific passages was further influenced by the fact that this book is part of a series on *Perspectives in Psychology*. Since I did not want to duplicate passages cited in other volumes of this series, relevant material will be found in some of the other books. I refer especially to additional excerpts on the nature of intelligence (Chs. 3 and 4) to be found in George A. Miller's *Mathematics and Psychology* and to passages relevant to the measurement of individual differences (Ch. 2) to be found in William Kessen's *The Child*.

A book of readings should be more than a substitute for a well-stocked library. Besides providing materials that may not be readily available, it should present an integrated view of the field. To this end, I perceive my function as that of a guide who takes the reader on a personally conducted tour of the literature. This I have tried to do through the selection and arrangement of excerpts, as well as through the introductory and connecting passages. It is the purpose of the editorial passages not only to show the significance of each study in the development of the topic, but also to provide critical evaluations of methodology and interpretation, when appropriate, and to cite other pertinent studies.

In a book of this type, the major contribution is that of the original authors whose writings are included. My thanks are extended to these authors and to their publishers, who graciously granted permission to reproduce selections from their works. In addition, I wish to express my appreciation to the series editors, William Kessen and George Mandler, who recognized and defined the place of individual differences in a series on *Perspectives in Psychology*. In fact, their recognition of individual differences is so genuine as to permit them to accept my own idiosyncracies of style and format in the preparation of this volume rather than insist on uniformity for the whole series. Dr. Mandler also read the entire manuscript and made valuable editorial contributions.

Finally, I wish to thank Vivienne Blache, Gayl Fowler, and Kathleen Gentile for their competent assistance in typing and proofreading.

ANNE ANASTASI

New York City

Contents

1 Sources of Differential Psychology   1

2 Measurement of Individual Differences   12

Inquiries into human faculty and its development   *Francis Galton*   13

Memories of my life   *Francis Galton*   21

Mental tests and measurements   *James McKeen Cattell*   24

Physical and mental measurements of the students of Columbia University   *James McKeen Cattell* and *Livingston Farrand*   26

The development of intelligence in children   *Alfred Binet* and *Theophile Simon*   30

3 Nature of Intelligence: Pioneer Research   45

"General intelligence," objectively determined and measured   *Charles Spearman*   46

The abilities of man: Their nature and measurement   *Charles Spearman*   51

Psychological implications of factor analysis   *Louis Leon Thurstone*   58

4 Nature of Intelligence: Later Developments   65

The structure of the mind: A review of the results of factor analysis   *Cyril Burt*   66

xii   Contents

The structure of human abilities   *Philip Ewart Vernon*   69
A developmental theory of intelligence   *Henry Edward Garrett*   73
The differentiation of intellectual ability   *Cyril Burt*   83
Three faces of intellect   *Joy Paul Guilford*   87

5 Behavior Genetics: Statistical Studies   106

On the laws of inheritance in man   *Karl Pearson*   108
Measurement of twins   *Edward Lee Thorndike*   120
Nature-nurture and intelligence   *Alice Mary Leahy*   132

6 Behavior Genetics: Selective Breeding   137

Genetic differences in maze-learning ability in rats   *Robert Choate Tryon*   138
Mass screening and reliable individual measurement in the experimental behavior genetics of lower organisms   *Jerry Hirsch* and *Robert Choate Tryon*   148
Sign of taxis as a property of the genotype   *Jerry Hirsch* and *Loise Erlenmeyer-Kimling*   155

7 Behavior Genetics: Theoretical Orientation   159

Heredity and environment in mammalian behaviour   *Donald Olding Hebb*   160
Heredity, environment, and the question "How?"   *Anne Anastasi*   170

8 Cultural Deprivation: Cross-Sectional Approaches   187

On the need for caution in establishing race norms   *Ada Hart Arlitt*   189
The intelligence of isolated mountain children   *Mandel Sherman* and *Cora Beale Key*   195

9   **Cultural Deprivation: Longitudinal Approaches   202**

A comparative study of the intelligence of East Tennessee mountain children   *Lester Rosin Wheeler*   **203**

Soldier intelligence in World Wars I and II   *Read Duncan Tuddenham*   **210**

The influence of schooling upon I.Q.   *Torsten Husén*   **218**

Early education of the mentally retarded: An experimental study   *Samuel Alexander Kirk*   **226**

10   **Nature of Genius: Early Exploration   237**

Hereditary genius: An inquiry into its laws and consequences   *Francis Galton*   **239**

The discovery and encouragement of exceptional talent   *Lewis Madison Terman*   **249**

11   **Nature of Genius: Focus on Creativity   264**

Current research on the nature of creative talent   *Ellis Paul Torrance*   **266**

The nature and nurture of creative talent   *Donald Wallace MacKinnon*   **282**

12   **Concluding Remarks   296**

Name Index   **299**

Sources of Differential Psychology[1]

Although it is likely that in practical dealings with his associates man has always been aware of individual differences, the scientific study of such differences is of relatively recent origin. Several developments in related fields and in psychology itself contributed to the rise of differential psychology—a field of psychology concerned with individual and group differences in behavior.

Curiously enough, it was in astronomy that the systematic collection of data on individual differences in a behavioral characteristic was first undertaken. In 1796 there occurred in the Greenwich Astronomical Observatory an incident that has been immortalized in the history of psychology. In that year Maskelyne, the astronomer royal at the Greenwich Observatory, discharged Kinnebrook, his assistant, because of what he regarded as excessive observational errors. Maskelyne found discrepancies of nearly a second between the times of stellar transits reported by himself and by his assistant. At that time, astronomers used what was known as the "eye-and-ear" method to make such observations. The observer read the time to the nearest second on a clock and then began to count seconds with the beats of the clock, at the same time watching the star as it crossed the field of the telescope. He noted the position of the star at the last

[1] References to original publications and more detailed discussion of material cited in this chapter can be found in Anne Anastasi. *Differential psychology* (3rd ed.). New York: Macmillan, 1958 (Ch. 1); Anne Anastasi. *Psychological testing* (2nd ed.). New York: Macmillan, 1961 (Ch. 1); and E. G. Boring. *A history of experimental psychology.* New York: Century, 1929.

beat just before it reached the critical line in the field and again at the first beat after it had crossed this line. From these observations, he estimated in tenths of a second the time when the star crossed the critical line. This procedure was generally assumed to be accurate to about one-tenth of a second. Kinnebrook's estimates, however, varied by as much as seven-tenths of a second from those of Maskelyne.

In 1816 Bessel, astronomer at Königsberg, read of the Kinnebrook incident in a history of the Greenwich Observatory and decided to look further into such observational errors. He sent to England for Maskelyne's complete report, studied the records of Kinnebrook's "error," and set out to discover whether such personal differences could be found among more experienced astronomical observers. He began by comparing his own observations with those of other well-known astronomers who recorded the time of transit of the same star. Finding even larger discrepancies than those between Maskelyne and his assistant, Bessel published his results in the form of a "personal equation" for every pair of observers. These equations gave the difference in seconds between the estimates of any two observers and could be used to "correct" the observations and make them comparable from one observer to another.

Other astronomers computed similar personal equations, not only for stellar transits but also for other astronomical observations. With the introduction of chronographs and chronoscopes in the second half of the nineteenth century, it became possible to obtain an absolute measure of each observer's personal equation, without reference to any other observer. By means of an artificial star whose transit could be automatically recorded on the chronograph, each observer's performance could be checked against "true values" and his absolute error recorded. Astronomers also became interested in the various conditions that affected the magnitude of the personal error, such as visual-versus-auditory modality, rate of movement of the stimulus, and the like. It was these questions, rather than the measurement of individual differences, that were followed up by the early experimental psychologists in their studies of reaction time.

In 1879, Wilhelm Wundt established the first laboratory of experimental psychology at Leipzig. Before this time, some psychological experiments had been performed by such well-known investigators as Weber, Fechner, and Holmholtz. But Wundt's laboratory was the first to be devoted exclusively to psychology and to provide facilities for training students in the methodology of the new science. Consequently, it played a major part in the development of early experimental psychology. Students from many nations were attracted to Wundt's laboratory and, after earning their doctorate at Leipzig, often established similar laboratories of experimental psychology in their own countries.

The first experimental psychologists had received their own training chiefly in physics and physiology. The influence of these sciences is clearly apparent in the nature of the problems investigated in the early psychological laboratories. Visual and auditory sensations, reaction time, and psychophysics were by far the principal areas of study. In their emphasis on general laws and uniformities of behavior, early experimental psychologists also reflected the approach typical of physicists and physiologists of their time. It was characteristic of these early psychologists either to ignore individual differences or to treat them simply as chance errors. The greater the individual variation in a phenomenon, the less accurate would be the generalizations regarding its nature. The extent of individual differences was therefore regarded as the margin of error to be expected in the application of general laws of psychology.

The rise of experimental psychology thus seemed to shift interest away from—rather than toward—the study of individual differences. Nevertheless, experimental psychology made some noteworthy contributions to the development of differential psychology. By investigating the many factors that influence even the simplest sensorimotor responses, experimental psychologists focused attention on the importance of controlling extraneous variables in measuring individual behavior. The standardization of testing materials and procedures undoubtedly owes much to these early experiments. An even more basic contribution is to be found in the demonstration that psychological phenomena are amenable to objective and quantitative investigation. Such a step was required before subjective speculation about individuals and groups could give way to empirical measurement of individual differences.

Several developments in the biological sciences during the late nineteenth century also helped to shape modern differential psychology. One of the by-products of Darwin's doctrine of evolution was the emergence of the comparative viewpoint, involving the observation of similar phenomena in different species. In the attempt to test some of the implications of evolutionary theory, Darwin and some of his contemporaries amassed the first large body of data on animal behavior. Beginning with anecdotal material and field observations, this search led eventually to the highly controlled animal experiments of the twentieth century. Differential psychology has profited in many ways from such investigations of animal behavior. An outstanding example of pertinent research is provided by the many controlled experiments on the effects of early experience on subsequent behavior development.

Another prominent influence in the history of differential psychology is found in the rise of modern genetics. The rediscovery of Mendel's laws of heredity in 1900 led to extensive research on the mechanisms of heredity. The investigation of the inheritance of physical traits in animals, as illustrated by the highly successful work on the fruit fly Drosophila, has contributed to differential psychology from several angles. First, it helped to clarify and refine the concept of heredity. Second, it provided a variety of genetic models in terms of which behavioral data could be examined. Third, it led directly to animal experiments on selective breeding and crossbreeding for behavioral traits. Finally, the development of human genetics suggested methods for the statistical analysis of family relationships that have been extensively applied to psychological data.

Of particular relevance to differential psychology is the work of Sir Francis Galton, an English biologist. It was Galton who first undertook to apply the Darwinian principles of variation, selection, and adaptation to the study of human populations. Galton's scientific pursuits were manifold, but they were unified by his underlying interest in heredity. In 1869 he published a book entitled "Hereditary Genius" in which, by the application of the now well-known family history method, he tried to demonstrate the inheritance of specific talents in various fields of work. This was followed in 1874 by a similar book on "English Men of Science." In a still later book, entitled "Natural Inheritance" (1889), Galton applied the same techniques to a sample of the general population. Data for this study were gathered through a published offer of cash prizes to persons submitting the best reports on their own family records. Usable records on approximately 150 families were received in response to this offer.

Many of Galton's activities were concerned with the direct measurement of physical and mental traits of large numbers of persons. For this purpose he devised several ingenious tests and measuring instruments and tried a variety of schemes for obtaining data. Among his best-known efforts was the establishment of an anthropometric laboratory where, for the payment of a small fee, the visitor could be examined in sensory discrimination, motor capacities, and other simple traits.

Arguing that all the information we receive about outward events reaches us through the senses, Galton regarded the measurement of sensory capacities as a promising method of gauging intellectual level. For this reason, tests of sensory discrimination were relatively prominent in his series of measuring instruments. Examples include the Galton bar for measuring visual discrimination of length, the Galton whistle for ascertaining the highest audible pitch, and a set of weights to be arranged in order of heaviness as a test of kinesthetic discrimination. In addition, the series included tests for measuring strength of movement, speed of simple reactions, and other sensorimotor functions. Galton also initiated the use of free association tests, a technique that was subsequently adopted and further developed by Wundt. Galton's extensive study of individual and group differences in mental imagery was another of his pioneer efforts. Utilizing questionnaire and rating procedures, this investigation foreshadowed many of the methodological problems now familiar in the use of these instruments.

Galton was keenly aware of the need for specialized statistical techniques for processing his data on individual differences. Accordingly he set out to adapt several mathematical procedures for this purpose. Chief among them were those dealing with the normal distribution curve and correlation. In connection with the latter, Galton carried out much of the spadework and evolved a measure that eventually led to the coefficient of correlation. It was his student and ardent admirer, Karl Pearson, however, who later worked out the mathematical details of correlation theory and proposed the correlation coefficient that bears his name. Pearson, in fact, was responsible for developing and systematizing what for many years constituted nearly the whole field of statistics.

Of equal importance with statistics as a tool of differential psychology is psychological testing. We have already identified the early beginnings of the testing movement in the pioneer work of Galton with simple sensorimotor tests. Another outstanding contributor to the development of psychological testing was the American psychologist, James McKeen Cattell. In Cattell we can see a convergence of two parallel movements: the rise of experimental psychology and the measurement of individual differences. For his doctorate at Leipzig, under Wundt, Cattell prepared a dissertation on individual differences in reaction time. Later he spent some time in England, where his interest in individual differences was strengthened by contact with Galton. Following his return to America, Cattell was active both in the establishment of psychological laboratories and in the development of the testing movement.

In an article published in 1890, Cattell[2] introduced the term "mental test" to the English psychological literature. The article described a series of tests that were being administered annually to college students in an effort to measure their intellectual level. The series included tests of muscular strength, speed of movement, sensitivity to pain, keenness of vision and hearing, weight discrimination, reaction time, and memory, among others. In his choice of tests, Cattell shared Galton's view that an estimate of intellectual functioning could be obtained through tests of sensory discrimination and reaction time. Cattell's preference for such tests was further supported by his conviction that simple functions could be measured with precision, while the more complex, "higher mental processes" could not.

Cattell's tests were typical of those found in several test series developed during the last decade of the nineteenth century. Some of these series did, however, try to tap more complex processes by including tests of reading, word association, memory, and simple arithmetic. Such tests were administered to school children, college students, and random samples of adults. At the Columbian Exposition held in Chicago in 1893, for example, Joseph Jastrow set up an exhibit at which visitors were invited to take tests of sensory, motor, and simple perceptual functions and then compare their skill with the norms. A few attempts to evaluate these early tests yielded discouraging results. The individual's performance showed little correspondence from one test to another, and it exhibited little or no

[2] J. McK. Cattell. Mental tests and measurements. *Mind*, 1890, **15**, 373–380.

correlation with independent estimates of intellectual level derived from teachers' ratings or school grades.

Similar test series were assembled by several European psychologists of the period, notably Oehrn, Kraepelin, and Ebbinghaus in Germany, and Guicciardi and Ferrari in Italy. In an article published in France in 1895, Binet and Henri[3] criticized most of the available test series because of their overemphasis on sensory functions and their undue concentration on simple and narrowly specialized abilities. They also argued that, since individual differences are larger in the more complex functions, a high degree of precision is not needed in the measurement of these functions. Binet and Henri then went on to describe their own test series, which covered such functions as memory, imagination, attention, comprehension, suggestibility, and esthetic judgment. In these tests we can recognize the forerunners of the famous Binet intelligence tests.

In 1904, the French Minister of Public Instruction appointed a commission to study the problem of retardation among public school children. As a direct outgrowth of his work for this commission, Binet, in collaboration with Simon, prepared the first intelligence scale designed to yield a global index of intellectual level. Their first revision of this scale, in which tests were grouped into age levels on the basis of empirical data, appeared in 1908. For example, in the four-year level were placed all tests that normal four-year-olds could pass, in the five-year level all tests passed by normal five-year-olds, and so on. A child's score on the scale could then be expressed as a mental age, that is, the age of normal children whose performance he equaled.

Even before the publication of the 1908 revision, the Binet–Simon scales were enthusiastically adopted by psychologists throughout the world. Translations and adaptations soon appeared in many countries. In America, several revisions were prepared, including the well-known Stanford-Binet developed by Terman and his associates at Stanford University. First published in 1916, the Stanford-Binet was revised in 1937 and brought up to date and further refined in 1960.

Another important milestone in the mental testing movement was the development of group tests. The Binet scales and their revisions

[3] A. Binet and V. Henri. La psychologie individuelle. *Année psychol.*, 1895, **2**, 411–463.

are individual tests, that is, they can be given to only one person at a time. In addition, these tests are of such a nature that they require a highly trained examiner to administer and score them. They are thus unsuited for large-scale testing and are now used chiefly as clinical instruments for the intensive study of individual cases. The advent of group intelligence tests was undoubtedly a major factor in the popularization of psychological testing. Group tests are not only designed for the simultaneous examination of large groups, but they are also relatively easy to administer and score.

The immediate stimulus for the development of group tests was provided in 1917, when the United States entered the first World War. At that time, the American Psychological Association appointed a committee, under the chairmanship of Robert M. Yerkes, to consider ways in which psychology could help in the conduct of the war. The committee recognized the preeminent need for the rapid classification of the million and a half recruits with respect to their general intellectual level. Such information was required for many administrative decisions, including rejection or discharge from military service, assignments to different types of service, and admission to officer training camps. The tests developed by the Army psychologists to meet these needs were the Army Alpha and the Army Beta. The Army Alpha was designed for general routine testing; the Army Beta was a nonlanguage test employed with illiterates and foreign-born draftees who were unable to take a test in English. Both tests were suitable for administration to large groups.

So far we have identified the antecedents of differential psychology in the growing interest in individual differences manifested in such diverse fields as astronomy and biology, as well as in the development of experimental psychology, genetics, statistics, and mental testing. By the turn of the century, differential psychology had begun to take definite shape. The previously cited article by Binet and Henri, published in 1895, was entitled "La psychologie individuelle." Besides describing their own test series, Binet and Henri presented therein the first systematic analysis of the aims, scope, and methods of differential psychology. Their opening sentence reflected the status of this field of psychology at the time. It read, "We broach here a new subject, difficult and as yet very meagerly explored."[4] They

[4] A. Binet and V. Henri. La psychologie individuelle. *Anné psychol.*, 1895, **2**, 411.

went on to discuss what they regarded as the two major problems of differential psychology. The first dealt with the nature and extent of individual differences in psychological functions. The second was concerned with the interrelationships of mental processes within the individual whence one may arrive at a classification of traits and establish which are the more basic functions.

In 1900 appeared the first edition of William Stern's book on differential psychology, "Uber Psychologie der individuellen Differenzen." Part I covered the nature, problems, and methods of differential psychology. Within this field, Stern included differences among individuals as well as among racial and cultural groups, occupational and social levels, and the two sexes. He considered the fundamental problem of differential psychology to be threefold. First, what is the nature and the extent of differences in the psychological life of individuals and groups? Second, what factors determine or affect these differences? In this connection he mentioned heredity, climate, social or cultural level, training, and adaptation, among others. Third, how are the differences manifested? Can they be detected by such indices as handwriting, facial conformation, etc.? Stern also discussed the concepts of psychological type, individuality, and normality-versus-abnormality. Under the methods of differential psychology, he considered introspection, objective observation, the use of material from history and poetry, the study of culture, quantitative testing, and experiment. Part II contained a survey of data on individual differences in various psychological traits, from simple sensory capacities to more complex mental functions and emotional traits. Stern's book appeared in a revised and enlarged edition in 1911, and again in 1921, under the title of "Die differentielle Psychologie in ihren methodischen Grundlagen."

In America, national organizations were becoming cognizant of the problems of individual differences. At its 1895 meeting, the American Psychological Association appointed a committee "to consider the feasibility of cooperation among the various psychological laboratories in the collection of mental and physical statistics."[5] The following year, the American Association for the Advancement of Science established a standing committee to organize an ethnographic

[5] J. McK. Cattell and L. Farrand. Physical and mental measurements of the students of Columbia University. *Psychol. Rev.*, 1896, **3**, 619.

survey of the white population of the United States. Cattell, who was a member of this committee, urged the inclusion of psychological tests in this survey and suggested that its work be coordinated with that proposed by the American Psychological Association.

Investigators were also beginning to administer the newly devised tests to various groups. R. L. Kelly in 1903 and Naomi Norsworthy in 1906 compared normal and mentally defective children in several sensorimotor and simple mental tests. Their findings highlighted the continuous gradation in ability between these groups, suggesting that mental defectives do not represent a distinct category. In 1903 appeared Helen B. Thompson's "The Mental Traits of Sex," the result of several years' testing of men and women with a variety of tests. This study was the first comprehensive investigation of sex differences in psychological traits.

Tests of sensory acuity, motor capacities, and a few simple mental processes were also being employed for the first time in the comparison of different racial groups. A few scattered investigations were conducted before 1900. In 1904, R. S. Woodworth and F. G. Bruner tested members of several racial groups at the St. Louis Exposition. Their findings called into question the prevalent belief that "primitive" man excelled "civilized" man in sensory capacities. Later research dispelled many other popular notions about racial differences. It was not until the 1920's, however, that the role of cultural factors in the mental test performance of different groups was systematically investigated. Studies of the intellectual development of culturally deprived groups—such as children reared in orphanages, gypsy camps, isolated mountain communities, and city slums—focused attention on the effects that early experience has upon intelligence test performance. These studies, together with research on the influence of schooling and other experiential factors, helped to clarify the results of the many comparative investigations of racial, national, and cultural groups conducted in the 1920's and 1930's.

From its inception, differential psychology has been concerned with the nature of intelligence and the identification of mental traits. An important landmark in this area of research was the publication in 1904 of an article by the British psychologist, Charles Spearman.[6]

[6] C. Spearman. "General intelligence" objectively determined and measured. *Amer. J. Psychol.*, 1904, **15**, 201–293.

In this article, Spearman proposed his Two-Factor theory of mental organization and introduced a statistical technique for investigating the problem. He thereby launched the empirical, quantitative study of trait relationships and opened the way for the modern techniques of factor analysis.

The passages reproduced in the remainder of this book were chosen to amplify this brief survey of the antecedents and development of differential psychology. With the exception of short transitional comments by the editor, the persons who have contributed to this development will speak for themselves, in their own words. Since any attempt to cite excerpts from all who have made significant contributions to the growth of differential psychology would require not a small book but several large volumes, coverage must necessarily be selective. Accordingly, five areas have been singled out for inclusion: measurement of individual differences, nature of intelligence, behavior genetics, cultural deprivation, and nature of genius.

These areas were chosen partly because they represent active foci of current research. It should thus be of interest to discover when, where, and under what circumstances psychologists began to investigate these contemporary problems. In addition, the concepts and findings within these areas appear to be more basic and far-reaching than those in other areas that might have been included. For example, data on sex, race, and other group differences can be better understood by reference to available knowledge regarding behavior genetics and cultural deprivation. In the effort to make a virtue of necessity and remain within the confines of the available space, we have thus tried to identify the more nearly "primary" topics of differential psychology.

2

Measurement of
Individual Differences

It is fitting that this survey should begin with the writings of Sir Francis Galton, a key figure in so many of the developments leading to modern differential psychology. The following passages from Galton's "Inquiries into Human Faculty and Its Development" illustrate a few of his many contributions. Beginning with his rationale for choosing sensory discrimination tests as an approach to the measurement of intelligence, Galton goes on to describe some of the tests he designed for this purpose. Among them are a weight discrimination test for measuring kinesthetic sensitivity and the Galton whistle for detecting the highest audible pitch. It is interesting to note that in choosing weights for the former, Galton applied Fechner's psychophysical law to obtain a series of equally perceptible intervals.

Francis Galton

Inquiries into Human Faculty and Its Development*

The only information that reaches us concerning outward events appears to pass through the avenue of our senses; and the more perceptive the senses are of difference, the larger is the field upon which our judgment and intelligence can act. . . . Two persons may be equally able just to hear the same faint sound, and they may equally begin to be pained by the same loud sound, and yet they may differ as to the number of intermediate grades of sensation. The grades will be less numerous as the organization is of a lower order, and the keenest sensation possible to it will in consequence be less intense. . . . The discriminative faculty of idiots is curiously low; they hardly distinguish between heat and cold, and their sense of pain is so obtuse that some of the more idiotic seem hardly to know what it is. . . . The trials I have as yet made on the sensitivity of different persons confirms the reasonable expectation that it would on the whole be highest among the intellectually ablest. . . .

I will now describe an apparatus I have constructed to test the delicacy with which weights may be discriminated by handling them. I do so because the principle on which it is based may be adopted in apparatus for testing other senses, and its description and the conditions of its use will illustrate the desiderata and difficulties of all such investigations.

* F. Galton. Inquiries into human faculty and its development. New York: Macmillan, 1883. (Pp. 27–29, 34–35, 38–39, 83–87, 378–380)

A series of test weights is a simple enough idea—the difficulty lies in determining the particular sequence of weights that should be employed. Mine form a geometric series, for the reason that when stimuli of all kinds increase by geometric grades the sensations they give rise to will increase by arithmetic grades, so long as the stimulus is neither so weak as to be barely felt, nor so strong as to excite fatigue. My apparatus . . . consists of a number of common gun cartridge cases filled with alternate layers of shot, wool, and wadding, and then closed in the usual way. They are all identical in appearance, and may be said to differ only in their specific gravities. They are marked in numerical sequence with the register numbers, 1, 2, 3, etc., but their weights are proportioned to the numbers of which 1, 2, 3, etc., are the logarithms, and consequently run in a geometric series. Hence the numbers of the weights form a scale of equal degrees of sensitivity. If a person can just distinguish between the weights numbered 1 and 3, he can also just distinguish between 2 and 4, 3 and 5, and any other pair of weights of which the register number of the one exceeds that of the other by 2. Again, his coarseness of discrimination is exactly double that of another person who can just distinguish pairs of weights differing only by 1, such as 1 and 2, 2 and 3, 3 and 4, and so on. The testing is performed by handing pairs of weights to the operatee until his power of discrimination is approximately made out, and then to proceed more carefully. It is best . . . to hand to the operatee sequences of three weights at a time, after shuffling them. These he has to arrange in their proper order, with his eyes shut, and by the sense of their weight alone. . . .

The use of tests, which, objectively speaking, run in a geometric series, and subjectively in an arithmetic one, may be applied to touch, by the use of wire-work of various degrees of fineness; to taste, by stock bottles of solutions of salt, etc., of various strengths; to smell, by bottles of attar of rose, etc., in various degrees of dilution. . . .

I contrived a small whistle for conveniently ascertaining
the upper limits of audible sound in different persons. . . .
I made a very small whistle from a brass tube whose internal
diameter was less than one-tenth of an inch in diameter. A
plug was fitted into the lower end of the tube, which could
be pulled out or pushed in as much as desired, thereby
causing the length of the bore of the whistle to be varied at
will. When the bore is long the note is low; when short, it is
high. The plug was graduated, so that the precise note
produced by the whistle could be determined by reading off
the graduations and referring to a table. . . .

On testing different persons, I found there was a remarkable falling off in the power of hearing high notes as age
advanced. The persons themselves were quite unconscious
of their deficiency so long as their sense of hearing low notes
remained unimpaired. It is an only too amusing experiment
to test a party of persons of various ages, including some
rather elderly and self-satisfied personages. They are indig-
nant at being thought deficient in the power of hearing, yet
the experiment quickly shows that they are absolutely deaf
to shrill notes which the younger persons hear acutely, and
they commonly betray much dislike to the discovery. Every
one has his limit, and the limit at which sounds become too
shrill to be audible to any particular person can be rapidly
determined by this little instrument. . . . .

Galton's classic study of mental imagery probably represents the
first systematic use of a questionnaire survey to gather data on
individual differences in a psychological trait. His references to the
difficulty of formulating suitable questions and to the likelihood of
biased sampling in the returns reveal an awareness of methodological
problems familiar today to anyone conducting consumer surveys or
public-opinion polls. A copy of the questionnaire itself is appended.
Note the thoroughness and fullness with which the respondent's
imagery is explored. The replies were arranged in rank order and
classified to yield a scale for rating an individual's imagery (e.g.,
falling at the median, upper or lower quartile points, etc.)

Anecdotes find their way into print, from time to time, of persons whose visual memory is so clear and sharp as to present mental pictures that may be scrutinised with nearly as much ease and prolonged attention as if they were real objects. I became interested in the subject and made a rather extensive inquiry into the mode of visual presentation in different persons, so far as could be gathered from their respective statements. It seemed to me that the results might illustrate the essential differences between the mental operations of different men, that they might give some clue to the origin of visions, and that the course of the inquiry might reveal some previously unnoticed facts. . . .

After the inquiry had been fairly started it took the form of submitting a certain number of printed questions to a large number of persons. There is hardly any more difficult task than that of framing questions which are not likely to be misunderstood, which admit of easy reply, and which cover the ground of inquiry. I did my best in these respects, without forgetting the most important part of all—namely, to tempt my correspondents to write freely in fuller explanation of their replies, and on cognate topics as well. These separate letters have proved more instructive and interesting by far than the replies to the set questions. . . .

The earliest results of my inquiry amazed me. I had begun by questioning friends in the scientific world, as they were the most likely class of men to give accurate answers concerning this faculty of visualising, to which novelists and poets continually allude, which has left an abiding mark on the vocabularies of every language, and which supplies the material out of which dreams and the well-known hallucinations of sick people are built.

To my astonishment, I found that the great majority of the men of science to whom I first applied protested that mental imagery was unknown to them, and they looked on me as fanciful and fantastic in supposing that the words "mental imagery" really expressed what I believed everybody supposed them to mean. They had no more notion of its true nature than a colour-blind man, who has not discerned his defect, has of the nature of colour. . . .

On the other hand, when I spoke to persons whom I met in general society, I found an entirely different disposition to prevail. Many men and a yet larger number of women, and many boys and girls, declared that they habitually saw mental imagery, and that it was perfectly distinct to them and full of colour. The more I pressed and cross-questioned them, professing myself to be incredulous, the more obvious was the truth of their first assertions. They described their imagery in minute detail, and they spoke in a tone of surprise at my apparent hesitation in accepting what they said. . . .

I have also received batches of answers from various educational establishments both in England and America, which were made after the masters had fully explained the meaning of the questions, and interested the boys in them. These have the merit of returns derived from a general census, which my other data lack, because I cannot for a moment suppose that the writers of the latter are a haphazard proportion of those to whom they were sent. Indeed I know of some who, disavowing all possession of the power, and of many others who, possessing it in too faint a degree to enable them to express what their experiences really were, in a manner satisfactory to them, sent no returns at all. Considerable statistical similarity was, however, observed between the sets of returns furnished by the school boys and those sent by my separate correspondents, and I may add that they accord in this respect with the oral information I have elsewhere obtained. The conformity of replies from so many different sources which was clear from the first, the fact of their apparent trustworthiness being on the whole much increased by cross-examination (though I could give one or two amusing instances of breakdown), and the evident effort made to give accurate answers, have convinced me that it is a much easier matter than I had anticipated to obtain trustworthy replies to psychological questions. . . .

Questionnaire

The object of these Questions is to elicit the degree in which different persons possess the power of seeing images in their mind's eye, and of reviving past sensations.

From inquiries I have already made, it appears that remarkable variations exist both in the strength and in the quality of these faculties, and it is highly probable that a statistical inquiry into them will throw light upon more than one psychological problem.

Before addressing yourself to any of the Questions on the opposite page, think of some definite object—suppose it is your breakfast-table as you sat down to it this morning—and consider carefully the picture that rises before your mind's eye.

1. *Illumination.* Is the image dim or fairly clear? Is its brightness comparable to that of the actual scene?

2. *Definition.* Are all the objects pretty well defined at the same time, or is the place of sharpest definition at any one moment more contracted than it is in a real scene?

3. *Colouring.* Are the colours of the china, of the toast, bread crust, mustard, meat, parsley, or whatever may have been on the table, quite distinct and natural?

4. *Extent of the field of view.* Call up the image of some panoramic view (the walls of your room might suffice). Can you force yourself to see mentally a wider range of it than could be taken in by any single glance of the eyes? Can you mentally see more than three faces of a die, or more than one hemisphere of a globe at the same instant of time?

5. *Distance of images.* Where do mental images appear to be situated? Within the head, within the eye-ball, just in front of the eyes, or at a distance corresponding to reality? Can you project an image upon a piece of paper?

6. *Command over images.* Can you retain a mental picture steadily before the eyes? When you do so, does it grow brighter or dimmer? When the act of retaining it becomes wearisome, in what part of the head or eye-ball is the fatigue felt?

7. *Persons.* Can you recall with distinctness the features of all near relations and many other persons? Can you at will cause your mental image of any or most of them to sit, stand, or turn slowly round? Can

you deliberately seat the image of a well-known person in a chair and see it with enough distinctness to enable you to sketch it leisurely (supposing yourself able to draw)?

8. *Scenery.* Do you preserve the recollection of scenery with much precision of detail, and do you find pleasure in dwelling on it? Can you easily form mental pictures from the descriptions of scenery that are so frequently met with in novels and books of travel?

9. *Comparison with reality.* What difference do you perceive between a very vivid mental picture called up in the dark, and a real scene? Have you ever mistaken a mental image for a reality when in health and wide awake?

10. *Numerals and dates.* Are these invariably associated in your mind with any peculiar mental imagery, whether of written or printed figures, diagrams, or colours? If so, explain fully, and say if you can account for the association.

11. *Specialties.* If you happen to have special aptitudes for mechanics, mathematics (either geometry of three dimensions or pure analysis), mental arithmetic, or chess-playing blindfold, please explain fully how far your processes depend on the use of visual images, and how far otherwise.

12. Call up before your imagination the objects specified in the six following paragraphs, numbered A to F, and consider carefully whether your mental representation of them, generally, is in each group very faint, faint, fair, good, or vivid and comparable to the actual sensation:

   A. *Light and colour.* An evenly clouded sky (omitting all landscape), first bright, then gloomy. A thick surrounding haze, first white, then successively blue, yellow, green, and red.
   B. *Sound.* The beat of rain against the window panes, the crack of a whip, a church bell, the hum of bees, the whistle of a railway, the clinking of tea-spoons and saucers, the slam of a door.
   C. *Smells.* Tar, roses, an oil-lamp blown out, hay, violets, a fur coat, gas, tobacco.
   D. *Tastes.* Salt, sugar, lemon juice, raisins, chocolate, currant jelly.
   E. *Touch.* Velvet, silk, soap, gum, sand, dough, a crisp dead leaf, the prick of a pin.
   F. *Other sensations.* Heat, hunger, cold, thirst, fatigue, fever, drowsiness, a bad cold.

13. *Music.* Have you any aptitude for mentally recalling music, or for imagining it?

14. *At different ages.* Do you recollect what your powers of visualising, etc., were in childhood? Have they varied much within your recollection?

General remarks. Supplementary information written here, or on a separate piece of paper, will be acceptable.

In his tireless efforts to gather data on individual differences among men and animals, Galton evolved many ingenious schemes. Social functions, lectures and other formal meetings, walks in the park, and visits to the zoo all provided him with opportunities for making observations and keeping records. He also made several attempts to set up systematic procedures for examining large samples of persons. In an article in the March 1882 issue of the Fortnightly Review, Galton asked, "When shall we have anthropometric laboratories, where a man may, when he pleases, get himself and his children weighed, measured, and rightly photographed, and have their bodily faculties tested by the best methods known to modern science?"[1] He then went on to describe what could be done along these lines with existing facilities and what more it was desirable to have. He tried to obtain the cooperation of schools for this purpose, but met with little success. His biographer, Karl Pearson, writes: "Failing the establishment of school anthropometric laboratories Galton determined to set one up at his own cost, and catch the world when on its leisurely and inquisitive peregrinations."[2] The operation of this anthropometric laboratory is described by Galton himself in the following excerpt. A poster directing the visitor to the laboratory in South Kensington Museum is also reproduced in Fig. 1.

[1] F. Galton. *Memories of my life.* London: Methuen, 1908. (Pp. 244–245.)
[2] K. Pearson. *The life, letters and labours of Francis Galton.* Vol. II. Cambridge: University Press, 1924. (P. 357.)

ANTHROPOMETRIC
LABORATORY
For the measurement in various ways of Human Form and Faculty.

Entered from the Science Collection of the S. Kensington Museum.

This laboratory is established by Mr. Francis Galton for the following purposes:—

1. For the use of those who desire to be accurately measured in many ways, either to obtain timely warning of remediable faults in development, or to learn their powers.

2. For keeping a methodical register of the principal measurements of each person, of which he may at any future time obtain a copy under reasonable restrictions. His initials and date of birth will be entered in the register, but not his name. The names are indexed in a separate book.

3. For supplying information on the methods, practice, and uses of human measurement.

4. For anthropometric experiment and research, and for obtaining data for statistical discussion.

Charges for making the principal measurements: THREEPENCE each, to those who are already on the Register. FOURPENCE each, to those who are not:— one page of the Register will thenceforward be assigned to them, and a few extra measurements will be made, chiefly for future identification.

The Superintendent is charged with the control of the laboratory and with determining in each case, which, if any, of the extra measurements may be made, and under what conditions.

H. & W. Brown, Printers, 20 Fulham Road, S.W.

FIG. 1 Poster announcing the establishment of Galton's Anthropometric Laboratory. (From K. Pearson, *The life, letters and labours of Francis Galton.* Cambridge: Cambridge University Press, 1924. Vol. II, p. 358).

Francis Galton

Memories of My Life*

When the International Exhibition of 1884 was under consideration, I offered to equip and maintain a Laboratory there, if a suitable place were given, the wood-work set up, and the security of it taken off my hands. This was done, and I arranged a long narrow enclosure with trellis-work, in front and at its ends. A table ran alongside the trellis-work on which the instruments were placed and where the applicants were tested, and a passage was left between the table and the wall. This gave a quasi-privacy, while it enabled outsiders to see a little of what was going on inside. A door-keeper stationed at one end admitted a single applicant at a time, who had to pay threepence. The superintendent took him through the tests in turn, and dismissed him at the other end with his schedule filled up. Sometimes I helped him; then two persons could be tested together, the one a little in advance of the other. The arrangement worked smoothly, and the Laboratory was seldom unemployed.

The measurements dealt with Keenness of Sight and of Hearing; Colour Sense; Judgment of Eye; Breathing Power; Reaction Time; Strength of Pull and of Squeeze; Force of Blow; Span of Arms; Height, both standing and sitting; and Weight. The ease of working the instruments that were used was so great that an applicant could be measured in all these respects, a card containing the results furnished him, and a duplicate made and kept for statistical purposes, at the total

* F. Galton. *Memories of my life.* London: Methuen, 1908. (Pp. 245–246, 249.)

cost of the threepenny fee, already described, for admission. That just defrayed the working expenses.

It is by no means easy to select suitable instruments for such a purpose. They must be strong, easily legible, and very simple, the stupidity and wrong-headedness of many men and women being so great as to be scarcely credible. I used at first the instrument commonly employed for testing the force of a blow. It was a stout deal rod running freely in a tube, with a buffer at one end to be hit with the fist and pressing against a spring at the other. An index was pushed by the rod as far as it entered the tube in opposition to the spring. I found no difficulty whatever in testing myself with it, but before long a man had punched it so much on one side, instead of hitting straight out, that he broke the stout deal rod. It was replaced by an oaken one, but this too was broken, and some wrists were sprained. . . .

After the Health Exhibition was closed in 1885, it seemed a pity that the Laboratory should also come to an end, so I asked for and was given a room in the Science Galleries of the South Kensington Museum. I maintained a Laboratory there during about six years. . . . Useful data were obtained from this Laboratory, but I found that it ought to be either in the hands of a trained scientific superintendent, who would be competent to undertake much more refined measurements than mine were intended for, or else that a great many more persons than I could tempt to attend should be roughly measured.

In America, James McKeen Cattell did much to disseminate Galton's influence. Besides introducing the term "mental test" into the psychologist's vocabulary, Cattell's 1890 article described a series of tests modeled in part on those devised by Galton but including also tests of a more distinctly "intellectual" nature. Of particular interest are the remarks by Francis Galton appended to this article. Here Galton makes a suggestion that underlies the Binet scales and other, later tests of intelligence—namely, that many different tasks should be sampled to measure the general level of the individual's capacities. Although it is doubtful that Binet himself saw this comment, Terman and Merrill cite it in their book on the 1937 revision of the Stanford-Binet.[3] In his remarks, Galton also foreshadows the concept of test validity as the correlation of test scores with a criterion.

James McKeen Cattell

Mental Tests and Measurements*

Psychology cannot attain the certainty and exactness of the physical sciences, unless it rests on a foundation of experiment and measurement. A step in this direction could be made by applying a series of mental tests and measurements to a large number of individuals. The results would be of considerable scientific value in discovering the constancy of mental processes, their interdependence, and their variation under different circumstances. Individuals, besides, would find their tests interesting, and, perhaps, useful in regard to training, mode of life or indication of disease. The scientific and practical value of such tests would be much increased should a uniform system be adopted, so that determinations made at different times and places would be compared and combined. With a view to obtaining agreement among those interested, I venture to suggest the following series of tests and measurements, together with methods of making them.

The first series of ten tests is made in the Psychological

* J. McK. Cattell. Mental tests and measurements. *Mind*, 1890, 15, 373–381. (Pp. 373, 380–381.)

[3] L. M. Terman and Maud A. Merrill. *Measuring intelligence: A guide to the administration of the new revised Stanford-Binet tests of intelligence.* Boston: Houghton Mifflin, 1937. (P. 4.)

Laboratory of the University of Pennsylvania on all who present themselves, and the complete series on students of Experimental Psychology. The results will be published when sufficient data have been collected. Meanwhile, I should be glad to have the tests, and the methods of making them, thoroughly discussed. The following ten tests are proposed:

     I. Dynamometer Pressure.
    II. Rate of Movement.
   III. Sensation-areas.[4]
   IV. Pressure causing Pain.
    V. Least noticeable difference in Weight.
   VI. Reaction-time for Sound.
  VII. Time for naming Colours.
 VIII. Bi-section of a 50 cm. line.
   IX. Judgment of 10 seconds time.
    X. Number of Letters remembered on once Hearing.

[Cattell also describes the longer list of 50 tests.—Ed.]

Remarks by Francis Galton

One of the most important objects of measurement is hardly if at all alluded to here and should be emphasised. It is to obtain a general knowledge of the capacities of a man by sinking shafts, as it were, at a few critical points. In order to ascertain the best points for the purpose, the sets of measures should be compared with an independent estimate of the man's powers. We thus may learn which of the measures are the most instructive. . . .

[4] Two-point threshold on the skin. (Ed.)

By 1896, Cattell's original test series had undergone some revision and had been applied to a larger number of students. At that time, the tests were routinely administered to entering freshmen at Columbia College, where Cattell had established a psychology laboratory along the same lines as the one he had founded earlier at the University of Pennsylvania. The following excerpts from an article by Cattell and Farrand include some general comments about the potential usefulness of the tests, as well as a copy of the record form. Cattell also employed a supplementary form on which the examiner could record additional observations and a questionnaire that the student could fill out at home. The original article contains detailed instructions for administering each test.

James McKeen Cattell and Livingston Farrand

Physical and Mental Measurements of the Students of Columbia University*

One of the present writers began the collection of physical and mental measurements of students of Cambridge University, the University of Pennsylvania and Bryn Mawr College in 1887–8, and some description of the tests was published in 1890. The methods have been gradually revised and we shall confine our present account to experiments made on students of Columbia University in 1894–5 and 1895–6. . . .

Our experience with these tests leads us to recommend that they be made a part of the work of every psychological laboratory. When used with freshmen on entering college the record is of interest to the man and may be of real value

*J. McK. Cattell and L. Farrand. Physical and mental measurements of the students of Columbia University. *Psychol. Rev.*, 1896, **3**, 618–648. (Pp. 620, 647–648.)

Laboratory of Psychology of Columbia College,

PHYSICAL AND MENTAL TESTS.

Name..Date of Birth..............................

Birthplace...........................of father...................of mother.....................

Class..................................Profession of father................................

Color of eyes................................ of hair..

Perception of size..........................Memory for size.............................

Height...Weight...

Breathing capacity $\begin{cases} 1 \\ 2 \end{cases}$ .... Size of head...................Right handed?..........

Strength of hand, right $\begin{cases} 1 \\ 2 \end{cases}$ .... Left $\begin{cases} 1 \\ 2 \end{cases}$ ....

Keenness of sight, right eye........................Left.........................

Keenness of hearing, right ear........................Left ....

Reaction-time $\begin{cases} \end{cases}$

	1	2	3	4	5	Av.

After-images..

Color vision...................................Perception of pitch...........................

Perception of weight 1........2........3........ Sensation areas 1........2........3........4........5........

Sensitiveness to pain $\begin{cases} \text{right hand} \\ \text{left hand} \end{cases}$ .... Preference for color....................

     1   2   3

Perception of time...

Accuracy of movement...........................Rate of perception and movement...............

Memory...

Imagery...

Are you willing to repeat these tests at the end of the Sophomore and Senior

years?.....................Do you wish to have a copy of these tests sent you?..................

Date of measurement ....Recorded by........................

FIG. 1 Record Form listing tests administered by Cattell to students at Columbia College. (From J. McK. Cattell and L. Farrand. Physical and mental measurements of the students of Columbia University. *Psychol. Rev.*, 1896, **3**, 622.)

to him. It is well for him to know how his physical development, his senses, his movements and his mental processes compare with those of his fellows. He may be able to correct defects and develop aptitudes. Then when the tests are repeated later in the college course and in subsequent life the record of progress or regression may prove of substantial importance to the individual. The making of the tests brings the psychological laboratory into relation with a large number of students and with other departments of the university, shows the modern methods of anthropometry and experimental psychology, and may lead to a more serious study of these on the part of a larger number of students.

The psychological laboratory can also be brought into mutually helpful relations with the community by extending the tests to any who wish to have them made. Children in the schools might be tested with special advantage. For this purpose tests are especially useful which can be made simultaneously on a large number of observers. Physicians might find it an advantage to have records made of their patients. The tests are well suited for civil service examinations. If a small fee were charged in these cases it might suffice to support an assistant, the larger part of whose time would be spent in scientific work. In any case the making of the tests is good practice for advanced students preliminary to, or in addition to, special research. By bringing the laboratory into relations with the community we add to its influence and at the same time secure the material needed for research.

We have only studied 100 individuals and regard this paper rather as an investigation of methods than as a summary of results. We think that an hour used in tests should be divided between physical, psycho-physical and mental measurements. . . .

Our own future work and that of others must proceed in two directions. On the one hand we must study the interrelations of the traits which we define and measure. To what extent are the several traits of body, of the senses and of mind interdependent? How far can we predict one thing from our knowledge of another? What can we learn from the tests of elementary traits regarding the higher intellectual and emotional life? On the other hand we must use our measurements to study the development of the individual and of the race, to disentangle the complex factors of heredity and environment. There is no scientific problem more important than the study of the development of man, and no practical problem more urgent than the application of our knowledge to guide this development

The tests of sensory discrimination and other simple processes devised by Galton, Cattell, and other early investigators proved to be disappointing as predictors of educational achievement and other practical indices of intellectual functioning. The correlations of these tests with each other as well as with external criteria were uniformly low. The French psychologist, Alfred Binet, departed from this approach and sought to measure intelligence more directly through the use of relatively complex tasks. In two articles published in 1905, Binet and his associate Simon presented the original version of the now famous "Binet tests." In the following excerpts from the first article, the authors describe the circumstances leading to the development of their tests and the need for such standardized measures in identifying and classifying the mentally retarded.

Alfred Binet and Theophile Simon

Upon the Necessity of Establishing a
Scientific Diagnosis of Inferior States of Intelligence*

We here present the first rough sketch of a work which was directly inspired by the desire to serve the interesting cause of the education of subnormals.

In October, 1904, the Minister of Public Instruction named a Commission which was charged with the study of measures to be taken for insuring the benefits of instruction to defective children. After a number of sittings, this Commission regulated all that pertained to the type of establishment to be created, the conditions of admission into the school, the teaching force, and the pedagogical methods to be employed. They decided that no child suspected of retardation should be eliminated from the ordinary school and admitted into a special class, without first being subjected to a pedagogical and medical examination from which it could be certified that because of the state of his intelligence, he was unable to profit, in an average measure, from the instruction given in the ordinary schools.

But how the examination of each child should be made, what methods should be followed, what observations taken, what questions asked, what tests devised, how the child should be compared with normal children, the Commission

*A. Binet and Th. Simon. Upon the necessity of establishing a scientific diagnosis of inferior states of intelligence. *Année psychol.*, 1905, 11, 163–191. (Translated by Elizabeth S. Kite and published in 1916 by Williams and Wilkins Co., Baltimore, under the auspices of The Training School at Vineland, N.J., in a book entitled *The development of intelligence in children.* Pp. 9–14, 23.) Reprinted through the courtesy of The Training School at Vineland, New Jersey.

felt under no obligation to decide. It was formed to do a work of administration, not a work of science.

It has seemed to us extremely useful to furnish a guide for future Commissions' examination. Such Commissions should understand from the beginning how to get their bearings. It must be made impossible for those who belong to the Commission to fall into the habit of making haphazard decisions according to impressions which are subjective, and consequently uncontrolled. Such impressions are sometimes good, sometimes bad, and have at all times too much the nature of the arbitrary, of caprice, of indifference. Such a condition is quite unfortunate because the interests of the child demand a more careful method. To be a member of a special class can never be a mark of distinction, and such as do not merit it, must be spared the record. Some errors are excusable in the beginning, but if they become too frequent, they may ruin the reputation of these new institutions. Furthermore, in principle, we are convinced, and we shall not cease to repeat, that the precision and exactness of science should be introduced into our practice whenever possible, and in the great majority of cases it is possible.

The problem which we have to solve presents many difficulties both theoretical and practical. It is a hackneyed remark that the definitions, thus far proposed, for the different states of subnormal intelligence, lack precision. These inferior states are indefinite in number, being composed of a series of degrees which mount from the lowest depths of idiocy, to a condition easily confounded with normal intelligence. Alienists have frequently come to an agreement concerning the terminology to be employed for designating the difference of these degrees; at least, in spite of certain individual divergence of ideas to be found in all questions, there has been an agreement to accept *idiot* as applied to the lowest state, *imbecile* to the intermediate, and *moron* (débile) to the state nearest normality. Still among the numerous alienists, under this common and apparently precise terminology, different ideas are concealed, variable and at the same time confused. The distinction between idiot, imbecile, and moron is not understood in the same way by all practitioners. We have abundant proof of this in the strikingly divergent medical diagnoses made only a few days apart by different alienists upon the same patient. . . .

What importance can be attached to public statistics of different countries concerning the percentage of backward children if the definition for backward children is not the same in all countries? How will it be possible to keep a record of the intelligence of pupils who are treated and instructed in a school, if the terms applied to them, feeble-minded, retarded, imbecile, idiot, vary in meaning according to the doctor who examines them? The absence of a common measure prevents comparison of statistics, and makes one lose all interest in investigations which may have been very laborious. But a still more serious fact is that, because of lack of methods, it is impossible to solve those essential questions concerning the afflicted, whose solution presents the greatest interest; for example, the real results gained by the treatment of inferior states of intelligence by doctor and educator; the educative value of one pedagogical method compared with another; the degree of curability of incomplete idiocy, etc. It is not by means of *a priori* reasonings, of vague considerations, of oratorical displays, that these questions can be solved; but by minute investigation, entering into the details of fact, and considering the effects of the treatment for each particular child. There is but one means of knowing if a child, who has passed six years in a hospital or in a special class, has profited from that stay, and to what degree he has profited; and that is to compare his certificate of entrance with his certificate of dismissal, and by that means ascertain if he shows a special amelioration of his condition beyond that which might be credited simply to the considerations of growth. But experience has shown how imprudent it would be to place confidence in this comparison, when the two certificates come from different doctors, who do not judge in exactly the same way, or who use different words to characterize the mental status of patients. . . .

The general belief seems to be that the confusion arises wholly from an absence of a uniform nomenclature. There is some truth in this opinion. . . . Undoubtedly it would be a good work to bring about a unification of this nomenclature as has been done for the standard of measurements and for electric units. But this reform in itself is not sufficient and we are very sure that they deceive themselves who think that at bottom this is only a question of terminology. It is very much more serious. . . .

In looking closely one can see that the confusion comes principally from a fault in the method of examination. When an alienist finds himself in the presence of a child of inferior intelligence, he does not examine him by bringing out each one of the symptoms which the child manifests and by interpreting all symptoms and classifying them; he contents himself with taking a subjective impression, an impression as a whole, of his subject, and of making his diagnosis by instinct. We do not think that we are going too far in saying that at the present time very few physicians would be able to cite with absolute precision the objective and invariable sign, or signs, by which they distinguish the degrees of inferior mentality. . . .

We are told for profound idiocy: *"There is here a fugitive attention."* What is that—a fugitive attention? In what does it consist? *"Motility exists a little."* What does "little" signify? We are assured that imbecility differs from idiocy in this: *"there is a gleam of intelligence";* in imbecility *"the intellectual faculties exist in a very incomplete degree."* We should like to know what difference must be established between "a gleam" of intelligence and "a very incomplete degree" of the intellectual faculties. We are again informed that in profound idiocy *"the attention is fugitive,"* while in imbecility, *"the attention is fleeting."* We are unable to grasp the distinctive shade of meaning. We are also ignorant of the value of the following symptoms which are noted in the definition of imbecility, *"defective speech," "limited language."* We admit that we have no idea what precise defect of articulation corresponds to "defective speech." There are people who stammer slightly, and others whose speech is scarcely intelligible. All have defective speech. The same remark is true for "limited language." Very many peasants have a limited language. What extent of vocabulary must one possess in order to have a "limited language?" . . .

In the following article, also published in 1905, Binet and Simon first described the thirty tests constituting their 1905 Scale and gave detailed instructions for their administration. These tests were arranged in order of difficulty on the basis of the number of children who were able to pass each. In the excerpts reproduced below, the authors emphasize the need for empirical tryouts in test development. Another noteworthy point is the central place the authors give to judgment and "practical sense" in their definition of intelligence and their repudiation of measures of sensory discrimination used by earlier testers. Of particular interest, too, are their recommendations for proper test administration—recommendations that underlie the procedures regularly followed today in giving individual tests.

Alfred Binet and Theophile Simon

New Methods for the Diagnosis of the Intellectual Level of Subnormals*

Before explaining these methods let us recall exactly the conditions of the problem which we are attempting to solve. Our purpose is to be able to measure the intellectual capacity of a child who is brought to us in order to know whether he is normal or retarded. We should therefore study his condition at the time and that only. We have nothing to do either with his past history or with his future; consequently we shall neglect his etiology, and we shall make no attempt to distinguish between acquired and congenital idiocy; for
• a stronger reason we shall set aside all consideration of pathological anatomy which might explain his intellectual deficiency. So much for his past. As to that which concerns his future, we shall exercise the same abstinence; we do not attempt to establish or prepare a prognosis, and we leave unanswered the question of whether this retardation is curable, or even improvable. We shall limit ourselves to ascertaining the truth in regard to his present mental state. . . .

To what method should we have recourse in making our diagnosis of the intellectual level? No one method exists, but

*A. Binet and Th. Simon. New methods for the diagnosis of the intellectual level of subnormals. *Année psychol.*, 1905, 11, 191–244. (Translated by Elizabeth S. Kite and published in 1916 by Williams and Wilkins Co., Baltimore, under the auspices of The Training School at Vineland, N. J., in a book entitled *The development of intelligence in children*. Pp. 37, 39–45.) Reprinted through the courtesy of The Training School at Vineland, New Jersey.

there are a number of different ones which should be used cumulatively, because the question is a very difficult one to solve, and demands rather a collaboration of methods. . . .

In order to recognize the inferior states of intelligence we believe that three different methods should be employed. We have arrived at this synthetic view only after many years of research, but we are now certain that each of these methods renders some service. These methods are:

1. *The medical method,* which aims to appreciate the anatomical, physiological, and pathological signs of inferior intelligence.

2. *The pedagogical method,* which aims to judge of the intelligence according to the sum of acquired knowledge.

3. *The psychological method,* which makes direct observations and measurements of the degree of intelligence.

From what has gone before it is easy to see the value of each of these methods. The medical method is indirect because it conjectures the mental from the physical. The pedagogical method is more direct; but the psychological is the most direct of all because it aims to measure the state of the intelligence as it is at the present moment. It does this by experiments which oblige the subject to make an effort which shows his capability in the way of comprehension, judgment, reasoning, and invention.

The Psychological Method

The fundamental idea of this method is the establishment of what we shall call a measuring scale of intelligence. This scale is composed of a series of tests of increasing difficulty, starting from the lowest intellectual level that can be observed, and ending with that of average normal intelligence. Each group in the series corresponds to a different mental level.

This scale properly speaking does not permit the measure of the intelligence, because intellectual qualities are not superposable, and therefore cannot be measured as linear surfaces are measured, but are on the contrary, a classification, a hierarchy among diverse intelligences; and for the necessities of practice this classification is equivalent to a measure. We shall therefore be able to know, after studying two individuals, if one rises above the other and to how many degrees, if one rises above the average level of other individuals considered as normal, or if he remains below. Understanding the normal progress of intellectual development among normals, we shall be able to determine how many years such an individual is advanced or retarded. In a word we shall be able to determine to what degree of the scale idiocy, imbecility, and moronity correspond.

The scale that we shall describe is not a theoretical work; it is the result of long investigations, first at the Salpêtrière, and afterwards in the primary schools of Paris, with both normal and subnormal children. These short psychological questions have been given the name of tests. The use of tests is today very common, and there are even contemporary authors who have made a specialty of organizing new tests according to theoretical views, but who have made no effort to patiently try them out in the schools. Theirs is an amusing occupation, comparable to a person's making a colonizing expedition into Algeria, advancing always only upon the map, without taking off his dressing gown. We place but slight confidence in the tests invented by these authors and we have borrowed nothing from them. All the tests which we propose have been repeatedly tried, and have been retained from among many, which after trial have been discarded. We can certify that those which are here presented have proved themselves valuable. . . .

But here we must come to an understanding of what meaning to give to that word so vague and so comprehensive, "the intelligence." Nearly all the phenomena with which psychology concerns itself are phenomena of intelligence; sensation, perception, are intellectual manifestations as much as reasoning. Should we therefore bring into our examination the measure of sensation after the manner of the psycho-physicists? Should we put to the test all of his psychological processes? A slight reflection has shown us that this would indeed be wasted time.

It seems to us that in intelligence there is a fundamental faculty, the alteration or the lack of which is of the utmost importance for practical life. This faculty is judgment, otherwise called good sense, practical sense, initiative, the faculty of adapting one's self to circumstances. To judge well, to comprehend well, to reason well, these are the essential activities of intelligence. A person may be a moron or an imbecile if he is lacking in judgment; but with good judgment he can never be either. Indeed the rest of the intellectual faculties seem of little importance in comparison with judgment. What does it matter, for example, whether the organs of sense function normally? Of what import that certain ones are hyperesthetic, or that others are anesthetic or are weakened? Laura Bridgman, Helen Keller, and their fellow-unfortunates were blind as well as deaf, but this did not prevent them from being very intelligent. Certainly this is demonstrative proof that the total or even partial integrity of the senses does not form a mental factor equal to judgment. We may measure the acuteness of the sensibility of subjects; nothing could be easier. But we should do this, not so much to find out the state of their sensibility, as to learn the exactitude of their judgment.

The same remark holds good for the study of the memory. At first glance, memory being a psychological phenomenon of capital importance, one would be tempted to give it a very conspicuous part in an examination of intelligence. But memory is distinct from and independent of judgment. One may have good sense and lack memory. The reverse is also common. Just at the present time we are observing a backward girl who is developing before our astonished eyes a memory very much greater than our own. We have measured that memory and we are not deceived regarding it. Nevertheless that girl presents a most beautifully classic type of imbecility.

As a result of all this investigation, in the scale which we present we accord the first place to judgment; that which is of importance to us is not certain errors which the subject commits, but absurd errors, which prove that he lacks judgment. We have even made special provision to encourage people to make absurd replies. In spite of the accuracy of this directing idea, it will be easily understood that it has been impossible to permit of its regulating exclusively our examinations. For example, one can not make tests of judgment on children of less than two years when one begins to watch their first gleams of intelligence. Much is gained when one can discern in them traces of coördination, the first delineation of attention and memory. We shall therefore bring out in our lists some tests of memory; but so far as we are able, we shall give these tests such a turn as to invite the subject to make absurd replies, and thus under cover of a test of memory, we shall have an appreciation of their judgment.

Measuring Scale of Intelligence

General Recommendations

The examination should take place in a quiet room, quite isolated, and the child should be called in alone without other children. It is important that when a child sees the experimenter for the first time, he should be reassured by the presence of someone he knows, a relative, an attendant, or a school superintendent. The witness should be instructed to remain passive and mute, and not to intervene in the examination either by word or gesture.

The experimenter should receive each child with a friendly familiarity to dispel the timidity of early years. Greet him the moment he enters, shake hands with him and seat him comfortably. If he is intelligent enough to understand certain words, awaken his curiosity, his pride. If he refuses to reply to a test, pass to the next one, or perhaps offer him a piece of candy; if his silence continues, send him away until another time. These are little incidents that frequently occur in an examination of the mental state, because in its last analysis, an examination of this kind is based upon the good will of the subject.

We here give the technique of each question. It will not suffice simply to read what we have written in order to be able to conduct examinations. A good experimenter can be produced only by example and imitation, and nothing equals the lesson gained from the thing itself. Every person who wishes to familiarize himself with our method of examination should come to our school. Theoretical instruction is valuable only when it merges into practical experience. Having made these reservations, let us point out the principal errors likely to be committed by inexperienced persons. There are two: the first consists in recording the gross results without making psychological observations, without noticing such little facts as permit one to give to the gross results their true value. The second error, equally frequent, is that of making suggestions. An inexperienced examiner has no idea of the influence of words; he talks too much, he aids his subject, he puts him on the track, unconscious of the help he is thus giving. He plays the part of pedagogue, when he should remain psychologist. Thus his examination is vitiated. It is a difficult art to be able to encourage a subject, to hold his attention, to make him do his best without giving aid in any form by an unskilled suggestion.

[The authors then give detailed instructions for administering and scoring each of the 30 tests—Ed.]

The following article describes the 1908 Binet-Simon scale, which represented the principal revision prepared by the original authors. Besides increasing the number of tests, in this revision Binet and Simon grouped the tests into year levels. It was in this scale that "mental age" was first employed as a means of expressing a child's test performance. It should be noted, however, that the scatter of successes and failures over several year levels, which Binet and Simon found to be so rare, is actually quite common and is now taken into consideration in computing mental age.

Alfred Binet and Theophile Simon

The Development of Intelligence in the Child*

This measurement is taken by means of a series of tests, the gradation of which constitutes what we call a "Measuring Scale of Intelligence." It is important, above all, to set forth these tests with sufficient precision to enable any one to repeat them correctly who will take the trouble to assimilate them. . . .

Always begin with the tests that fit the child's age. If one gives him too difficult work at first he is discouraged. If, on the contrary, it is too easy it arouses his contempt, and he asks himself if he is not being made fun of, and so makes no effort. We have seen manifestations of this misplaced self-esteem. . . .

*A. Binet and Th. Simon. The development of intelligence in the child. *Année psychol.*, 1908, 14, 1–90. (Translated by Elizabeth S. Kite and published in 1916 by Williams and Wilkins Co., Baltimore, under the auspices of The Training School at Vineland, N. J., in a book entitled *The development of intelligence in children.* Pp. 184, 236–239, 250–252, 272–273.) Reprinted through the courtesy of The Training School at Vineland, New Jersey.

Classification of the Tests according to Age

We here give the series of tests ranged according to the ages at which the majority of children succeed in them. This constitutes our measuring scale of intelligence. Those who adopt our method will very often need to refer to it.

Three years
Show eyes, nose, mouth.
Name objects in a picture.
Repeat 2 figures.
Repeat a sentence of 6 syllables.
Give last name.

Four years
Give sex.
Name key, knife, penny.
Repeat 3 figures.
Compare 2 lines.

Five years
Compare 2 boxes of different weights.
Copy a square.
Repeat a sentence of 10 syllables.
Count 4 sous.
Put together two pieces in a "game of patience."

Six years
Repeat a sentence of 16 syllables.
Compare two figures from an esthetic point of view.
Define by use only, some simple objects.
Execute 3 simultaneous commissions.
Give one's age.
Distinguish morning and evening.

Seven years
Indicate omissions in drawings.
Give the number of fingers.
Copy a written sentence.
Copy a triangle and a diamond.
Repeat 5 figures.
Describe a picture.
Count 13 single sous.
Name 4 pieces of money.

Eight years
Read selection and retain two memories.
Count 9 sous. (3 single and 3 double).
Name four colors.
Count backward from 20-0.
Compare 2 objects from memory.
Write from dictation.

Nine years
Give the date complete (day, month, day of the month, year).
Name the days of the week.
Give definitions superior to use.
Retain 6 memories after reading.
Make change, 4 sous from 20 sous.
Arrange 5 weights in order.

Ten years
Name the months.
Name 9 pieces of money.
Place 3 words in 2 sentences.
Answer 3 comprehension questions.
Answer 5 comprehension questions.

Eleven years
Criticize sentence containing absurdities.
Place 3 words in 1 sentence.
Find more than 60 words in 3 minutes.
Give abstract definitions.
Place disarranged words in order.

Twelve years	*Thirteen years*
Repeat 7 figures.	Paper cutting.
Find 3 rhymes.	Reversed triangle.
Repeat a sentence of 26 syllables.	Give differences of meaning.
Interpret pictures.	
Problems of facts.	

— — —

First of all, it will be noticed that our tests are well arranged in a real order of increasing difficulty. It is as the
result of many trials that we have established this order; we
have by no means imagined that which we present. If we
had left the field clear to our conjectures, we should certainly
not have admitted that it required the space of time comprised between four and seven years for a child to learn to
repeat 5 figures in place of 3. Likewise we should never have
believed that it is only at ten years that the majority of
children are able to repeat the names of the months in
correct order without forgetting any; or that it is only at ten
years that a child recognizes all the pieces of our money.

In order to make perfectly clear the real hierarchy of our
tests, we have made a very simple calculation and one easy
to explain. We have already said that when a child passed all
but one of the tests of a certain age, he has the intellectual
level of that age. Let us see if it happens that, according to
this rule, a child may lack the level of a given age but
at the same time reach that of a higher age. If such a case
presented itself, it would be an argument against the hierarchy that we have admitted. Let us suppose that such a case
could present itself; the independence of the intellectual
faculties is great enough to explain this. But is such a case
often presented? Out of 70 children whose replies we have
examined from this point of view, the hierarchical depre-
ciation mentioned has not presented itself a single time. Let
us conclude that it must therefore be very rare. Let us also
conclude that this forms a first experimental confirmation
of the order we have established in our tests.

We have a second means of learning if our measuring scale of intelligence is gauged accurately. This means consists in trying out a large number of children of all ages and seeing if on the average they pass the intellectual tests of their age. . . . We have studied 203 children individually, each of whom was examined during a period lasting a half hour at the least. . . . [Of these], 103 pupils are at age, have exactly the mental level that we attribute to their age; 44 are advanced; 56 are retarded. We have here a confirmation, which is greater even than we had supposed *a priori*. In fact we should not have thought that so large a proportion of children of normal intelligence could exist, that is to say, having the intelligence of their age, and that those advanced or retarded should form such a small minority. . . .

These examples to which we could add many others show that the methods of measuring the individual intelligence have not a speculative interest alone; by the direction, by the organization of all the investigations, psychology has furnished the proof (we do not say for the first time but in a more positive manner than ever before), that it is in a fair way to become a science of great social utility.

3

Nature of Intelligence:

Pioneer Research

In a classic paper published in 1904, the British psychologist Charles Spearman reported the first attempt to investigate the structure of intelligence by empirical, quantitative methods. The rudimentary statistical techniques described in this article underwent considerable revision during the next two decades and eventually led to the development of modern factor analysis. Spearman took issue with the conclusions of early mental testers, who obtained low and negligible correlations between laboratory tests and practical estimates of intelligence. He attributed their negative findings to unreliability of measuring instruments, sampling errors, and other methodological deficiencies.

In his own research, Spearman began with an analysis of correlations among tests of sensory discrimination (pitch, brightness, weight) and estimates of intelligence derived from school grades and ratings by teachers and classmates. By applying the formula for the correction of correlation coefficients for attenuation,[1] which he had himself

[1] The formula is: $r'_{pq} = \dfrac{r_{pq}}{\sqrt{r_{pp}r_{qq}}}$, in which

r'_{pq} = estimated correlation between common elements in sensory and intellective measures (found by Spearman to be close to 1.00).

r_{pq} = mean of correlations between each sensory and each intellective measure.

r_{pp} = mean of intercorrelations among sensory tests.

r_{qq} = mean of intercorrelations among intellective measures.

devised, Spearman demonstrated an almost perfect correlation between the common element in the sensory tests and the common element in the intellectual measures. This finding led him to suggest that all correlations among mental functions may be the result of a single intellective factor, which later came to be known as the **g** (general) factor. Spearman further argued that, if this hypothesis is correct, it should be possible to arrange the intercorrelations among a set of variables into a consistent hierarchy. In other words, if the variables are arranged in decreasing order on the basis of their saturation with the general factor, the correlations of each variable with all the others will decrease in the same order. This hierarchical arrangement of a correlation table represents the first statistical test of Spearman's theory of the unity of intelligence.

Charles Spearman

"General Intelligence," Objectively Determined and Measured*

The present article . . . advocates a "Correlational Psychology," for the purpose of positively determining all psychical tendencies, and in particular those which connect together the so-called "mental tests" with psychical activities of greater generality and interest. These will usually belong to that important class of tendencies produced by community of organism, whereby sufficiently similar acts are almost always performed by any one person in much the

*C. Spearman. "General intelligence," objectively determined and measured. *Amer. J. Psychol.*, 1904, **15**, 201–292. (Pp. 205–206; 219–220; 224–225; 274–277.)

same manner; if, for example, he once proves good at dis-
criminating two musical tones, he may be expected to manifest this talent on any subsequent occasion, and even in
another portion of the scale.

For finding out the classes and limits of these individual
functions, modern psychology seems to have mainly con-
tented itself with borrowing statements from the discredited
"faculties" of the older school, and then correcting and ex-
panding such data by inward illumination. The following
work is an attempt at the more fatiguing procedure of
eliciting verifiable facts; the good intention and the difficulty
of such an enterprise may, perhaps, be allowed to palliate
the short-comings in its execution. Our particular topic will
be that cardinal function which we can provisionally term
"General Intelligence"; first, there will be an inquiry into its
exact relation to the Sensory Discrimination of which we
hear so much in laboratory work; and then—by the aid of
information thus coming to light—it is hoped to determine
this Intelligence in a definite objective manner, and to discover means of precisely measuring it. . . .

After surveying relevant published studies, Spearman comments:

Here, then, is a strange enough answer to our question.
When Laboratory and Life, the Token and the Betokened,
are at last objectively and positively compared as regards
one of the most important Functional Uniformities, they
would seem to present no correspondence whatever with
one another. Either we must conclude that there is no such a
thing as general intelligence, but only a number of mental
activities perfectly independent of one another except for
this common word to designate them, or else our scientific
"tests" would appear to have been all so unhappily invented
as to lie outside the widest limits of those very faculties of
which they are supposed to form a concentrated essence. . . .

An analysis of the methodological deficiencies of these studies, however, leads Spearman to the following conclusion:

Under all these circumstances, in spite of the many previous inconclusive and negatory verdicts, the question of correspondence between the Tests of the Laboratory and the Intelligence of Life cannot yet be regarded as definitely closed. The only thing so far demonstrated is that the old means of investigation are entirely inadequate. The present undertaking, therefore, has only ventured once more to approach the problem, because believing to have elaborated a new and reasonably complete methodological procedure, such as appears capable of at last bringing light upon this and innumerable other important regions hitherto inexplorable. . . .

Following his presentation of the nearly perfect correlations he found between the common elements in the sensory and in the intellective functions, Spearman goes on to outline his hierarchical criterion.

The Theorem of Intellective Unity leads us to consider a corollary proceeding from it logically, testing it critically, and at once indicating some of its important practical uses. This corollary may be termed that of the Hierarchy of the Specific Intelligences.

For if we consider the correspondence between the four branches of school study, a very remarkable uniformity may be observed. English and French, for instance, agree with one another in having a higher correlation with Classics than with Mathematics. Quite similarly, French and Mathematics agree in both having a higher correlation with Classics than with English. And the same will be found to be the case when any other pair is compared with the remainder. The whole thus forms a *perfectly constant Hierarchy* in the following order: Classics, French, English, and Mathematics. This unbroken regularity becomes especially astonishing when we regard the minuteness of the variations involved, for the four branches have average correlations of .77, .72, .70, and .67, respectively.

When in the same experimental series we turn to the Discrimination of Pitch, we find its correlations to be of slightly less magnitude (raw) but in precisely the same relative rank, being: .66 with Classics, .65 with French, .54 with English, and .45 with Mathematics. Even in the crude correlations furnished by the whole school without excluding the non-musicians, exactly the same order is repeated, though with the general diminution caused by the impurity: Classics .60, French .56, English .45, and Mathematics .39.

Just the same principle governs even Musical Talent, a faculty that is usually set up on a pedestal entirely apart. For it is not only correlated with all the other functions, but once again in precisely the same order: with Classics .63, with French .57, with English .51, with Mathematics .51, and with Discrimination .40. Ability for music corresponds substantially with Discrimination of tones, but nevertheless not so much as it does with algebra, irregular verbs, etc.

The actual degree of uniformity in this Hierarchy can be most conveniently and summarily judged from the following table of correlation; the values given are those actually observed (theoretical correction would modify the relative order, but in no degree affect the amount of Hierarchy or otherwise). Each number shows the correlation between the faculty vertically above and that horizontally to the left; except in the oblique line italicized, the value always becomes smaller as the eye travels either to the right or downwards.

	Classics	French	English	Mathem.	Discrim.	Music
Classics	.87	.83	.78	.70	.66	.63
French	.83	.84	.67	.67	.65	.57
English	.78	.67	.89	.64	.54	.51
Mathematics	.70	.67	.64	.88	.45	.51
Discrimination	.66	.65	.54	.45	*	.40
Music	.63	.57	.51	.51	.40	*

* No reliability coefficient available—Ed.

Altogether, we have a uniformity that is very nearly perfect and far surpasses the conceivable limits of chance coincidence. When we consider that the probable error varies between about .01 for the ordinary studies to about .03 for music, it is only surprising that the deviations are not greater. The general Hierarchy becomes even more striking when compared with the oblique line, which is no measure of the central Function and where consequently the gradation abruptly and entirely vanishes. . . .

In the above Hierarchy one of the most noticeable features is the high position of languages; to myself, at any rate, it was no small surprise to find Classics and even French placed unequivocally above English (note that this term does not refer to any study of the native tongue, but merely to the aggregate of all the lessons conducted therein, such as History, Geography, Dictation, Scripture, and Repetition).

However it may be with these or any other special facts, here would seem to lie the long wanted general rational basis for public examinations. Instead of continuing ineffectively to protest that high marks in Greek syntax are no test as to the capacity of men to command troops or to administer provinces, we shall at last actually determine the precise accuracy of the various means of measuring General Intelligence, and then we shall in an equally positive objective manner ascertain the exact relative importance of this General Intelligence as compared with the other characteristics desirable for the particular post which the candidate is to assume. . . . Thus, it is to be hoped, we shall eventually reach our pedagogical conclusions, not by easy subjective theories, nor by the insignificant range of personal experiences, nor yet by some catchpenny exceptional cases, but rather by an adequately representative array of established facts.

Spearman's theory of intelligence was eventually designated as the Two-Factor theory, since it analyzed all intellectual functions into two classes of factors—a general (g) factor and specific (s) factors. His statistical procedure for testing this theory evolved through several stages, beginning with the original hierarchical criterion. Its final and most widely employed form was that of the "tetrad equation," in which variables were analyzed in sets of four. This "tetrad criterion" was described in 1927 in Spearman's "The Abilities of Man," a book which also provides the fullest discussion of his theory and of the evidence in support of it.

Charles Spearman

The Abilities of Man: Their Nature and Measurement*

Criterion of "Tetrad Differences"

The start of the whole inquiry was a curious observation made in the correlations calculated between the measurements of different abilities (scores for tests, marks for school subjects, or estimates made on general impression). These correlations were noticed to tend towards a peculiar arrangement, which could be expressed in a definite mathematical formula. And the formula thus originally reached has ever since been maintained without any essential change. Only from time to time, for convenience, it has been converted from one form to some other that is mathematically equivalent.

The form recently preferred is given below. In it, as usual, the letter r stands for any correlation, whilst its two sub-

*C. Spearman. *The abilities of man: Their nature and measurement.* New York: Macmillan, 1927. (Pp. 73–77; 197–198; 414.)

scripts indicate the two abilities (tests, school marks, etc.) that are correlated.

$$r_{ap} \times r_{bq} - r_{aq} \times r_{bp} = 0$$

This formula has been termed the *tetrad equation* and the value constituting the left side of it the *tetrad difference*.

An illustration may be afforded by the following imaginary correlations between mental tests (actually observed correlations will be given in abundance later on):

	Opposites	Completion	Memory	Discrimination	Cancellation
Opposites		.80	.60	.30	.30
Completion	.80		.48	.24	.24
Memory	.60	.48		.18	.18
Discrimination	.30	.24	.18		.09
Cancellation	.30	.24	.18	.09	

For instance, let us try the effect of making:

a denote Opposites.
b denote Discrimination.
p denote Completion.
q denote Cancellation.

From the table of correlations above, we see that r_{ap} will mean the correlation between Opposites and Completion, which is .80. Obtaining in a similar fashion the other three correlations needed, the whole tetrad equation becomes

$$.80 \times .09 - .30 \times 24 = 0$$

which is obviously correct. And so will be found any other application whatever of the tetrad equation to this table.

The Two Factors

So far, the business is confined to matters of observation; we simply try out the tetrad equation on any table of actually observed correlations and examine whether it fits.

The next step, however, is not observational, but purely mathematical; we have to ask how, if at all, this equation between the correlations bears upon the individual measurements of the correlated abilities. The answer is that there has been shown to exist a very remarkable bearing indeed. It is to the effect that, whenever the tetrad equation holds throughout any table of correlations, and *only* when it does so, then every individual measurement of every ability (or of any other variable that enters into the table) can be divided into two independent parts which possess the following momentous properties. The one part has been called the "general factor" and denoted by the letter g; it is so named because, although varying freely from individual to individual, it remains the same for any one individual in respect of all the correlated abilities. The second part has been called the "specific factor" and denoted by the letter s. It not only varies from individual to individual, but even for any one individual from each ability to another. The proof of this all-important mathematical theorem has gradually evolved through successive stages of completeness, and may now be regarded as complete.[2]

Although, however, both of these factors occur in every ability, they need not be equally influential in all. On the contrary, the very earliest application of this mathematical theorem to psychological correlations showed that there the g has a much greater relative influence or "weight" in some of the abilities tested than in others. Means were even found of measuring this relative weight. At one extreme lay the talent for classics, where the ratio of the influence of g to that of s was rated to be as much as 15 to 1. At the other extreme was the talent for music, where the ratio was only 1 to 4.

Here at once we have before us the essence of the whole doctrine, the seedling from which all else has sprung. But

[2] The proof was given in the Appendix to *The Abilities of Man*, pp. i–vi. (Ed.)

notice must be taken that this general factor g, like all measurements anywhere, is primarily not any concrete thing but only a value or magnitude. Further, that which this magnitude measures has not been defined by declaring what it is like, but only by pointing out where it can be found.

It consists in just that constituent—whatever it may be—which is common to all the abilities inter-connected by the tetrad equation. This way of indicating what g means is just as definite as when one indicates a card by staking on the back of it without looking at its face.

Such a defining of g by site rather than by nature is just what was meant originally when its determination was said to be only "objective." Eventually, we may or may not find reason to conclude that g measures something that can appropriately be called "intelligence." Such a conclusion, however, would still never be the definition of g, but only a "statement about" it.

Suggested Universality of g

The vital problem, in respect of empirical observation, is as to how far and how regularly our tetrad equation actually holds good. In the original work, an extremely wide generalization was adventured. The suggestion was made that "all branches of intellectual activity have in common one fundamental function (or group of functions), whereas the remaining or specific elements seem in every case to be wholly different from that in all the others." Here, then, lies the justification for attributing so much importance to g, despite its purely formal character. The view is put forward that this g, far from being confined to some small set of abilities whose intercorrelations have actually been measured and drawn up in some particular table, may enter into all abilities whatsoever.

Such a universal law could only be advanced very tenta-

tively. The express caution was added that "it must acquire
a much vaster corroborative basis before we can accept it
even as a general principle and apart from its inevitable
corrections and limitations."

This caution was the more impressive, seeing that the law
not only had such a tremendous scope, but moreover came
into sharp conflict with the most authoritative psychology
then prevailing, the latter being at that time wedded to the
doctrine of independence. . . .

Theorem of Indifference of Indicator

A corollary—more practical than theoretical—to be derived from the universality of g is what may be called the
theorem of the indifference of the indicator. This means
that, for the purpose of indicating the amount of g possessed
by a person, any test will do just as well as any other, provided only that its correlation with g is equally high. With
this proviso, the most ridiculous "stunts" will measure the
self-same g as will the highest exploits of logic or flights of
imagination.

Another consequence of the indifference of the indicator
consists in the significance that should be attached to personal estimates of "intelligence" made by teachers and others.
However unlike may be the kinds of observation from which
these estimates may have been derived, still insofar as they
have a sufficiently broad basis to make the influence of g
dominate over that of the s's, they will tend to measure precisely the same thing.

And here, it should be noticed, we come at last upon the
secret why all the current tests of "general intelligence" show
high correlation with one another, as also with g itself. The
reason lies, not in the theories inspiring these tests (which
theories have been most confused), nor in any uniformity of
construction (for this has often been wildly heterogeneous),

but wholly and solely in the above-shown "indifference of the indicator." Indeed, were it worth while, tests could be constructed which had most grotesque appearance, and yet after all would correlate quite well with all the others.

— — —

So far, we have carefully restricted ourselves to the bare facts that have been definitely ascertained. In particular, we have introduced no hypothesis as to the essential nature of what is measured by g. . . . Indeed, save for some particular and cogent evidence to the contrary, it might even have been some mathematical function of a large number of elements distributed by "chance." And we are under no absolute necessity of going beyond these actually established facts. But for scientific ends, there is much advantage in doing so. For the purpose of building up an intelligible whole, and also for that of inspiring further investigation, there is urgent need of framing—however tentatively and provisionally— some or other explanatory hypothesis.

Now, out of all that have been suggested hitherto, one and only one appears to fit all the facts known at present. This is to regard g as measuring something analogous to an "energy"; that is to say, it is some force capable of being transferred from one mental operation to another different one. Even on the physiological side, there are some grounds for hoping that some such energy will sooner or later be discovered in the nervous system, especially the cerebral cortex.

Even before the publication of "The Abilities of Man," Spearman and his followers recognized the inadequacy of a single general factor to account for all correlation among test scores. More and more research was beginning to reveal "group factors," narrower in scope than g but broader than s factors. Although Spearman and other British psychologists identified a few group factors in their own studies, the intensive investigation of such group factors has been more characteristic of American research. In a book entitled "Crossroads in the Mind of Man" (Stanford University Press, 1928), published only a year after Spearman's book, Truman L. Kelley outlined a method for using tetrad equations to locate group factors and presented evidence for five such factors in addition to a general factor. The five factors, which he identified in samples of seventh grade, third grade, and kindergarten children, were described as verbal, number, memory, spatial, and speed factors.

Spearman's methodology was later replaced by more sophisticated techniques of factor analysis. The most widely used procedure is that developed by L. L. Thurstone at the University of Chicago. First described in a 1931 article,[3] Thurstone's method underwent continuing refinement and extension and was most fully reported in a 1947 book, "Multiple Factor Analysis" (University of Chicago Press). Following the application of these factor-analytic procedures to test scores obtained by samples of college students and of children at different age levels, Thurstone proposed a small set of group factors, which he called "primary mental abilities." These abilities, which show some resemblance to Kelley's group factors, are described in the following excerpts from a 1948 article by Thurstone. In the same article, Thurstone suggests an interpretation of Spearman's **g** as a second-order factor, identified by analyzing the intercorrelations among the previously established group factors.

[3] L. L. Thurstone. Multiple factor analysis. *Psychol. Rev.*, 1931, **38**, 406–427.

Louis Leon Thurstone

*Psychological Implications of Factor Analysis**

Factor analysis originated in an epoch-making paper by
Spearman in 1904. Spearman probably saw important implications in that paper but it seems doubtful whether he could
have realized at that time the superstructure that was to be
built on his first observations on what he called hierarchy.
For a quarter of a century the journals were full of controversy about Spearman's single-factor theory of intelligence. His hypothesis and his uni-dimensional methods
were extended to the n-dimensional case in 1930. In the last
seventeen years, multiple-factor analysis has seen a very fast
development so that even in this short period there have
been published several thousand papers on multiple-factor
theory and experimental results.

Our purpose here is to review some psychological implications of multiple-factor analysis and to make only incidental
reference to the factorial methods as such. It is time that we
take stock more frequently of how the factorial methods are
affecting psychological concepts, and how these in turn affect
the development of appropriate factorial methods. It should
be emphasized that factor analysis is a scientific method
that must be adjusted to each problem. It is not merely a
statistical method, and it is not a routine that can be applied
fruitfully to every correlation table in sight. . . .

* L. L. Thurstone. Psychological implications of factor analysis. *Amer. Psychologist*, 1948, **3**,
402–408. (Pp. 402–404; 406–407.) Reprinted by permission of the American Psychological
Association.

Most of the factorial studies that have been done so far have been concerned with the cognitive domain. Previous work had discovered a number of group factors such as the verbal, the numerical, and the visual. These were more clearly revealed by the more powerful multiple-factor methods. The further breakdown of the cognitive intellective functions into primary factors has revealed that the cognitive field represents a large number of functional unities or factors. We no longer speak of "the" verbal factor as if it were unitary. At least three verbal factors are known and several additional verbal factors are clearly indicated. One of these verbal factors has been denoted V and it represents facility in understanding verbal material. Another verbal factor has been denoted Word Fluency W and it represents facility in finding words to represent restricted context. A third verbal factor F represents ideational fluency with words. There is indication that a naming factor exists which is independent of the three that have been mentioned. In some forms of aphasia we seem to be dealing with patients who have one or more of these verbal factors intact while they are lacking in other verbal factors. Without understanding the differences between the several distinct verbal factors, one is at a loss to understand why the patient can do certain verbal tests while he fails on other verbal tests. This field should be experimentally investigated more intensively in the light of factorial results.

The ability to memorize has been found to be a primary factor that is independent of other cognitive functions. Incidental memory seems to be an ability that is distinct from the ability to memorize intentionally. There is good indication that auditory memory is not the same ability as visual memory.

One of the most important of the primary abilities is that of visualizing space which has been denoted the Space factor S. It is involved in all thinking about solid objects and flat objects in space.

The perceptual functions have been broken down into a number of distinct primary factors. Among the most interesting are those which represent facility in perceptual closure in which there are very large individual differences. Perceptual closure has been found in a battery of visual tests and also in a battery of twenty-eight auditory tests that were specially designed for factorial analysis. It is a curious circumstance that we do not yet know whether the closure factor in visual material is the same as the closure factor in auditory material. In order to solve that problem, it will be necessary to include both visual and auditory tests of closure in the same factorial analysis. It will then be interesting to ascertain whether perceptual closure is a primary factor that transcends the visual and auditory modalities. If so, then closure is a central factor that may be of considerable importance in the human intellect. On the other hand, it may be found that closure is represented by two or more factors that are specific for each modality. . . .

When we consider the increasing number of distinct functional unities into which the field of cognition is being divided, we find that it is necessary to revise very fundamentally our notions about general intelligence. Factorial results make it imperative that we describe each individual in terms of a profile of mental abilities instead of by a single index such as the IQ.

With further progress in this field we shall have a profile for each person with a very large number of columns. It is our present belief that if we knew the twenty most important primary factors we should be able to undertake educational and vocational counseling with more confidence than at present. Even in the present state of knowledge with about ten of these factors identified, we certainly can do much better in appraising the intellective assets of a person than by the older methods by which each person was described in terms of a single IQ.

Factorial work raises interesting questions about the general intellective factor of Spearman. According to his hypothesis, general intelligence is mediated by a central intellective factor which he denoted "g." This hypothesis has been the subject of much controversy in the last forty years. When the multiple-factor methods began to isolate quite a number of primary factors in the cognitive domain, it looked at first as if the Spearman single-factor hypothesis would have to be discarded, but that does not seem to be necessary. It was found that the primary factors of cognition were positively correlated. For adults, most of these correlations are under +.30. When the positive correlations between the primary factors are examined factorially, there appear second-order factors, and the most conspicuous of these second-order factors agrees well with Spearman's hypothesis. Here we have a clue to an interpretation that may unify the early work of Spearman and the later work with multiple-factor analysis. The interpretation that seems plausible at this time is that the primary factors represent different kinds of mental facilities such as several kinds of memory, several kinds of perceptual closure, several visualizing factors, and several verbal factors. These primary abilities may be regarded as media for the expression of intellect and people differ markedly in the effectiveness with which they can express themselves in these different media. The second-order factors may represent parameters that are more central in character and more universal in the sense that they are not determined by the efficiency of each modality or imagery type. The first-order primary factors may be regarded as separate organs, in a general sense, while the second-order or general factors represent parameters which influence the activities of the several organs or primary factors. The general factors may then be expected to have no particular locus whereas some of the primary factors may eventually be rather definitely localized.

This attempt to unify Spearman's work with the later multiple-factor work seems to be plausible in terms of the findings of recent factorial studies but it should not be taken very literally. We can make only a tentative sketch of the underlying order at this early stage of knowledge of the organization of human intellect. If Spearman's general intellective factor is the same as the second-order inductive factor, then we can now determine that general factor uniquely. That is something which Spearman was never able to do. I have spoken of second-order factors in the plural. The reason is that we seldom find a single second-order general factor which would be indicated by Spearman's original hypothesis. Such complications are to be expected with the development of any science and it should not be interpreted as a discredit to Spearman's early work on which all of us have built.

In introducing our speculation about the relation of Spearman's general intellective factor "g" to later multiple-factor studies, we have noted that the primary factors are positively correlated. This also introduces a conflict between our statistical habits and psychological judgment. Some students of factorial theory bring to this subject their statistical habits and they sometimes insist that factors must be uncorrelated in order to be meaningful and useful. This is a curious situation. We deal all the time with meaningful measures that are correlated such as height and weight, but when we turn to the mental abilities, we are told that we must force them to be uncorrelated. Scientific judgment dictates that we report the correlation between primary factors as they are actually found, irrespective of statistical convenience. . . .

Some of the implications of recent factorial work are of educational significance. A factorial study has been made with seventy psychological tests that were given to several hundred five-year-old children. Since most children at that age cannot read, it was necessary to design all of the tests in pictorial form. The results of that study indicated essentially the same primary mental abilities that have been found among high school students and adults. The mental profiles of five-year-old children show the same great variation as adults. The number factor in children of this age seems to be more inductive than in adults so that it can be called quantitative thinking. It seems to be possible to identify the space factor in children even at the age of three or four. For example, if a very young child shows interest in jigsaw puzzles, one can probably make the inference that he is a good visualizer. It certainly is evident that young children are capable of more complex reasoning than we ordinarily give them credit for. As adults, we are so accustomed to the verbal medium that we are likely to misjudge the reasoning powers of young children who have not yet developed adult vocabulary. The frequent early development of quantitative thinking at the kindergarten age makes one question the current practice of delaying instruction in arithmetic until a later age. . . .

Since the primary mental abilities have been isolated as functionally distinct, even at the kindergarten age, one naturally raises the question of differential growth in the primary factors. It is still a question of fact whether children differ markedly in the rate of development of the different primary factors. If there are great individual differences in the primary mental abilities themselves, it would not be surprising to find that there are also individual differences in the rate of growth of the different factors. Besides the possible individual differences in rate of growth, we already know that some factors mature much sooner than others. Perceptual closure seems to mature at the age of nine or ten, so that there are no differences between nine-year-olds and adults in mean performance. The verbal comprehension factor V probably matures more slowly than any of the others. The growth of verbal comprehension is difficult to appraise because the estimation of this factor is more influenced by schooling and experience than some of the other primary factors. Instead of worrying about the constancy of the IQ we shall probably find ourselves worrying about the relative constancy of the profile throughout the life span. . . .

In educational and vocational guidance it has been the practice to find by trial and error those tests which are diagnostic for different curricula and for different occupations. With increasing knowledge of primary abilities it may be expected that job analyses will be made in terms of these abilities. When jobs are so described, the selection tests can be prepared rationally instead of by crudely empirical methods and we shall then predict with confidence that the selection tests will have validity for the jobs. The same reasoning applies to the more complex fields of vocations and professions. We shall then have rational vocational guidance instead of trial and error search for valid tests for each job.

Mental profiles have been determined for over half a million high school children in Chicago and it has been found that all possible combinations occur in the profiles. The records show many hundreds of interesting case histories. A boy who was a poor reader was considered to be a dunce by his teachers. His mental profile showed that he had the highest score on Space and Reasoning, and high scores in all other factors except the verbal factor V. His teachers changed their attitudes when they saw that his handicap was quite specific. An amusing case was a girl who talked herself out of a number of situations involving truancy and misbehavior by fantastic but plausible stories. When her lies were eventually discovered, it was also found that her mental profile was very low in all factors except one, namely, verbal fluency. If the profile had been seen earlier, her teachers would have been warned about the possibilities of such a strange profile. It requires often considerable insight of the examiner to relate the mental profile to the circumstances of each case, but there is no question but that the profile is more helpful than the IQ in the interpretation of educational and behavior problems.

4

Nature of Intelligence:
Later Developments

The widespread application of factor analysis in the 1940's led to a rapid proliferation of factors. In the selection reproduced in Chapter 3, Thurstone referred to about ten major cognitive factors that had been clearly identified to date, and he anticipated that some twenty would ultimately be sufficient for purposes of educational and vocational counseling. The latter number was soon exceeded, however, by the mounting accumulation of factors identified in published studies. In the attempt to introduce order into this growing complexity, some psychologists proposed systematic schemas for the organization of intellectual factors. An arrangement that is widely accepted — particularly among British psychologists — is the hierarchical schema[1] suggested by Cyril Burt. In a comprehensive survey of published research, Burt undertook to fit previously identified factors into this hierarchy. The summary of this rather lengthy article is reproduced below.

[1] Burt's schema is not to be confused with Spearman's hierarchical criterion for demonstrating the operation of a general factor. Spearman's hierarchy refers to correlation coefficients; Burt's refers to factors or traits.

Cyril Burt

The Structure of the Mind: A Review of the Results of Factor Analysis*

In the survey of the results of factor analysis which I attempted some twenty-three years ago, I suggested that there were four main questions which such investigations might hope to answer. (1) First, can the mind be analysed into anything like the list of faculties which the traditional psychology assumed, e.g., the "special aptitudes" of Galton and Binet, and the "group factors" of later writers? (2) If so, what precisely are these faculties or factors, and how does their nature differ from the traditional conception? (3) In particular, are they to be regarded as innate or inheritable tendencies or abilities, and, if not, how far is each the product of innate constitution or environmental and cultural influences? And finally (4) what is the general structure of the mind as thus empirically revealed? To each of these four questions the accumulated results of later research should now enable us to give at least a tentative answer.

1. After an impartial survey of the evidence I have collected in the foregoing pages, there can, I imagine, no longer be any doubt about the existence of group factors. In my survey of 1926, I named eleven such factors on the cognitive side as resting each on at least one sound experimental study,

* C. Burt. The structure of the mind: A review of the results of factor analysis. Brit. J. educ. Psychol., 1949, **19**, 100–111; 176–199. (Pp. 198–199.) Reprinted by permission of the publisher.

and I noted that several appeared to split into further sub-factors. All these factors and sub-factors have since been amply confirmed. At least eighteen can now be cited as established by three or more independent investigators. Five factors—all of them of special importance in educational work, the verbal, the arithmetical, the spatial, the memory, and the speed factors—have been independently corroborated by more than a dozen investigators, British, Colonial, and American, often belonging to quite different schools. Hitherto, in the controversies of the existence of group factors—with the supporters of the old three factor theory on the one side and the adherents of Spearman's two factor theory on the other—the relative merits of either hypothesis have commonly been discussed on purely theoretical or abstract grounds. Those who feel that such arguments have not proved conclusive either one way or the other will, I hope, be convinced by the actual list of concrete factors for which so much empirical evidence now exists.

2. As regards the general structure of the mind, a systematic comparison of the various factors I have described, and of their relations both to each other and to the mental processes into which they enter, throws an unexpected light on this fundamental problem. Spearman's attractive picture of a single fund of cognitive "energy," operating a large number of highly specific cortical "mechanisms," now appears much too simple. Thurstone's theory of "simple structure," which represents the mind as containing a miscellaneous number of primary abilities, collected together with no definite or intelligible relations, begins to look still more inadequate. Both these hypotheses seem out of accord with what is now known of mental activities and of the architecture of the central nervous system or "brain." Taken together, the facts I have just reviewed suggest a far more complex and systematic type of structure; and go far to confirm the notion that the mind is organized on what may be called a hierarchical basis. As we have seen, there is, first a compre-

hensive general factor, covering all cognitive activities; next
a comparatively small number of broad group factors, covering different activities classified according to their form or
content; these in turn sub-divide into narrower group factors;
and the whole series appears to be arranged on successive
levels, the factors on the lowest level being the most specific
and the most numerous of all.

3. The nature of the factors so far established, and their
general classification and arrangement, are in many ways
suggestive of the traditional schemes of mental "powers" or
"faculties." These, it will be remembered, were grouped into
genera and *species,* and assigned to three or four main
intellectual levels. Much the same is true of the factors here
reported. But at least two important distinctions between
"mental factors" and "mental faculties" now seem clear. A
factor is not to be regarded as a simple, isolated, causal en-
tity, much less as an elementary capacity, inherited as such,
and capable of spontaneous maturation, regardless of environmental influence (except perhaps when the environment
is definitely abnormal). A factor is primarily a principle of
classification; it is thus, not so much a concrete cause as an
abstract component. Moreover, unlike "faculties," "primary
abilities," or "unitary traits," the factors discovered by the
more recent methods of analysis prove to be in no way
atomic or indivisible. On the contrary, they tend to split up
into sub-factors, and these sub-factors into narrower factors
still.

4. Probably all the more important broad group factors
have now been approximately identified. But there is still
room for further research on their precise specification and
nature, and still more on the various sub-factors into which
each of them may be sub-divided. However, from the standpoint of the educationist, the most urgent problem, calling for
experimental study, is the influence of heredity, or rather
of genetic constitution. Every measurable ability is the
product of a genetic potentiality interacting with certain

postnatal and environmental conditions. But these two groups of influences, though not capable of actual separation as popular psychology is apt naively to assume, can nevertheless themselves be treated as distinguishable components, and their relative influence determined and measured. Lastly, I should repeat that the list I have here brought forward is by no means final or complete; it is rather to be regarded as a working basis for current practice and a provisional scheme for future research.

In the next selection, another British psychologist, Philip E. Vernon, further discusses the hierarchical schema and elaborates it with special reference to those factors of practical significance in educational and vocational guidance. Vernon's comments also illustrate the emphasis that British psychologists characteristically place upon g, in contrast to the much greater weight attributed to group factors by American psychologists.

Philip Ewart Vernon

The Structure of Human Abilities*

In this country, where most work was done on less selected samples of the population such as Navy and Army conscript recruits, the importance of g was amply confirmed. In eight analyses, g was found to cover more than twice as much variance as all group factors combined. . . . After the removal of g, tests tend to fall into two main groups: the

* P. E. Vernon. *The structure of human abilities.* London: Methuen (New York: Wiley), 1950. (Pp. 22–23, 25–28.) Reprinted by permission of the publisher.

verbal-numerical-educational on the one hand (referred to as *v:ed* factor), and the practical-mechanical-spatial-physical on the other hand (referred to as *k:m* factor). If the analysis is sufficiently detailed, i.e. if sufficient tests are included, these types themselves subdivide. The *v:ed* factor gives minor *v* and *n* (number) group factors. In other analyses *k:m* splits similarly into mechanical information, spatial, and manual subfactors. Thus a first approximation to mental structure is provided by the hierarchical diagram of Fig. 1, resembling a genealogical tree. . . .

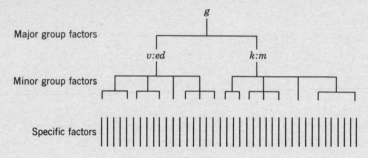

Fɪɢ. 1   Diagram illustrating hierarchical structure of human abilities.

The strict hierarchical picture of mental structure is an over-simplification. For the results of any factor analysis depend largely on the composition of the population tested (e.g. its degree of selection), and on the number and kind of tests studied. Since by choosing suitable tests almost any specific factor can be turned into a group factor, it is suggested that only those group factors shown to have significant practical value in daily life are worth incorporating in the picture. . . . A diagram such as Fig. 1 would be obtained only if an extensive battery of tests, covering—or at least sampling —most of the varieties of human abilities, could be applied to a very large and representative sample of the population. With one or two hundred testees the correlations are usually too unreliable for more than two-to-four group factors to be established at a time. In general a minimum of three tests is needed to define a factor, hence only a few factors can be resolved in any one investigation with a limited battery of tests. Further, if such a battery consists only, or predominantly, of a specialized type of test (e.g. all tests of sensory-motor abilities), the g and major group factors may fail to reveal themselves. The diagram is, in other words, a hypothetical integration of all the factorial investigations that have been carried out, rather than an established fact. . . .

An important problem, as yet unsolved, is how broad a group factor should be before it is accepted as a useful element in our picture of mental structure. Some of the primary factors of Thurstone, Guilford, and others—rote memory, for example—are so narrow in content that it may be more harmful than helpful to name them. It is unlikely that the rote memory tests which make up Thurstone's M factor have any predictive value for the rote memory in which teachers are interested. Only if it were possible to establish a common factor (over and above g and v:ed) in rote memory tests and in the learning of spellings, multiplication tables, and poetry would the notion of a rote memory group factor be acceptable. The same structure holds for most of the manual dexterity, sensory-motor, and coordination factors that have so far been proposed. At the present moment the writer cannot think of any objective basis for distinguishing between acceptable group factors, and narrow factors confined to the highly specialized types of test which psychologists delight in constructing. But he would suggest that factors which fail to contribute at least 5 per cent to the variance of some measure of educational or occupational proficiency or other capacity in daily life should be relegated to the latter category. . . .

The hierarchical group-factor viewpoint implies that most of the variance of human abilities in daily life is attributable to g and to highly specific (or very small group) factors, and that the role of the broader group factors is rather meagre. If our diagram could be worked out completely to cover all human abilities, the g-variance might amount to about 40 per cent, the major and minor group factors to some 10 per cent each, and the remaining 40 per cent would consist of very narrow group factors and unreliability. This means that fairly good predictions of ability in education, industry, or everyday life can be achieved by g tests alone, and that somewhat more ground can be covered by tests of the main group factors. But only by much more detailed experimentation on tests relevant to particular jobs, or by work-sample methods (i.e. trying candidates out on the actual work), can much more than 50 per cent accuracy be obtained. This explains why Stanford-Binet or Terman-Merrill IQ, or all-round intelligence as measured by reliable group tests, have considerable practical value both among children and adults, whereas more specialized tests add something but not very much in educational and vocational guidance.

Comparison of trait relationships found among subjects differing in age, education, occupation, and other personal characteristics has suggested hypotheses regarding the origins and development of psychological traits. As early as 1919, for example, Cyril Burt presented evidence for the increasing differentiation of intellectual ability with age. This hypothesis was strongly supported in a series of studies conducted at Columbia University between 1930 and 1945, under the direction of Henry E. Garrett. The results of these studies are brought together in the following article by Garrett, who proposes a developmental approach to the nature of intelligence.

Henry Edward Garrett

A Developmental Theory of Intelligence*

It is the thesis of this paper that intelligence . . . changes in its organization with increasing maturity. In 1938 I proposed a differentiation hypothesis[2] with respect to the growth of intelligence which I shall now present in greater detail. My hypothesis runs as follows: Abstract or symbol intelligence changes in its organization as age increases from a fairly unified and general ability to a loosely organized group of abilities or factors. If this hypothesis is true, the measurement of intelligence must perforce change in its methods and objectives with increase in age.

Over a period of ten years and more, we conducted at Columbia University a long-range program designed to test out the differentiation hypothesis. Our work has dealt for the most part with children of school age, as symbol intelligence is obviously not readily measurable until the child can use language with some facility. In the remainder of this paper I shall cite our own and other relevant data in support of the differentiation hypothesis. I shall then try to present the implications of this formulation for mental measurement generally.

* H. E. Garrett. A developmental theory of intelligence. Amer. Psychologist, 1946, 1, 372–378. (Pp. 373–377.) Reprinted by permission of the author and the American Psychological Association.

[2] H. E. Garrett. Differentiable mental traits. Psychol. Rec., 1938, 2, 259–298.

Evidence for the Differentiation Hypothesis

In a general way, our method has been (1) to analyze tables of intercorrelations for the presence of ability-clusters or factors, and (2) to study the changing relationship of such factors, i.e., their organization, with age. I shall first consider the results of four investigations carried out upon subjects differing fairly widely in age.

In a study of mental organization among school children, Schiller[3] administered 12 tests to 189 third and fourth grade boys, averaging nine years of age. Four of these tests were classified as verbal, three as numerical, and five as spatial-non-language. Evidence for the existence of ability-clusters described, respectively, as verbal, numerical, and spatial, appeared clearly in the correlation tables. There was, however, considerable overlap as between categories. The average correlation between the verbal and number tests, for example, was .63; between the verbal and spatial tests, .33, and between the number and spatial tests, .41. When the 12 test vectors were rotated into a three-dimensional space by the centroid method of factor analysis, there was a clear separation of the verbal, number, and spatial test groupings. Since the reference axes were oblique, the three primary factors were of necessity correlated. Vectors through the verbal and number test clusters were close together so that correlation of the verbal and number factors was quite high (.83). The correlations of the verbal and spatial factors, and of the number and spatial factors, were much lower (.27 and .30, respectively). From these results it seemed clear that at the nine-year level, verbal and numerical tests taken together constitute a homogenous general factor which is fairly independent of the abilities employed in the spatial

[3] Belle Schiller. Verbal, numerical, and spatial abilities of young children. *Arch. Psychol.*, 1934, No. 161.

tests. The high correlation of verbal and number abilities for nine-year-old boys is in interesting contrast to the r of .26 between the verbal and number factors found by Schneck[4] at the college level. Schneck's nine tests, five verbal and four numerical, were administered to 210 college men, 18 to 21 years old.

The same decrease in intercorrelation within a test battery as we go from children to adults is found in the work of Bryan[5] and Anastasi.[6] Bryan administered 11 tests of immediate memory to 100 five-year-old boys. The tests made use of pictures, objects, forms, colors, and blocks. All were given individually. For our purposes, the most significant finding is that these memory tests were as closely related to vocabulary (i.e., verbal ability) as they were to each other—indicating a considerable degree of homogeneity in the abilities utilized by these young children in dealing with symbols. In contrast, Anastasi's study of memory with adult subjects reports the correlation of the verbal factor with memory to be —.085; of the number factor with memory, .00. Anastasi administered four tests of memory, as well as two verbal and two number tests, to 140 college women, 16 to 28 years old. Anastasi also verified the low correlation for adults between verbal and number abilities found by Schneck, her correlation between these factors being .24.

These four studies agree in showing that for children, at least, skills in verbal and numerical tasks possess greater homogeneity than they do for adults. Other investigations have obtained essentially the same results. In Thorndike's CAVD,[7] for example, the correlation of level V (vocabulary)

[4] M. R. Schneck. The measurement of verbal and numerical abilities. *Arch. Psychol.*, 1929, No. 107.
[5] Alice I. Bryan. Organization of memory in young children. *Arch. Psychol.*, 1934, No. 162.
[6] Anne Anastasi. Further studies on the memory factor. *Arch. Psychol.*, 1932, No. 142.
[7] E. L. Thorndike. *The measurement of intelligence*. New York: Teachers College, Columbia University, Bureau of Publications, 1926. (P. 429.)

and level A (arithmetic) for 126 fifth grade children was .52, while the correlation between level V (vocabulary) and level A (arithmetic) for 100 college students was .23. In the same two groups the correlations between levels C (completion) and A (arithmetic) were .64 and .23, respectively. I have verified these correlations among the parts of the Thorndike CAVD examination in a group of 313 college freshman women.[8] The correlation of levels A and V in this adult group was .21, of levels C and A also .21. The Thurstones have carried out two extensive investigations of ability organization at different ages. In one study[9] 60 tests involving words, numbers, spatial problems, diagrams, dot patterns, pictures, and mazes were administered to 1154 eighth grade children. By means of the centroid method of factor analysis, ten factors (later reduced to six primaries) were extracted from the correlational matrix. These factors were called, respectively, N (number), W (word fluency), V (verbal), S (spatial), M (memory), and I (induction or reasoning). Our present interest lies in the correlations found among the six primary factors. Some correlation was to be expected among these factors since oblique transformations were used in rotating the test vectors. From the table of interfactor correlations a general factor emerged, called by the Thurstones "a second-order general factor," and identified by them as probably equivalent to Spearman's "g." This general factor was most highly correlated with the verbal and word fluency factors (.715 and .615) suggesting that it is intrinsically "linguistic." In a further study on a smaller sample of 438 children in which 21 tests selected from the original 60 were employed, the same second-order general factor again strongly emerged. Its correlations with the verbal and word fluency factors (.676 and .686) offer confirmatory evidence

[8] H. E. Garrett. A study of the CAVD intelligence examination. *J. educ. Res.*, 1930, **21**, 103–108.
[9] L. L. Thurstone and Thelma G. Thurstone. Factorial studies of intelligence. *Psychometr. Monogr.*, 1941, No. 2.

as to its linguistic and abstract nature and substantiate the first finding. The highest r in the second study was that between the general factor and induction or reasoning (namely, .843), the tests of which category demand the ability to understand and manipulate verbal symbols.

In an earlier study[10] of an older group, Thurstone administered 56 tests to 240 student volunteers, ranging in age from 16 to 25. The intercorrelations among the primary factors found in this study were quite negligible, the median of 72 r's being .03 and the largest r .24. It should be noted that the intercorrelations of these 56 tests gave almost the same factorial matrix whether the transformations were oblique or orthogonal. It thus appears that the primary factors extracted are essentially independent and that no second-order general factor was present. As stated above, in the study of eighth grade children transformations were oblique rather than orthogonal. While the use of oblique reference axes makes correlation among the primary abilities inevitable, the fact that oblique transformations gave the clearest result (closest approximation to simple structure) suggests that the second-order general factor is not an artifact introduced by the method.

To sum up, it seems clear that when we compare the extent of generality in tables of correlations obtained from subjects well separated in age, greater differentiation appears at the upper age levels. Criticism may be made of this finding on the grounds that the tests employed at successive age levels were not identical (though they involve the same materials) and that sampling differences may account for some or all of the difference found. Again, it may be argued that the use of oblique rather than orthogonal transformations allows the *method* rather than the data to determine the final result.

To meet these objections a second approach to the prob-

[10] L. L. Thurstone. Primary mental abilities. *Psychometr. Monogr.*, 1938, No. 1.

78 Individual Differences

lem of changing mental organization with age can be made which will at least in part overcome these difficulties. This method is to compute intercorrelations of the same set of tests at successive age levels and note the change in correlations if such is present. Care must be exercised, of course, to have the subjects at different age levels comparable, and tests must have sufficient range to prevent skewness in the younger or older age groups.

Several comparative studies of this sort were included in our program. In 1935, Garrett, Bryan, and Perl[11] administered ten carefully selected tests designed to measure memory, verbal, and number abilities, to groups of public school boys and girls at three age levels. In all, 646 children were examined, 225 at age 9, 196 at age 12, and 225 at age 15. Considerable effort was made to obtain comparable samples; precautions taken to this end are given in detail in the monograph (pp. 16–18). With one exception, the intercorrelations among the memory, verbal, and number tests showed a regular tendency to decrease with age from 9 to 12 and from 12 to 15. The average intercorrelation at ages 9, 12, and 15 were, for boys, .30, .21 and .18; for girls, .27, .30, and .10. A multiple factor analysis of the correlations at each age level—boys and girls kept separate—substantiated (as was to be expected) the correlational evidence. The proportion of variance accounted for by the first unrotated factor (roughly equivalent to "g") at ages 9, 12, and 15 was, for boys, .31, .32, and .12; for girls, .31, .24, .19. This regular fall in the trend of relationship with age was verified by Asch[12] who retested 161 of Schiller's subjects (originally tested at age 9) after a period of three years. From age 9 to 12 the average correlation for boys dropped from .56 to .41, for girls from .59 to .51; the correlation of the verbal and numerical tests

---

[11] H. E. Garrett, Alice I. Bryan, and Ruth Perl. The age factor in mental organization. *Arch Psychol.*, 1935, No. 176.
[12] S. Asch. A study of change in mental organization. *Arch. Psychol.*, 1936, No. 195.

dropped from .57 to .36 (boys) and from .64 to .49 (girls). Again we note a loss in generality with increasing maturity.

Two recent studies made upon different groups and with different tests substantiate further this general finding. In 1944 Clark[13] administered the Chicago Tests of Primary Mental Abilities to 320 boys, roughly 100 each at ages 11, 13, and 15. Subjects were drawn from the public schools and were from the same social and economic levels. Scores in each of six primary factors, V, N, S, W, M, and R, when correlated at each age level, showed a regular tendency to drop with age. Average factor correlations (excluding M which was very unreliable) were as follows at ages 11, 13, and 15: N and the battery, .55, .44, and .43; V and the battery, .62, .55, and .49; S and the battery, .48, .47, and .35. These results confirm the existence of the second-order general factor found by the Thurstones, and show, moreover, that it gradually weakens with age. Reichard[14] has in part verified Clark's findings, though the evidence from her work is not entirely clear. Reichard administered eight tests designed to measure verbal, numerical, and spatial abilities of 542 subjects, 280 girls and 262 boys, in public schools of suburban New York. Three age levels, 9, 12, and 15, were represented. Intercorrelations dropped sharply from age 12 to age 15 (.43 to .38 for the boys and .51 to .37 for the girls), but rose from age 9 to age 12—for both boys and girls. A reasonable explanation of this reversal seems to lie in the content of the tests which favored the nine year old group. This group, too, was probably somewhat superior to average nine year olds in performance level.

From these various studies I believe we can predict a steady drop in correlation among tests involving verbal, numerical, and spatial concepts from about age 8 to age 18.

13 Mamie P. Clark. Changes in primary mental abilities with age. *Arch. Psychol.,* 1944, No. 291.
14 Suzanne Reichard. Mental organization and age level. *Arch. Psychol.,* 1944, No. 295.

With increasing age there appears to be a gradual break-down of an amorphous general ability into a group of fairly distinct aptitudes. It seems highly probable that maturation has much to do with this differentiating process, but increasing experience and diverging interests must also contribute heavily. . . .

Implication of the Differentiation Hypothesis for Theory and Practice

Implications for Theory

The differentiation hypothesis has implications of a theoretical as well as of a practical nature. On the theoretical side, it seems to effect a rapprochement between the Spearman General Factor and the Group Factor theories. Over the elementary school years we find a functional generality among tests at the symbol level. Later on this general factor or "g" breaks down into the quasi-independent factors reported by many investigators.

It seems likely that the "g" factor which appears strongly at the elementary school level is, in large part, verbal or linguistic in nature. If the school child can read well, he can very probably do the rest of his school work well. Solving arithmetic problems is contingent upon ability to read and understand directions; hence a fifth grade child high in verbal facility may do as well in arithmetic as a child of much greater native aptitude for numbers. This notion is not entirely speculative. Thurstone found that in the seventh and eighth grades his second-order general factor entered with greatest weight into the reading and composition tests. Kelley[15] reports the general factor to be stronger in power tests of reading and arithmetic for third than for seventh

15 T. L. Kelley. *Crossroads in the mind of man.* Stanford, Calif.: Stanford University Press, 1928. (Chs. 5 and 6.)

grade children. In the group of 126 fifth grade children men tioned above, the general factor in the CAVD had the following correlations with the four parts of the examination: with Completion, .90; with Arithmetic, .70; with Vocabulary, .86; and with Directions, .88. It is evident that the general factor at this age level is quite strong and is largely verbal. The "g" factor in CAVD for 313 freshman women had correlations of .70 with Completion, .45 with Arithmetic, .74 with Vocabulary, and .76 with Directions. Although still verbal, the general factor is considerably weaker at this age level and is much less highly related to arithmetic. The conclusion which I draw from these data is that the overall ability ("g") which looms large during the elementary school years becomes progressively less important at the high school and college level, where factor studies have shown it to be negligible or quite small. . . .

Implications for Practice

The differentiation hypothesis has definite practical implication for the interpretation of intelligence test scores over a wide age range. The best individual tests of abstract intelligence (e.g., the Stanford-Binet) are most useful over the age range from 6 to 15 years. To know that a boy of 10 has a Stanford-Binet MA of 12 and an IQ of 120 is to have valid and useful information. From his MA and IQ we can predict how well this boy will do in school and how well he might do (if not seriously handicapped in other ways) in occupations requiring the comprehension and use of symbols in the solution of problems. I do not think that at the elementary school level we should attempt, except very tentatively, to fractionate the IQ into, say, language ability, number ability, reasoning, and the like. The test items which might reasonably be classified under each of these heads are too few to permit a definitive judgment as to specific abilities. This does not mean, of course, that for a given child one should not look for sharp deviations in performance upon significant items, or that one should not take note of the child's distinctive strengths and weaknesses with the test situations. But we should always remember that the total score on an individual intelligence test is a better measure of general ability than part scores on the same test can possibly be measures of more specific functions. . . .

At the high school and college levels, abstract intelligence breaks down, as we have seen, into a number of relatively independent factors. It would seem to be theoretically more defensible, therefore, and practically more useful, to measure verbal, numerical, perceptual, or spatial ability, and perhaps other factors at these ages, than to give the subject a single over-all score. Perhaps some may wonder why, if this is true, total scores and not part scores were computed for the Army General Classification Test. I believe that the use of total scores for the AGCT was justified by reason of the wide range in schooling (and presumably in abstract intelligence) reported by the 8,000,000 or so men who took this test. In large samples, correlations among the three parts of the AGCT were quite high, indicating substantial homogeneity within this examination. This probably resulted from the fact that many soldiers were undoubtedly closer to the elementary school child than to the superior adult in the facility with which they handled abstract test material. Correlations among the three parts of the AGCT would almost certainly be lower if computed separately for high school and college graduates.

Factor scores have been shown to be useful predictors of college achievement in science, literature, and other fields.[16] For highly selected students the part scores shown on the profile of such a test as the Graduate Record Examination are more useful in guidance than is a single omnibus score. In the case of adults tests designed to measure aptitude for

[16] I. Chein. An empirical study of verbal, numerical, and spatial factors in mental organization. *Psychol. Rec.*, 1939, **3**, 71–94.

special kinds of work are to be preferred to blanket measures of general ability. Profiles are useful as one means of presenting the structural patterns which part scores exhibit. Such typology is at first primarily utilitarian—a useful scheme of classification—though it is to be hoped that more fundamental relations may eventually be revealed.

Several investigations conducted after Garrett's 1946 paper reported contradictory results, which called the differentiation hypothesis into question. A detailed examination of these studies, however, led Burt to the conclusion that their contradictory findings arose from improper choice of subjects, tests, or statistical techniques of factor analysis, as well as from other methodological weaknesses. In a 1954 article, Burt reaffirmed his original differentiation hypothesis in the light of all the evidence then available. Both Burt and Garrett attribute the differentiation of abilities chiefly to maturation. It should be noted, however, that the results can be explained equally well in terms of education, since the older groups in these studies had received more education than the younger.

Cyril Burt

The Differentiation of Intellectual Ability*

In some of the earlier surveys I carried out in London schools, an endeavour was made to test representative groups with standardized tests of scholastic abilities at each successive year of school life; and the correlations thus obtained

* C. Burt. The differentiation of intellectual ability. Brit. J. educ. Psychol., 1954, **24** (2), 76–90. (Pp. 80–83; 85.) Reprinted by permission of the publisher.

were subjected to a factorial analysis. At every age both a general factor and several group factors were discovered; but there was a marked tendency for the group factors to become increasingly predominant with increasing age. The conclusions drawn were summed up as follows: "The application of such methods through all the classes in all the departments, infants as well as senior, shows that the relative influence of the more general capacity (so-called "intelligence") is far greater in earlier years as contrasted with later. With younger children, one can often demonstrate little but the influence of the general factor; with older children, and particularly with college students, little but specific abilities or specialized interests. During early childhood, specialization is the exception rather than the rule."[17] This, so far as I am aware, was the first explicit statement of the hypothesis in precise factorial terms.

TABLE 1. Contributions of General and Special Factors to Total Individual Variability at Different Ages

Factor	Age 8 +	Age 10 +	Age 12 +
1. General	52.1	35.6	27.8
2. Verbal	7.3	9.3	10.7
3. Arithmetical	3.1	3.0	13.4
4. Manual	2.5	5.9	6.5

Table 1, which I reproduce from the initial report, perhaps expresses the change most succinctly. The figures are based on the application of standardized educational tests to the same individuals (294 boys and 252 girls) at two-yearly intervals, and show the relative importance (expressed as a percentage) of the factors named. "Up to the age of about ten the general factor of intelligence (g) almost swamps the influence of the more specialized factors: nevertheless, the

[17] Report of the L. C. C. Psychologist on "The bearing of the factor theory on the organization of schools and classes" (1919). Reprinted in: C. Burt. *Mental and scholastic tests.* London: King, 1921. (Memo. III, p. 266.)

verbal factor (v) is clearly discernible even at the age of eight; about the age of twelve the special arithmetical factor (n) becomes more conspicuous, though the general factor is still twice as important; the manual factor (m or k) remains obscurely in the background, even at the later ages". . . . (*loc. cit*).

The conclusions announced in my 1921 Report at once aroused a good deal of controversy. Most of the early criticisms came from adherents of Spearman's "two factor theory," who doubted the very existence of special abilities or group factors. Several "longitudinal studies" were started; but little factual evidence was available for some years. . . .

Here Burt briefly summarizes confirmatory evidence provided by Garrett and his co-workers in America and by investigators in other countries.

Nevertheless, investigators are far from unanimous; and of late there has been a marked inclination to question the hypothesis of differentiation. Rarely, if ever, do the various critics discuss the neurological or biological evidence; most of them, indeed, seem hardly aware of it. The facts on which they chiefly rely consist either of the negative findings of recent American factorists or of a re-analysis of results obtained with tests constructed primarily in connection with the problem of re-allocation at 11 plus. . . .

There follows a survey and critical evaluation of contradictory findings, all of which Burt attributes to methodological flaws.

Judging from my own data, I should readily agree that, after the age of puberty, it is not easy to find evidence for further differentiation of *abilities*, though a specialization of *interests* is often discernible. That, however, cannot affect the hypothesis with which we are here concerned—namely, that, *between late infancy and early adolescence, there is a* definite increase in specialization in ability due, not to education, but to maturation. At the same time, it would be gross over-simplification to describe mental development exclusively in terms of a single sweeping principle—whether of increasing differentiation or of increasing integration—or to assume that any such principle must hold good of all mental processes and of every individual. Certain capacities, after gradually maturing and even for a while dominating the child's mental life, often seem to atrophy in later years; a striking example is seen in the way many children between the ages of six and ten—especially boys—tend increasingly to carry out their thinking in pictorial form, and then gradually lose the power, or at least the habit, of concrete visualization.

Summary and Conclusions

1. Biological, neurological, and statistical evidence all appears strongly to support the view that with increasing age intellectual ability tends to become more and more specialized. Thus, the general factor accounts for a distinctly smaller proportion of the total amount of individual variation, while group factors play an increasingly predominant part.

2. Changes of this kind are shown most clearly in tests of scholastic attainments, but may here be due in some degree to environmental influences and to a specialization of interest rather than of ability. Similar changes, however, are also found with tests of mental capacities such as are less likely to be affected by extraneous conditions, and must, therefore, at least in part, be the result of intrinsic processes of maturation.

3. Many of the investigations commonly cited as bearing on this problem are vitiated by defects in the way the experiments have been planned and the resulting data analysed. An ordinary summational or centroid analysis is inconclusive;

a group factor analysis is essential. The tests employed must be such as will elicit special abilities; and the most satisfactory results are obtained by testing the same individuals at different stages of their school life.

The most recent development in the factorial analysis of intelligence comes from the long-range research of J. P. Guilford and his associates at the University of Southern California. Beginning with an investigation of reasoning and creative thinking, this project led Guilford to a re-examination and reformulation of the structure of intellect as a whole. Accepting the fact that intelligence is complex, Guilford anticipates the identification of more than 120 distinct intellectual abilities. His three-dimensional, cubical model for organizing this multiplicity of factors is described in the following article. The same article introduces and illustrates a number of new tests of creative abilities and "divergent thinking" which Guilford and his associates have contributed to the psychometrician's armamentarium.

Joy Paul Guilford

Three Faces of Intellect*

Our knowledge of the components of human intelligence has come about mostly within the last 25 years. The major sources of this information in this country have been L. L. Thurstone and his associates, the wartime research of psychologists in the United States Air Forces, and more recently the Aptitudes Project at the University of Southern Cali-

*J. P. Guilford. Three faces of intellect. *Amer. Psychologist,* 1959, **14**, 469–479. (Pp. 469–477.) Reprinted by permission of the author and the American Psychological Association.

fornia, now in its tenth year of research on cognitive and
thinking abilities. The results from the Aptitudes Project that
have gained perhaps the most attention have pertained to
creative-thinking abilities. These are mostly novel findings.
But to me, the most significant outcome has been the development of a unified theory of human intellect, which organizes
the known, unique, or primary intellectual abilities into a
single system called the "structure of intellect." It is to this
system that I shall devote the major part of my remarks. . . .

Although each factor is sufficiently distinct to be detected
by factor analysis, in very recent years it has become apparent that the factors themselves can be classified because
they resemble one another in certain ways. One basis of
classification is according to the basic kind of process or
operation performed. This kind of classification gives us five
major groups of intellectual abilities: factors of cognition,
memory, convergent thinking, divergent thinking, and evaluation.

Cognition means discovery or rediscovery or recognition.
Memory means retention of what is cognized. Two kinds of
productive-thinking operations generate new information
from known information and remembered information. In
divergent-thinking operations we think in different directions, sometimes searching, sometimes seeking variety. In
convergent thinking the information leads to one right answer or to a recognized best or conventional answer. In
evaluation we reach decisions as to goodness, correctness,
suitability, or adequacy of what we know, what we remember, and what we produce in productive thinking.

A second way of classifying the intellectual factors is according to the kind of material or content involved. The
factors known thus far involve three kinds of material or
content: the content may be figural, symbolic, or semantic.
Figural content is concrete material such as is perceived
through the senses. It does not represent anything except
itself. Visual material has properties such as size, form, color,

location, or texture. Things we hear or feel provide other examples of figural material. Symbolic content is composed of letters, digits, and other conventional signs, usually organized in general systems, such as the alphabet or the number system. Semantic content is in the form of verbal meanings or ideas, for which no examples are necessary.

When a certain operation is applied to a certain kind of content, as many as six general kinds of products may be involved. There is enough evidence available to suggest that, regardless of the combinations of operations and content, the same six kinds of products may be found associated. The six kinds of products are: units, classes, relations, systems, transformations, and implications. So far as we have determined from factor analysis, these are the only fundamental kinds of products that we can know. As such, they may serve as basic classes into which one might fit all kinds of information psychologically.

The three kinds of classifications of the factors of intellect can be represented by means of a single solid model, shown in Figure 1. In this model, which we call the "structure of intellect," each dimension represents one of the modes of variation of the factors. Along one dimension are found the various kinds of operations, along a second one are the various kinds of products, and along the third are various kinds of content. Along the dimension of content a fourth category has been added, its kind of content being designated as "behavioral." This category has been added on a purely theoretical basis to represent the general area sometimes called "social intelligence." More will be said about this section of the model later.

In order to provide a better basis for understanding the model and a better basis for accepting it as a picture of human intellect, I shall do some exploring of it with you systematically, giving some examples of tests. Each cell in the model calls for a certain kind of ability that can be described in terms of operation, content, and product, for each

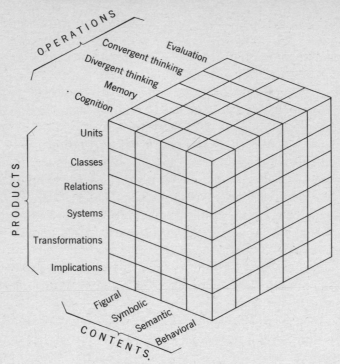

FIG. 1   A cubical model representing the structure of intellect.

cell is at the intersection of a unique combination of kinds of operation, content, and product. A test for that ability would have the same three properties. In our exploration of the model, we shall take one vertical layer at a time, beginning with the front face. The first layer provides us with a matrix of 18 cells (if we ignore the behavioral column for which there are as yet no known factors) each of which should contain a cognitive ability.

The Cognitive Abilities

We know at present the unique abilities that fit logically into 15 of the 18 cells for cognitive abilities. Each row presents a triad of similar abilities, having a single kind of product in common. The factors of the first row are concerned with the knowing of units. A good test of the ability to cognize figural units is the Street Gestalt Completion Test. In this test, the recognition of familiar pictured objects in silhouette form is made difficult for testing purposes by blocking out parts of those objects. There is another factor that is known to involve the perception of auditory figures — in the form of melodies, rhythms, and speech sounds — and still another factor involving kinesthetic forms. The presence of three factors in one cell (they are conceivably distinct abilities, although this has not been tested) suggests that more generally, in the figural column, at least, we should expect to find more than one ability. A fourth dimension pertaining to variations in sense modality may thus apply in connection with figural content. The model could be extended in this manner if the facts call for such an extension.

The ability to cognize symbolic units is measured by tests like the following:

Put vowels in the following blanks to make real words:

P ____W____R
M____RV____L
C____RT____N

Rearrange the letters to make real words:

R A C I H
T V O E S
K L C C O

The first of these two tests is called Disemvoweled Words, and the second Scrambled Words.

The ability to cognize semantic units is the well-known factor of verbal comprehension, which is best measured by means of a vocabulary test, with items such as:

GRAVITY means _____
CIRCUS means _____
VIRTUE means _____

From the comparison of these two factors it is obvious that recognizing familiar words as letter structures and knowing what words mean depend upon quite different abilities.

For testing the abilities to know classes of units, we may present the following kinds of items, one with symbolic content and one with semantic content:

Which letter group does not belong?

    XECM   PVAA   QXIN   VTRO

Which object does not belong?

    clam   tree   oven   rose

A figural test is constructed in a completely parallel form, presenting in each item four figures, three of which have a property in common and the fourth lacking that property.

The three abilities to see relationships are also readily measured by a common kind of test, differing only in terms of content. The well-known analogies test is applicable, two items in symbolic and semantic form being:

| JIRE : KIRE : : FORA : | KORE | KORA | LIRE | GORA | GIRE |
| poetry : prose : : dance : | music | walk | sing | talk | jump |

Such tests usually involve more than the ability to cognize relations, but we are not concerned with this problem at this point.

The three factors for cognizing systems do not at present appear in tests so closely resembling one another as in the case of the examples just given. There is nevertheless an underlying common core of logical similarity. Ordinary space tests, such as Thurstone's Flags, Figures, and Cards or Part V (Spatial Orientation) of the Guilford-Zimmerman Aptitude Survey (GZAS), serve in the figural column. The system involved is an order or arrangement of objects in space. A system that uses symbolic elements is illustrated by the Letter Triangle Test, a sample item of which is:

$$\frac{\overline{\quad}}{d}$$

```
              ___
       d      ___
   b      e      ___
 a    c      f      ? 
```

What letter belongs at the place of the question mark?

The ability to understand a semantic system has been known for some time as the factor called general reasoning. One of its most faithful indicators is a test composed of arithmetic-reasoning items. That the phase of understanding only is important for measuring this ability is shown by the fact that such a test works even if the examinee is not asked to give a complete solution; he need only show that he structures the problem properly. For example, an item from the test Necessary Arithmetical Operations simply asks what operations are needed to solve the problem:

A city lot 48 feet wide and 149 feet deep costs $79,432. What is the cost per square foot?

A. add and multiply
B. multiply and divide
C. subtract and divide
D. add and subtract
E. divide and add

Placing the factor of general reasoning in this cell of the structure of intellect gives us some new conceptions of its nature. It should be a broad ability to grasp all kinds of systems that are conceived in terms of verbal concepts, not restricted to the understanding of problems of an arithmetical type.

Transformations are changes of various kinds, including modifications in arrangement, organization, or meaning. In the figural column for the transformations row, we find the factor known as visualization. Common measuring instruments for this factor are the surface-development tests, and an example of a different kind is Part VI (Spatial Visualization) of the GZAS. A test of the ability to make transformations of meaning, for the factor in the semantic column, is called Similarities. The examinee is asked to state several ways in which two objects, such as an apple and an orange, are alike. Only by shifting the meanings of both is the examinee able to give many responses to such an item.

In the set of abilities having to do with the cognition of implications, we find that the individual goes beyond the information given, but not to the extent of what might be called drawing conclusions. We may say that he extrapolates. From the given information he expects or foresees certain consequences, for example. The two factors found in this row of the cognition matrix were first called "foresight" factors. Foresight in connection with figural material can be tested by means of paper-and-pencil mazes. Foresight in connection with ideas, those pertaining to events, for example, is indicated by a test such as Pertinent Questions:

> In planning to open a new hamburger stand in a certain community, what four questions should be considered in deciding upon its location?

The more questions the examinee asks in response to a list of such problems, the more he evidently foresees contingencies.

The Memory Abilities

The area of memory abilities has been explored less than some of the other areas of operation, and only seven of the potential cells of the memory matrix have known factors in them. These cells are restricted to three rows: for units, relations, and systems. The first cell in the memory matrix is now occupied by two factors, parallel to two in the corresponding cognition matrix: visual memory and auditory memory. Memory for series of letters or numbers, as in memory span tests, conforms to the conception of memory for symbolic units. Memory for the ideas in a paragraph conforms to the conception of memory for semantic units.

The formation of associations between units, such as visual forms, syllables, and meaningful words, as in the method of paired associates, would seem to represent three abilities to remember relationships involving three kinds of content. We know of two such abilities, for the symbolic and semantic columns. The memory for known systems is represented by two abilities very recently discovered.[18] Remembering the arrangement of objects in space is the nature of an ability in the figural column, and remembering a sequence of events is the nature of a corresponding ability in the semantic column. The differentiation between these two abilities implies that a person may be able to say where he saw an object on a page, but he might not be able to say on which of several pages he saw it after leafing through several pages that included the right one. Considering the blank rows in the memory matrix, we should expect to find abilities also to remember classes, transformations, and implications, as well as units, relations, and systems.

The Divergent-Thinking Abilities

The unique feature of divergent production is that a *variety* of responses is produced. The product is not completely determined by the given information. This is not to say that divergent thinking does not come into play in the total process of reaching a unique conclusion, for it comes into play wherever there is trial-and-error thinking.

The well-known ability of word fluency is tested by asking the examinee to list words satisfying a specified letter requirement, such as words beginning with the letter "s" or words ending in "-tion." This ability is now regarded as a

[18] R. E. Christal. Factor analytic study of visual memory. *Psychol. Monogr.*, 1958, **72**, No. 13 (Whole No. 466).

facility in divergent production of symbolic units. The parallel semantic ability has been known as ideational fluency. A typical test item calls for listing objects that are round and edible. . . .

The divergent production of class ideas is believed to be the unique feature of a factor called "spontaneous flexibility." A typical test instructs the examinee to list all the uses he can think of for a common brick, and he is given eight minutes. If his responses are: build a house, build a barn, build a garage, build a school, build a church, build a chimney, build a walk, and build a barbecue, he would earn a fairly high score for ideational fluency but a very low score for spontaneous flexibility, because all these uses fall into the same class. If another person said: make a door stop, make a paper weight, throw it at a dog, make a bookcase, drown a cat, drive a nail, make a red powder, and use for baseball bases, he would also receive a high score for flexibilty. He has gone frequently from one class to another.

A current study of unknown but predicted divergent-production abilities includes testing whether there are also figural and symbolic abilities to produce multiple classes. An experimental figural test presents a number of figures that can be classified in groups of three in various ways, each figure being usable in more than one class. An experimental symbolic test presents a few numbers that are also to be classified in multiple ways.

A unique ability involving relations is called "associational fluency." It calls for the production of a variety of things related in a specified way to a given thing. For example, the examinee is asked to list words meaning about the same as "good" or to list words meaning about the opposite of "hard." In these instances the response produced is to complete a relationship, and semantic content is involved. Some of our present experimental tests call for the production of varieties of relations, as such, and involve figural and symbolic content also. For example, given four small digits, in how many ways can they be related in order to produce a sum of eight?

One factor pertaining to the production of systems is known as expressional fluency. The rapid formation of phrases or sentences is the essence of certain tests of this factor. For example, given the initial letters:

W_____c_____e_____n_____

with different sentences to be produced, the examinee might write "We can eat nuts" or "Whence came Eve Newton?" In interpreting the factor, we regard the sentence as a symbolic system. By analogy, a figural system would be some kind of organization of lines and other elements, and a semantic system would be in the form of a verbally stated problem or perhaps something as complex as a theory.

In the row of the divergent-production matrix devoted to transformations, we find some very interesting factors. The one called "adaptive flexibility" is now recognized as belonging in the figural column. A faithful test of it has been Match Problems. This is based upon the common game that uses squares, the sides of which are formed by match sticks. The examinee is told to take away a given number of matches to leave a stated number of squares with nothing left over. Nothing is said about the sizes of the squares to be left. If the examinee imposes upon himself the restriction that the squares that he leaves must be of the same size, he will fail in his attempts to do items like that in Figure 2. Other odd kinds of solutions are introduced in other items, such as overlapping squares and squares within squares, and so on. In another variation of Match Problems the examinee is told to produce two or more solutions for each problem.

A factor that has been called "originality" is now recognized as adaptive flexibility with semantic material, where there must be a shifting of meanings. The examinee must produce the shifts or changes in meaning and so come up with novel, unusual, clever, or farfetched ideas. The Plot Titles Test presents a short story, the examinee being told

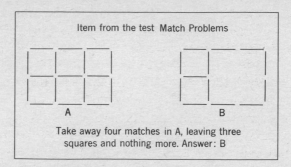

FIG. 2 · A sample item from the test Match Problems. The problem in this item is to take away four matches and leave three squares. The solution is given.

to list as many appropriate titles as he can to head the story. One story is about a missionary who has been captured by cannibals in Africa. He is in the pot and about to be boiled when a princess of the tribe obtains a promise for his release if he will become her mate. He refuses and is boiled to death.

In scoring the test, we separate the responses into two categories, clever and nonclever. Examples of nonclever responses are: African Death, Defeat of a Princess, Eaten by Savages, The Princess, The African Missionary, In Darkest Africa, and Boiled by Savages. These titles are appropriate but commonplace. The number of such responses serves as a score for ideational fluency. Examples of clever responses are: Pot's Plot, Potluck Dinner, Stewed Parson, Goil or Boil, A Mate Worse Then Death, He Left a Dish for a Pot, Chaste in Haste, and A Hot Price for Freedom. The number of clever responses given by an examinee is his score for originality, or the divergent production of semantic transformations.

Another test of originality presents a very novel task so that any acceptable response is unusual for the individual. In the Symbol Production Test the examinee is to produce a simple symbol to stand for a noun or a verb in each short sentence, in other words to invent something like pictographic symbols. Still another test of originality asks for writing the "punch lines" for cartoons, a task that almost automatically challenges the examinee to be clever. Thus, quite a variety of tests offer approaches to the measurement of originality, including one or two others that I have not mentioned.

Abilities to produce a variety of implications are assessed by tests calling for elaboration of given information. A figural test of this type provides the examinee with a line or two, to which he is to add other lines to produce an object. The more lines he adds, the greater his score. A semantic test gives the examinee the outlines of a plan to which he is to respond by stating all the details he can think of to make the plan work. A new test we are trying out in the symbolic area presents two simple equations such as $B - C = D$ and $z = A + D$. The examinee is to make as many other equations as he can from this information.

The Convergent-Production Abilities

Of the 18 convergent-production abilities expected in the three content columns, 12 are now recognized. In the first row, pertaining to units, we have an ability to name figural properties (forms or colors) and an ability to name abstractions (classes, relations, and so on). It may be that the ability in common to the speed of naming forms and the speed of naming colors is not appropriately placed in the convergent-thinking matrix. One might expect that the thing to be produced in a test of the convergent production of figural units would be in the form of figures rather than words. A better test of such an ability might somehow specify the need for one particular object, the examinee to furnish the object.

A test for the convergent production of classes (Word Grouping) presents a list of 12 words that are to be classified in four, and only four, meaningful groups, no word to appear in more than one group. A parallel test (Figure Concepts Test) presents 20 pictured real objects that are to be grouped in meaningful classes of two or more each.

Convergent production having to do with relationships is represented by three known factors, all involving the "eduction of correlates," as Spearman called it. The given information includes one unit and a stated relation, the examinee to supply the other unit. Analogies tests that call for completion rather than a choice between alternative answers emphasize this kind of ability. With symbolic content such an item might read:

pots   stop   bard   drab   rats   __?__

A semantic item that measures eduction of correlates is:

The absence of sound is _____.

Incidentally, the latter item is from a vocabulary-completion test, and its relation to the factor of ability to produce correlates indicates how, by change of form, a vocabulary test may indicate an ability other than that for which vocabulary tests are usually intended, namely, the factor of verbal comprehension.

Only one factor for convergent production of systems is known, and it is in the semantic column. It is measured by a class of tests that may be called ordering tests. The examinee may be presented with a number of events that ordinarily have a best or most logical order, the events being presented in scrambled order. The presentation may be pictorial, as in the Picture Arrangement Test, or verbal. The pictures may be taken from a cartoon strip. The verbally presented events may be in the form of the various steps needed to plant a new lawn. There are undoubtedly other kinds of systems than temporal order that could be utilized for testing abilities in this row of the convergent-production matrix.

In the way of producing transformations of a unique variety, we have three recognized factors, known as redefinition abilities. In each case, redefinition involves the changing of functions or uses of parts of one unit and giving them new functions or uses in some new unit. For testing the ability of figural redefinition, a task based upon the Gottschaldt figures is suitable. Figure 3 shows the kind of item for such a test. In recognizing the simpler figure within the structure of a more complex figure, certain lines must take on new roles.

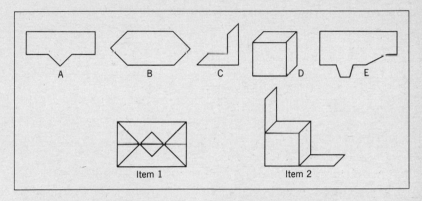

Fig. 3   Sample items from a test Hidden Figures, based upon the Gottschaldt figures. Which of the simpler figures is concealed within each of the two more complex figures?

In terms of symbolic material, the following sample items will illustrate how groups of letters in given words must be re-adapted to use in other words. In the test Camouflaged Words, each sentence contains the name of a sport or game:

> I did not know that he was ailing.
> To beat the Hun, tin goes a long way.

For the factor of semantic redefinition, the Gestalt Transformation Test may be used. A sample item reads:

From which object could you most likely make a needle?
    A. a cabbage
    B. a splice
    C. a steak
    D. a paper box
    E. a fish

The convergent production of implications means the drawing of fully determined conclusions from given information. The well-known factor of numerical facility belongs in the symbolic column. For the parallel ability in the figural column, we have a test known as Form Reasoning, in which rigorously defined operations with figures are used. For the parallel ability in the semantic column, the factor sometimes called "deduction" probably qualifies. Items of the following type are sometimes used.

> Charles is younger than Robert
> Charles is older than Frank
> Who is older: Robert or Frank?

Evaluative Abilities

The evaluative area has had the least investigation of all the operational categories. In fact, only one systematic analytical study has been devoted to this area. Only eight evaluative abilities are recognized as fitting into the evaluation matrix. But at least five rows have one or more factors each, and also three of the usual columns or content categories. In each case, evaluation involves reaching decisions as to the accuracy, goodness, suitability, or workability of information. In each row, for the particular kind of product of that row, some kind of criterion or standard of judgment is involved.

In the first row, for the evaluation of units, the important decision to be made pertains to the identity of a unit. Is this unit identical with that one? In the figural column we find the factor long known as "perceptual speed." Tests of this factor invariably call for decisions of identity, for example, Part IV (Perceptual Speed) of the GZAS or Thurstone's Identical Forms. I think it has been generally wrongly thought that the ability involved is that of cognition of visual forms. But we have seen that another factor is a more suitable candidate for this definition and for being in the very first cell of the cognitive matrix. It is parallel to this evaluative ability but does not require the judgment of identity as one of its properties.

In the symbolic column is an ability to judge identity of symbolic units, in the form of series of letters or numbers or of names of individuals.

Are members of the following pairs identical or not:

           825170493_____825176493
           dkeltvmpa_____dkeltvmpa
      C. S. Meyerson_____C. E. Meyerson

Such items are common in tests of clerical aptitude.

There should be a parallel ability to decide whether two ideas are identical or different. Is the idea expressed in this sentence the same as the idea expressed in that one? Do these two proverbs express essentially the same idea? Such tests exist and will be used to test the hypothesis that such an ability can be demonstrated.

No evaluative abilities pertaining to classes have as yet been recognized. The abilities having to do with evaluation where relations are concerned must meet the criterion of logical consistency. Syllogistic-type tests involving letter symbols indicate a different ability than the same type of test involving verbal statements. In the figural column we might expect that tests incorporating geometric reasoning or proof would indicate a parallel ability to sense the soundness of conclusions regarding figural relationships.

The evaluation of systems seems to be concerned with the internal consistency of those systems, so far as we can tell from the knowledge of one such factor. The factor has been called "experiential evaluation," and its representative test presents items like that in Figure 4 asking "What is wrong with this picture?" The things wrong are often internal inconsistencies.

A semantic ability for evaluating transformations is

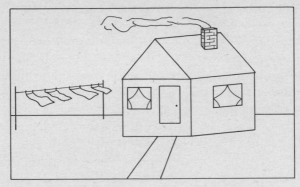

Fig. 4   A sample item from the test Unusual Details. What two things are wrong with this picture?

thought to be that known for some time as "judgment." In typical judgment tests, the examinee is asked to tell which of five solutions to a practical problem is most adequate or wise. The solutions frequently involve improvisations, in other words, adaptations of familiar objects to unusual uses. In this way the items present redefinitions to be evaluated.

A factor known first as "sensitivity to problems" has become recognized as an evaluative ability having to do with implications. One test of the factor, the Apparatus Test, asks for two needed improvements with respect to each of several common devices, such as the telephone or the toaster. The Social Institutions Test, a measure of the same factor, asks what things are wrong with each of several institutions, such as tipping or national elections. We may say that defects or deficiencies are implications of an evaluative kind. Another interpretation would be that seeing defects and deficiencies are evaluations of implications to the effect that the various aspects of something are all right. . . .

The structure of intellect is a theoretical model that predicts as many as 120 distinct abilities, if every cell of the model contains a factor. Already we know that two cells contain two or more factors each, and there probably are actually other cells of this type. Since the model was first conceived, 12 factors predicted by it have found places in it. There is consequently hope of filling many of the other vacancies, and we may eventually end up with more than 120 abilities. . . .

The structure of intellect as I have presented it to you may or may not stand the test of time. Even if the general form persists, there are likely to be some modifications. Possibly some different kind of model will be invented. Be that as it may, the fact of a multiplicity of intellectual abilities seems well established.

There are many individuals who long for the good old days of simplicity, when we got along with one unanalyzed intelligence. Simplicity certainly has its appeal. But human nature is exceedingly complex, and we may as well face that fact. The rapidly moving events of the world in which we live have forced upon us the need for knowing human intelligence thoroughly. Humanity's peaceful pursuit of happiness depends upon our control of nature and of our own behavior; and this, in turn, depends upon understanding ourselves, including our intellectual resources.

5

Behavior Genetics:
Statistical Studies

In the interpretation of individual and group differences in psychological traits, a persistent question has been that of heredity and environment. To what extent are behavioral differences the result of hereditary factors, and to what extent are they the result of the environmental conditions to which the developing organism has been exposed?

The earliest attempts to study human heredity were based on the analysis of family resemblances. Although many versions and modifications of this procedure have been employed, interpretation of results is often difficult. The chief source of confusion is that the family is a cultural as well as a biological unit. Related persons usually live together, sharing a common environment. While the psychological environment is by no means uniform for all members of a family, their environments nevertheless have major features in common, such as socioeconomic level and cultural milieu. In general, the closer the degree of hereditary relationship, the greater are these environmental similarities.

In addition, family members constitute a part of each other's environments. Family interaction thus provides many opportunities for mutual influence. A third important factor is that of social expectancy. The child is often reminded of the special talents and defects of his forebears and any chance display of similar traits on his part will be augmented by such references. What is expected of an individual helps to shape his self concept, which in turn is likely to affect his subsequent development.

It follows that to demonstrate family resemblance in a psychological trait does not in itself constitute proof of its hereditary origin. In the effort to disentangle the contribution of hereditary and environmental factors to behavior development, special familial relationships have been investigated, including twins and foster children. Even in these studies, however, we shall see that certain methodological difficulties remain.

A major landmark in the measurement of family resemblance was Karl Pearson's study of sibling relationships in physical and psychological traits. In his approach, Pearson reflects the influence of Galton, for whom he had unbounded admiration. Pearson described his investigation in the Fourth Annual Huxley Lecture, which he delivered before the British Anthropological Institute in 1904. A modern touch is provided by Pearson's acknowledgment of financial support for the study, received from both governmental and private sources. This is certainly one of the earliest recorded instances of such grants for psychological research. It must be admitted, however, that one of the sponsors of Pearson's study, the Worshipful Company of Drapers, sounds more picturesque than the foundations familiar to today's researchers!

Like some of Galton's earlier work, Pearson's study utilized questionnaire and rating procedures. It pioneered not only in the application of the statistical techniques of regression and correlation to the study of human heredity, but also in the use of large-scale surveys for gathering data on human variation. Note also Pearson's empirical check of rater reliability in a pilot study. Pearson computed degree of relationship between siblings by measuring the slope of the regression line. Since this regression line is plotted in standard scores, its slope is equal to the index subsequently known as the Pearson Product-Moment Correlation Coefficient and it may be interpreted as such.

It should be noted that Pearson bases his argument for the importance of heredity in psychological development on the similarity of sibling correlations in physical and psychological traits. He considers it improbable that environmental factors alone or in combination with heredity would yield psychological trait correlations so close to those obtained with such physical traits as eye color, whose variation is attributable wholly to heredity. We know now, however, that sibling correlations in psychological traits do not reveal such striking uniformity, but vary from trait to trait. In Pearson's data, a spurious uniformity of sibling correlations may have resulted at least in part from halo effect and suggestion, since many of the sibling pairs were undoubtedly rated by the same teachers, who were aware of the children's family relationship.

When Pearson writes, "We inherit our parents' tempers, our parents' conscientiousness, shyness and ability, even as we inherit their stature, forearm and span," he is expressing a conviction that prevailed in psychology during the first quarter of the twentieth century and continued to find exponents until midcentury. This is the view that heredity accounts for the major variations among individuals and groups and that the effects of environment are minor.

Karl Pearson

On the Laws of Inheritance in Man*

Since the publication of Francis Galton's epoch-making books, *Hereditary Genius* and *English Men of Science,* it is impossible to deny *in toto* the inheritance of mental characters. But we require to go a stage further and ask for an exact quantitative measure of the inheritance of such characters and a comparison of such measure with its value for the physical characters.

Accordingly some six or seven years ago I set myself the following problem: What is the quantitative measure of the inheritance of the moral and mental characters in man, and

* K. Pearson. On the laws of inheritance in man. II. On the inheritance of the mental and moral characters in man, and its comparison with the inheritance of the physical characters. *Biometrika,* 1904, **3**, 131–190. (Pp. 132, 134, 145, 147–149, 155–156, 158–159.)

how is it related to the corresponding measure of the inheritance of the physical characters? . . .

In order to carry out this investigation I sought and received aid from the Government Grant Committee of the Royal Society. I have further to acknowledge the assistance I have received, in the task of reduction and computation, from a grant made to my department at University College, by the Worshipful Company of Drapers.

I had deemed it desirable to measure not only the mental and moral characters, but a wide range of physical characters also. These would act as a check on the whole work, for we knew perfectly well what the inheritance of these physical characters might be expected to be. . . .

Schedules were then, after much consideration and some experimenting, prepared, in which teachers could briefly note the chief characteristics of the children under their charge. These schedules were white for a pair of brothers, pink for a pair of sisters, and blue for a brother and sister. Additional brothers were given on attached white, and additional sisters on attached pink sheets. With the schedules were distributed (a) printed directions for the use of the headspanner; (b) general directions as to the estimation of both the physical and mental characters; and (c) two additional series of lithographed instructions, which were suggested by special inquiries of the teachers who first began the observations. Copies of the schedule and the general directions are printed in Appendix 1 [not herein reproduced—Ed.]

The material took upwards of five years to collect. Appeal was made through the columns of the educational journals to teachers of all kinds, and our observations were made not only in the great boys' public schools, in the girls' high schools and the grammar schools of the country, but in modern mixed schools, in national and elementary schools of all kinds, in board schools and private schools throughout the kingdom. Some 6000 schedules were distributed and between 3000 and 4000 returned with more or less ample data. . . .

I now come to the fundamental idea of my comparison of the psychical and physical resemblance of brothers. Suppose we assume that moral and mental qualities in man, like the physical, follow a normal law of distribution, and that the regression is linear. What results shall we obtain by thus assuming perfect continuity between the physical and the psychical? No doubt the drums will begin to beat the tattoo, we shall hear talk of the hopeless materialism of some men of science. But to use Huxley's appropriate words: "One does not battle with drummers." I cannot free myself from the conception that underlying every psychical state there is a physical state, and from that conception follows at once the conclusion that there must be a close association between the succession or the recurrence of certain psychical states, which is what we judge mental and moral characteristics by, and an underlying physical confirmation be it of brain or liver. Hence I put to myself the problem as follows: Assume the fundamental laws of distribution which we know to hold for the physical characters in man, and see whither they lead us when applied to the psychical characteristics. They must: (a) Give us totally discordant results. If so, we shall conclude that these laws have no application to the mental and moral attributes. Or, (b) Give us accordant results. If so, we may go a stage further, and ask how these results compare with those for the inheritance of the physical characters: Are they more or less or equally subject to the influence of environment? Here are the questions before us. Let us examine how they are to be answered. As an illustration I take *Ability in Girls.* I measured intelligence by the following seven classes. (i) *Quick Intelligent;* (ii) *Intelligent;* (iii) *Slow Intelligent;* (iv) *Slow;* (v) *Slow Dull;* (vi) *Very Dull;* and a quite distinct category (vii) *Inaccurate-Erratic.* Some explanation of these terms is given in Appendix IA [not herein reproduced —Ed.], which contains the general instructions for observation, and the terms themselves were practically formulated by a schoolmaster of considerable pedagogic and psychological experience.

My next stage was to ask two or three different teachers in several schools to apply the classification to 30 to 50 pupils known to each of them. The classifications were made quite independently, often by teachers of quite different subjects, and a comparison of the results showed that 80 to 85 per cent of the children were put into the same classes by the different teachers, while about 10 per cent more only differed by one class. This gave one very great confidence not only in the value of this scale, but of other psychical classifications when used by observant teachers. The next stage was to obtain exactly, as in the case of *Health*, a general scale of intelligence.

Figure 1 gives the normal distribution of intelligence in a population of 2014 girls. It is a curious if a common result of experience to find that the modal ability is on the borderland between the *Intelligent* and *Slow Intelligent*. We have here for the first time a quantitative scale of intelligence, and we can at once apply it to the problem of the degree of resemblance between sisters as regards ability. Just as in the case of *Health*, all the girls of a given class are taken, say the *Slow Intelligents*, and at the average value of this class, is plotted upon this scale of intelligence, the average value of the intelligence of the sisters of these girls on the same scale. We thus obtain the six points of Figure 2, all well within the limits of random sampling, lying on the straight line found from the fourfold division of the data. The slope of this line is .47 or 47, close to 50, in the 100. There can, I think, be small doubt that *Intelligence* or *Ability* follows precisely the same laws of inheritance as *General Health*, and both the same laws as *Cephalic Index*, or any other physical character. . . .

You have in Table 1 the mean of the physical measurements of our school records—16 series in the first, 24 series

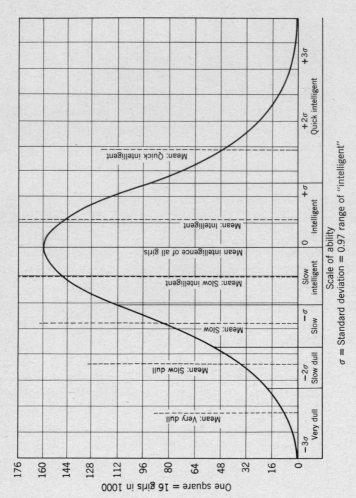

FIG. 1.   Distribution of intelligence in 2,014 girls.

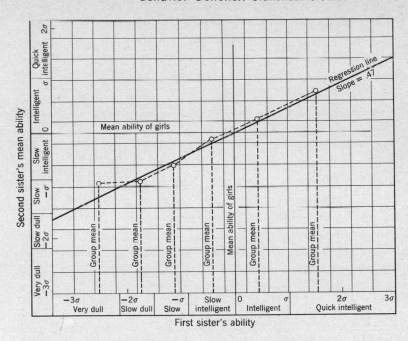

Fig. 2   Resemblance of sisters in ability.

TABLE 1. *Inheritance of the Physical Characters*
(School Observations on Children)

Character	Correlation		
	Brothers	Sisters	Brother and Sister
Health	.52	.51	.57
Eye colour	.54	.52	.53
Hair colour	.62	.57	.55
Hair curliness	.50	.52	.52
Cephalic index	.49	.54	.43
Head length	.50	.43	.46
Head breadth	.59	.62	.54
Head height	.55	.52	.49
Mean	.54	.53	.51
Athletic power	.72	.75	.49

in the latter. I venture to say that remembering the possible slips in measurement and in classification, there is not the slightest doubt that those two series absolutely confirm each other, and give a mean degree of resemblance of nearly .5 between children of the same parents for physical characters. How much of that physical resemblance is due to home environment? You might at once assert that size of head and size of body are influenced by nurture, food, and exercise. It is quite true; even curliness may be subject to home influences. But what is the broad effect of such environment on our coefficients of heredity? Can any possible home influence be brought to bear on cephalic index,[1] on hair colour, or eye colour? I fancy not, and yet these characters are within broad lines inherited exactly like the characters directly capable of being influenced by nurture and exercise. I am compelled to conclude that the environmental influence on physical characters, however great in some cases, is not to the first approximation a great disturbing factor when we consider coefficients of fraternal resemblance in man. I do not believe it to be at all comparable with the irregularities that arise from random sampling and occasional carelessness in measurement or in appreciation of character.

Now turn to Table 2 giving the degree of resemblance in the mental and moral characters. What do we find in it? Perhaps slightly more irregularity in the values than in the case of the physical characters. The judgment required is much finer; and the classification is much rougher. Let me frankly admit the difficulties of the task, both for observers and computers. I will lay no weight whatever, if you like, on the second place of decimals. But what is the obvious conclusion? Why, that the values of the coefficient again cluster round .5. If anything, the average degree of resemblance for the psychical is rather less than for the physical, it certainly

[1] It has now been demonstrated that cephalic index is in fact subject to considerable modification by cradling, binding, and other culturally determined infant-rearing practices—Ed.

TABLE 2.   Inheritance of the Mental Characteristics
(School Observations on Children)

Character	Correlation		
	Brothers	Sisters	Brother and Sister
Vivacity	.47	.43	.49
Assertiveness	.53	.44	.52
Introspection	.59	.47	.63
Popularity	.50	.57	.49
Conscientiousness	.59	.64	.63
Temper	.51	.49	.51
Ability	.46	.47	.44
Handwriting	.53	.56	.48
Mean	.52	.51	.52

is not greater. Personally I would lay not a grain's weight on the difference.

I have illustrated the whole result in Figure 3. The two lines representing physical and psychical qualities go bobbing up and down, and cutting and re-cutting one another. No wise man, however, would venture to assert that one or other is sensibly uppermost, or that any of those rises or falls have real significance. We are forced absolutely to the con-

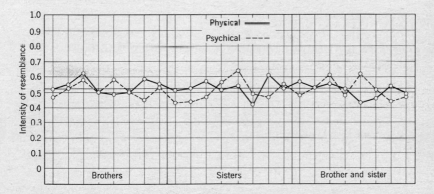

Fig. 3   Comparison of resemblance for physical and psychical characters.

clusion that the degree of resemblance of the physical and mental characters in children is one and the same.

It has been suggested that this resemblance in the psychical characters is compounded of two factors, inheritance on the one hand and training or environment on the other. If so, you must admit that inheritance and environment make up the resemblance in the physical characters. Now these two sorts of resemblance being of the same intensity, either the environmental influence is the same in both cases, or it is not. If it is the same, we are forced to the conclusion that it is insensible, for it cannot influence eye colour. If it is not the same, then it would be a most marvellous thing, that with varying degrees of inheritance, some mysterious force always modifies the extent of home influence, until the resemblance of brothers or sisters is brought sensibly up to the same intensity! Occam's razor will enable us at once to cut off such a theory. We are forced, I think literally forced, to the general conclusion that the physical and psychical characters in man are inherited within broad lines in the same manner, and with the same intensity. The average home environment, the average parental influence is in itself part of the heritage of the stock and not an extraneous and additional factor emphasising the resemblance between children from the same home.

But we are not yet at the end of our conclusions. By assuming our normal distribution for the psychical characters we have found, not only self-consistent results—linear regression, for example, as in the case of the inheritance of intelligence—but we have found the *same* degree of resemblance between physical and psychical characters. That *sameness* surely involves something additional. *It involves a like heritage from parents.* The degree of resemblance between children and parents for the physical characters in man may be applied to the degree of resemblance between children and parents for psychical characters. We inherit our parents' tempers, our parents' conscientiousness, shyness and ability, even as we inherit their stature, forearm and span . . . .

We see the man, not only physically, but morally and mentally, the product of a long line of ancestry. We realise that evolution and selection play no greater and play no less a part in the production of the psychical character than in the production of the physique of man. Once fully realise that the psychic is inherited in the same way as the physical, and there is no room left to differentiate one from the other in the evolution of man. Realise all this, and two mysteries have been linked into one mystery, but the total mystery is no less in magnitude, and no more explicable than it was before. We know not why living forms vary, nor why either physical or psychical characters are inherited, nor wherefore the existence at all of living forms, and their subjection to the great principle of selective evolution. We have learnt only a law common to the physical and the psychical; we have not raised the one or debased the other, because in a world where the ultimate source of change is utterly inexplicable, whether you strive to perceive it through matter like a physicist, through the lower living forms like the biologist, or through man like the anthropologist, all terminology like higher and lower is futile. Where the mystery is absolute in all cases, there can be no question of grade.

But I would not leave you with a mere general declaration that all is mystery, that scientific ignorance of the ultimate is profound. Rather I would emphasise what I have endeavoured to show you tonight, that the mission of science is not to explain but to bring all things, as far as we are able, under a common law. Science gives no real explanation, but provides comprehensive description. In the narrower field it has to study how its general conceptions bear on the comfort and happiness of man. Herein, I think, lies especially the coming function of anthropology. Anthropology has in the first place to study man, to discover the sequence of his evolution from his present comparative stages and from his past history. But it cannot halt here; it must suggest how those laws can be applied to render our own human society both more stable and more efficient. In this function it becomes at least the handmaiden of statecraft, if indeed it were not truer to call it the preceptor of statesmen.

If the conclusion we have reached tonight be substantially a true one, and for my part I cannot for a moment doubt that it is so, then what is its lesson for us as a community? Why simply that geniality and probity and ability may be fostered indeed by home environment and by provision of good schools and well equipped institutions for research, but that their origin, like health and muscle, is deeper down than these things. They are bred and not created. That good stock breeds good stock is a commonplace of every farmer; that the strong man and woman have healthy children is widely recognized too. But we have left the moral and mental faculties as qualities for which we can provide amply by home environment and sound education.

It is the stock itself which makes its home environment; the education is of small service, unless it be applied to an intelligent race of men.

The special advantages of twins as subjects for the study of human heredity were recognized by Galton. In his "Inquiries into Human Faculty and Its Development" (1883), Galton discusses data on the resemblances of twins, which he had gathered through a questionnaire survey. He concentrates particularly on the developmental history of 35 pairs of twins who had been very similar in childhood and 20 pairs described as very dissimilar in childhood. Galton himself refers to the existence of two types of twins, one with identical heredity and the other no more alike in heredity than ordinary siblings, but he had no data permitting the genetic classification of his own cases. Much of his discussion pertains to the fact that the similar twins retained their close similarity throughout life, despite frequent divergence in their living conditions as adults. Conversely, the dissimilar twins remained dissimilar, even though exposed to a common home environment in childhood.

Galton's material on twins was purely anecdotal and no attempt was made to quantify it. The first quantitative study of twin resemblance in psychological traits was conducted by Edward L. Thorndike. Working with 50 pairs of twins enrolled in New York City public schools, Thorndike correlated the scores obtained by the twins in each pair on a series of simple psychological tests. For comparative purposes, similar correlations were computed for a group of siblings attending the same schools. Among the twins, comparisons were likewise made between correlations obtained with younger and with older twins, with mental and with physical traits, and with those mental functions in which training is customarily provided (such as multiplication) and those in which it is not. The rationale underlying Thorndike's interpretations of the results obtained in each of these comparisons can be questioned. For example, it cannot be assumed that the environments of siblings are psychologically as similar as the environments of twins. Because of their identical age and similar appearance, twins are more likely to have common experiences and to be treated alike than are siblings.

Thorndike did not subdivide his twin cases into identical and fraternal—in fact, he did not accept the distinction between these two types of twins. Later investigators,[2] however, have found that fraternal twin correlations fall approximately midway between sibling correlations and identical twin correlations. In intelligence tests, such as the Stanford-Binet, for example, identical twin correlations are close to .90, fraternal twin correlations fall between .60 and .70, and sibling correlations cluster around .50. It should be noted that the difference between the sibling and fraternal correlations must result from the greater environmental similarity of the twins, since degree of hereditary relationship is the same in both cases. The difference between fraternal and identical twin correlations, on the other hand, has been frequently attributed to heredity. Even some of this difference, however, may reflect the still greater environmental similarity of identical as compared to fraternal twins, for which there is some empirical data. Since they are always of the same sex and

[2] For further discussion and references, see Anne Anastasi. *Differential psychology.* 3rd ed. New York: Macmillan, 1958. (Ch. 9.)

physically more alike than fraternal twins, identical twins tend to be closer to each other and to share more experiences.

Early investigations on the inheritance of human traits, such as those of Pearson and Thorndike, serve to remind us that a particular study can contribute significantly to the development of an area of research even when its own conclusions may later be questioned or disproved.

Edward Lee Thorndike

Measurements of Twins*

The General Argument

We inquire concerning those causes which make one of a twin pair resemble the other. We mean by resemblance any greater likeness than would be found in a pair of children of the same age and sex picked at random from the school population of New York City. . . . These measures of resemblance will be presented in the form of Pearson coefficients of correlation corrected for attenuation by the methods described by Spearman.

If now these resemblances are due to the fact that the two members of any twin pair are treated alike at home, have the same parental models, attend the same school, and are subject in general to closely similar environmental conditions, then (1) twins should, up to the age of leaving home, grow more and more alike, and in our measurements the twins 13 and 14 years old should be much more alike than those 9 and 10 years old. Again (2) if similarity in training is

* E. L. Thorndike. Measurements of twins. Arch. Philos., Psychol., scient. Meth., 1905, No. 1. (Pp. 1–2, 6–12.)

the cause of similarity in mental traits, ordinary fraternal[3] pairs not over four or five years apart in age should show a resemblance somewhat nearly as great as twin pairs, for the home and school condition of a pair of the former will not be much less similar than those of a pair of the latter. Again, (3) if training is the cause, twins should show greater resemblance in the case of traits much subject to training, such as ability in addition or in multiplication, than in traits less subject to training, such as quickness in marking off the A's on a sheet of printed capitals, or in writing the opposites of words.

On the other hand, (1) the nearer the resemblance of young twins comes to equaling that of old, (2) the greater the superiority of twin resemblance to ordinary fraternal resemblance is, and (3) the nearer twin resemblance in relatively untrained capacities comes to equaling that in capacities at which the home and school direct their attention, the more must the resemblances found be attributed to inborn traits. . . .

The Resemblances of Twins and of Siblings

From the information at hand, which is not so satisfactory as information I hope to obtain during the next few years, the resemblance of twins in mental traits is roughly twice that of ordinary siblings; according to the actual figures of my measurements of siblings, more than twice. I have reason, however, to believe that the correlation coefficients obtained for siblings are affected by constant errors which make them too low; namely, the selection of mentally unlike pairs by the conditions of the methods of obtaining siblings and the absence of suitable data to make sufficient correction for attenuation. Table 1 gives the facts.

[3] Thorndike uses this term to refer to siblings, not to fraternal twins—Ed.

TABLE 1. *The Resemblances of Twins and Siblings Compared*

Ability	Coefficients of Correlation	
	Twins	Siblings
A test	.69	.32
Word test	.71	.29
Opposites test	.90	.30

In this and following sections I shall use the words *"resemblance of"* and *"likeness of"* as synonyms for *"coefficient of correlation between."* A resemblance of .50 means then a Pearson correlation coefficient of .50. I shall use the terms A test, word test, misspelled word test, opposites test, addition, and multiplication to mean the tests, or at times the abilities measured by the tests. . . .

The Resemblances of Young and of Old Twins

The older twins show no closer resemblance than the younger twins, and the chances are surely four to one that

TABLE 2. *The Resemblances of Young and Old Twins Compared*

Ability	In Corrected Coefficients		In Raw Coefficients	
	Twins 9–11	Twins 12–14	Twins 9–11	Twins 12–14
1. A test	.66	.73	.58	.67
2. Word test	.81	.62	.62	.49
3. Misspelled word test	.76	.74	.76	.74
4. Addition	.90	.54	.83	.46
5. Multiplication	.91	.69	.81	.53
6. Opposites	.96	.88	.79	.78
Marks in (1), (2), and (3) combined			.71	.69
Marks in (4), (5), and (6) combined			.90	.75
Averages	.83	.70	.75	.64

with an infinite number of twins tested the 12–14 year olds would not show a resemblance .15 greater than the 9–11 year olds. The facts are given in Table 2.

The Resemblances in Traits Little and in Traits Much Subject to Training

The variations in the closeness of resemblance of the twins in the different traits show little, and possibly no, direct correlation with the amount of opportunity for environmental influences. The traits most subject to training (addition and multiplication) do show closer resemblances than the traits least subject to training (the A test and word test); but on the other hand show less close resemblances than the traits moderately subject to training (the misspelled word test and opposites test). The hypothesis that the true resemblance varies in amount *inversely* with the amount of opportunity for environmental influence would not be irreconcilable with the facts, and the hypothesis that the differences between the different traits are due to chance (including in that term the variable errors of the measurements and the possibility of the unequal inheritance of different traits) is the most probable of all. The difference between the traits most sub-

TABLE 3. *The Resemblances of Twins in Traits Little and in Traits Much Subject to Training*

Ability	Coefficients of Correlation	Averages
1. A test	.69	.70
2. Word test	.71	
3. Misspelled word test	.80	.85
6. Opposites test	.90	
4. Addition	.75	.795
5. Multiplication	.84	
Marks in (1), (2), and (3) combined	.70 (raw)	
Marks in (4), (5), and (6) combined	.82 (raw)	

ject and those least subject to training is no greater than the median difference between any one trait of the six and any other. Surely there is no evidence here of any large contribution from similarity of training to similarity of achievement. The facts are given in Table 3.

The Resemblances in Mental Traits Compared with the Resemblances in Physical Traits

It is highly probable from the facts given that the similarity of twins in ancestry and conditions of conception and birth accounts for almost all of their similarity in mental achievement,—that only a small fraction of it can be attributed to similarity in training. On general principles it is also highly probable that similarity of ancestry and conditions of conception will produce equal similarity in original physical nature and in original mental nature. Certain resemblances in original physical nature are in all probability neither increased nor decreased by such similarities and differences of home training as act upon twins and non-related children, respectively, within a group such as ours; e.g., resemblances in cephalic index, ratio of height sitting to total height, eye color, and hair color. Other resemblances in original physical nature are so increased and decreased slightly and perhaps

TABLE 4.   The Resemblances of Twins in Mental and in Physical Traits

In Mental Traits		In Physical Traits	
1. A test	.69	11. Cephalic index	.76
2. Word test	.71	12. Ht. sitting/ht.	.76
3. Misspelled word test	.80	13. Height	.78
4. Addition	.75	14. Height sitting	.83
5. Multiplication	.84	15. Circ. of head	.75
6. Opposites	.90	16. Width of head	.86
7. Combined mark in 1–3	.70	17. Arm length	.72
8. Combined mark in 4–6	.82	18. Finger length	.71

not at all; e.g., circumference of head, length of head, width of head, length of forearm, and length of finger joints.

If then the resemblances of twins were almost entirely due to original nature, we should expect them to be only slightly in excess of the resemblances in physical traits. The existence of the latter as a fact may properly be taken as a partial verification of the former as a general hypothesis. The evidence of its existence is given in Table 4.

Summary and Criticism

The facts . . . prove that among one hundred twins living and attending school in New York City in 1903–4, the mental resemblances of a twin pair are about twice as great as those of a pair of siblings similarly chosen, are as great or nearly as great in the case of the younger as of the older half of the group, are as great or nearly as great in the case of the A, word, misspelled word, and opposites tests as in the case of addition and multiplication, and are only slightly, if at all, greater than resemblances in physical traits which could have been caused, in some cases, only by original nature.

The facts are easily, simply, and completely explained by one simple hypothesis: namely, that the natures of the germ cells—the conditions of conception—cause whatever similarities and differences exist in the original natures of men, that these conditions influence body and mind equally, and that in life the differences in modification of body and mind produced by such differences as obtain between the environments of present-day New York City public school children are slight. . . .

It may be said that all that has been proved of the twins is that the environmental conditions from 9 to 14 years count little; that the similarities in environment *in utero* and during childhood are left as possible causes of the resemblances found; and that these are the real causes. But that the conditions *in utero* are the cause of the resemblances of related individuals is disproved by the fact that paternal is as great as maternal resemblance in the case of those traits where parents and offspring have been compared; and that similarities in environment from 0 to 9 years should produce a far greater effect on the children's abilities to add, multiply, mark misspelled words, and write opposites than do similarities in environment from 9 to 15 is a notion utterly devoid of probability.

It is equally difficult to accept original nature as a cause of a moderate amount of the resemblance found and to explain the rest as due to training. Suppose, for instance, that someone assumes that the force of the germ-natures—of the conditions of conception—is sufficient to produce a resemblance of .20 in siblings and .40 in twins in mental traits. He must then be willing to believe that the likeness in training of a twin pair is enough greater than the likeness in training of a sibling pair, two or three years apart in age, to make the .40 rise to .80, whereas the .20 rises only to .40 or less. He must also be willing to believe either that inborn mental make-up is inherited by a totally different law from that regulating inborn physical make-up or else that the similarities in training of twins will raise .40 to .80 in physical traits such as cephalic index, and that the similarities in training of siblings will raise the .20 only to .40 or .50. He must also place the bulk of influence of this training previous to the tenth year and assume that it is of such a generalized sort as would raise the resemblances in marking A's or words containing *r* and *e* as much as that in multiplication.

Doubtless we all feel a repugnance to assigning so little efficacy to environmental forces as the facts of this study seem to demand; but common opinion also feels a repugnance to believing that the mental resemblances of twins, however caused, are as great as the physical resemblances. Yet they are. I cannot here discuss the general facts and detailed studies which bear upon the question of the amount of influence of such likenesses and differences in environment as existed in the case of these twins.

I shall also spend but little time in comments upon the application of the facts so far presented to theories of education and human action and to the practical problems of social control. The inferences with respect to the enormous importance of original nature in determining the behavior and achievements of any man in comparison with his fellows of the same period of civilization and conditions of life are obvious. All theories of human life must accept as a first principle the fact that human beings at birth differ enormously in mental capacities and that these differences are largely due to similar differences in their ancestry. All attempts to change human nature must accept as their most important condition the limits set by original nature to each individual.

We must be careful, however, not to confuse two totally different things: (1) the power of the environment—for instance, of schools, laws, books, and social ideals—to produce differences in the relative achievements of men, and (2) the power of the environment to produce differences in absolute achievement. It has been shown that the relative differences in certain mental traits which were found in these one-hundred children are due almost entirely to differences in ancestry, not in training; but this does not in the least deny that better methods of training might improve all their achievements fifty per cent or that the absence of training, say in spelling and arithmetic, might decrease the corresponding achievements to zero. . . .

The argument has been limited entirely to the causes which make one person differ from another in mental achievements *under the same general conditions of life at the beginning of the twentieth century in New York City as pupils in its school system.* If the resemblance of twins had been measured in the case of a group made up partly of New York City school children and partly of children of equal capacity brought up in the wilds of Africa, the variability of the group in addition and multiplication would have increased and the correlation coefficients would rise. They would then measure the influence of original nature plus the now much increased influence of the environment.

The relative impotence of such similarities of home training as existed in our fifty pairs of twins to create similarities of achievement does, however, make one suspect that the magnitude of the influence of the training given by schools, periods of civilization, and the like has been exaggerated. For other reasons, also, I imagine this to be the case, but to prove or disprove it, one would need data quite different from the records of these hundred twins.

It is then folly to conclude that the inheritance of mental capacities from immediate ancestry implies the futility of education and social control in general—the wisdom of fatalism and *laissez faire.* Such studies as this merely prove the existence of and measure one determinant of human intellect and character and demonstrate that the influences of the environment are differential, the product varying not only in accord with the environmental force itself but also in accord with the original nature upon which it operates. We may even expect that education will be doubly effective, once society recognizes the advantages given to some and denied to others by heredity. That men have different amounts of capacity does not imply any the less advantage from or need of wise investment. . . .

To the real work of man for man—the increase of achievement through the improvement of the environment—the influence of heredity offers no barrier. But to the popular demands from education and social reforms it does. For the common man does not much appreciate absolute happiness or absolute betterment. He does not rejoice that he and his children are healthier, happier, and more supplied with noble pleasures than were his ancestors of a thousand years ago.

His complaint is that he is not so well off as some of those about him; his pride is that he is above the common herd. The common man demands *relative superiority*—to be above those of his own time and locality. If his son leads the community, he does not mind his real stupidity; to be the handsomest girl in the county is beauty enough. Social discontent comes from the knowledge or fancy that one is below others in welfare. The effort of children in school, of men in labor, and of women in the home is, except as guided by the wise instincts of nature or more rarely by the wisdom of abstract thought, to rise above someone who seems higher. Thus the prizes which most men really seek are after all in large measure given or withheld by original nature. In the actual race of life, which is not to get ahead, but to get ahead of somebody, the chief determining factor is heredity.

Another approach to the heredity-environment problem was provided by the study of foster children. Like twin research, this approach seemed to offer promise of disentangling the roles of heredity and environment in behavior development. But it, too, proved to have methodological complications that precluded definitive interpretation of results.

Early studies of foster children were concerned chiefly with practical questions of the educational and social adjustment of such children. It was not until 1928, when the National Society for the Study of Education devoted its Twenty-seventh Yearbook to the topic of "Nature and Nurture," that reports of quantitative, controlled research on foster children first appeared. This Yearbook included an investigation of foster children conducted at Stanford University by Burks,[4] under the general direction of Terman, and another

[4] Barbara S. Burks. The relative influence of nature and nurture upon mental development; a comparative study of foster parent–foster child resemblance and true parent–true child resemblance. *27th Yearb., Nat. Soc. Stud. Educ.*, 1928, Pt. I, 219–316.

conducted at the University of Chicago by Freeman and his associates.[5] The controversial nature of the problem is reflected in the fact that the two studies reached opposite conclusions—Burks emphasizing the contribution of heredity and Freeman the contribution of environment. In the next decade, Leahy[6] at the University of Minnesota repeated Burks' study with some methodological improvements and reached essentially the same conclusion, as will be seen in the next selection. Skodak and Skeels,[7] working at the University of Iowa, conducted still another study of foster children and again emphasized the role of home environment in their interpretations.

That different investigators can reach such sharply divergent conclusions is an indication of the complex methodological problems inherent in research with foster children. When results are ambiguous, the investigator's theoretical orientation is likely to color his interpretations. And when no experimental design completely avoids pitfalls, the data of each study are subject to different sources of error.

Some of the limitations of research with foster children stem from the procedures necessarily followed by placement agencies. It is a common policy of such agencies, for example, to try to "fit the child to the home" on the basis of any available knowledge about the child or his background. Such selective placement may produce spurious correlations between a child's IQ and the characteristics of the foster parents or foster home. On the other hand, it is also standard practice to place children only in the more desirable foster homes. Consequently, the cultural range of foster homes is narrower than that of the general population. With such a restricted range, the effect of environmental differences will be underestimated. For that matter, any estimate of the "proportional contribution" of heredity or environment to individual differences could be obtained,

[5] F. N. Freeman, K. J. Holzinger, and B. C. Mitchell. The influence of environment on the intelligence, school achievement, and conduct of foster children. *27th Yearb., Nat. Soc. Stud. Educ.*, 1928, Pt. I, 103–217.

[6] Alice M. Leahy. Nature-nurture and intelligence. *Genet. Psychol. Monogr.*, 1935, **17**, 236–308.

[7] Marie Skodak. Children in foster homes: A study of mental development. *Univer. Iowa Stud. Child Welf.*, 1939, **16**, No. 1. Marie Skodak and H. M. Skeels. A final follow-up study of one hundred adopted children. *J. genet. Psychol.*, 1950, **77**, 3–9.

ranging from 0 to 100 per cent, depending on the range of hereditary and environmental variation included in the investigation. This is one reason why such estimates of proportional contribution have subsequently been challenged. Still another reason is their assumption that hereditary and environmental influences combine in an additive fashion. Interaction is now generally regarded as a more appropriate model for their operation. These more basic theoretical issues will be considered further in Chapter 7.

Still other complications arise from the influence of the pre-adoption environment on the foster child's psychological development. If the child has lived either with his own parents or relatives or in an institution prior to adoption, such experiences represent uncontrolled factors in the study. With children adopted in early infancy, as in Leahy's study, there still remain the important contributions of prenatal and natal conditions. A growing body of data indicates that medical complications of pregnancy and parturition as well as deficiencies in maternal diet—all of which are more prevalent in culturally deprived populations—are significantly associated with intellectual retardation and other behavioral handicaps in children.

Mention should also be made of the nature of the family relationship in foster homes. The attitudes of parents toward a foster child are likely to differ in essential ways from the attitudes of parents toward their own children. Knowledge of adoption may also affect the child's own attitudes. Social expectancy, which tends to augment parent-child resemblance in ordinary families, would operate differently with foster children. It is difficult to estimate the possible effects of such attitudinal and motivational factors on the child's development.

Alice Mary Leahy

Nature-Nurture and Intelligence*

Variation in human intelligence is universally recognized. But experimentation to discover the causes which affect this variation has moved slowly. The reasons are obvious. First, conditions which permit the control of either heredity or environment are difficult to secure, and secondly, our tools for measurement are limited and crude. Although identical twins provide an absolute control of heredity, their separate location in diverse environments is rare. Experimentation involving the control of environment, on the other hand, is not entirely possible. Measures are available for only certain of its features. For its dynamic attributes we have no measures. Hence, what may appear to be similar environments are only approximately identical. However, the individual mental examination has been demonstrated to be fairly reliable [as a measure] of what may be called test intelligence.

The present investigation approaches the problem by a comparison of two groups of children living in approximately identical environments. In one group, the children are unrelated by blood or marriage to the persons shaping the environment. They are adopted children. In the other group, the children are the offspring of the persons who have shaped the environment. Both heredity and environment are

* Alice M. Leahy. Nature-nurture and intelligence. *Genet. Psychol. Monogr.*, 1935, **17**, 236–308. (Pp. 241, 255–258, 282–284, 304–305.) Reprinted by permission of the author and The Journal Press.

operative in the latter group, while in the former, only environment. . . .

In order that the least possible ambiguity exist in our results, the experimental group was limited to:

1. *Children placed in their adoptive homes at the age of 6 months or younger* (The mean age of placement was 2.5 months). At this early age precise judgments of mental ability on the basis of test performance, physical development, or overt behavior are highly improbable. Further, this criterion assures from early infancy an environment that is no more or less changing in character than that enjoyed by children in general. Moreover, it definitely avoids the difficulties which would arise in attempting to measure the influence of environment previous to the adoptive one under consideration.

2. *Only those adopted children who were known to be of white race, non-Jewish, north-European extraction.* This prerequisite tends to reduce the possibilities of a fortuitous resemblance between adoptive parent and child on the basis of racial regression. In addition it minimizes the possibility of a spurious heterogeneity arising from uncontrolled factors relating to race. Further, it limits the group to one which is similar in composition to the one on which the Stanford-Binet test was standardized.

3. *Children who were not less than 5 nor more than 14 years of age at the time of investigation.* This age range is conceded to give the most reliable test results.

4. *Children reared in communities of 1000 or more.* In this way we attempted to equalize the influence of such environmental factors as churches, clubs, and schools. No farm children are included. Ninety-five per cent of the group have been reared in communities of over 10,000.

5. *Children who were legally adopted by married persons.* Thus we secured a group where the legal relationship and

responsibility between parent and child was the same as that of true parent and offspring.

6. *Adoptive parents who were of white race, non-Jewish, north-European extraction.* With this criterion we attempted to reduce the possibility of adventitious resemblance and further reduced the possibility of securing non-English-speaking homes.

By adhering rigidly to the foregoing criteria it is believed that we have controlled the element of selective placement to a point beyond the facilities of earlier investigators and to the highest possible degree that present day child adoption permits. . . .

With the primary purpose of a control group serving as a check upon the validity of our methods, each *adopted* child was matched with an *own* child as follows:

1. *For sex.*
2. *Within an age range of plus or minus 6 months.*
3. *Whose fathers' occupations fell in the same group on the Minnesota Occupational Scale.*
4. *Whose fathers' school attainments agreed within plus or minus one school grade level.*
5. *Whose mothers' school attainments agreed within plus or minus one school grade level.*
6. *Whose parents were white race, non-Jewish, north-European extraction.*
7. *Whose residence has been in communities of 1000 or more.*

— — —

The relationship between test intelligence of children and various attributes of their home environment is shown in Table 1. . . . For the Adopted children [the correlations] are consistently low, about .20. In the Control group they maintain the level usually found for hereditary physical charac-

TABLE 1.   Child's IQ Correlated with Other Factors (r corrected for unequal range in child's IQ)*

Correlated Factor	Adopted		Control	
	N	r	N	r
Father's Otis score	178	.19	175	.51
Mother's Otis score	186	.24	191	.51
Mid-parent Otis score	177	.21	173	.60
Father's Stanford-Binet vocabulary	177	.26	168	.47
Mother's Stanford-Binet vocabulary	185	.24	190	.49
Mid-parent Stanford-Binet vocabulary	174	.29	164	.56
Environmental status score	194	.23	194	.53
Cultural index of home	194	.26	194	.51
Child training index	194	.22	194	.52
Economic index	194	.15	194	.37
Sociality index	194	.13	194	.42
Father's education	193	.19	193	.48
Mother's education	192	.25	194	.50
Mid-parent education	193	.24	194	.54
Father's occupational status	194	.14	194	.45

* Although these correlations were corrected for unequal ranges in IQ of adopted and control children, no correction was made for the wider variability in home environment found in the control group. See W. D. Wallis. Observations on Dr. Alice M. Leahy's "Nature-nurture and intelligence." J. genet. Psychol., 1936, 49, 315–324—Ed.

teristics, .50. In the case of the latter group heredity and environment are both operative. Hence variance in intelligence is accounted for by variance in heredity and environment combined to the extent of about 25 per cent (square of r .50). In the Adopted group, however, where environment is functioning independently of heredity, variance in intelligence is accounted for by variance in environment only to the extent of about 4 per cent (square of r .20). If we neglect whatever artificial heredity selective placement of adopted children may have introduced into the data, these coefficients are clear evidence of maximum variance in intelligence with variance in environment. Apparently environment cannot compensate for the lack of blood relationship in creating mental resemblance between parent and child. Heredity persists. . . .

Conclusions

By methods which allowed the effects of environment to be studied separately from those of heredity in combination with environment, this study attempted to discover the influence of environment and heredity on intellectual variation. As stated in the opening section, the tendencies observed in this study are valid only for populations which are similar to the experimental population in composition. However, the consistency with which a coefficient of .50 was secured for parent and offspring suggests that the restricted range in both the hereditary and environmental variables was reciprocal and hence no serious distortion in our results exists. The main conclusions are as follows:

1. Variation in IQ is accounted for by variation in home environment to the extent of not more than 4 per cent; 96 per cent of the variation is accounted for by other factors.

2. Measurable environment does not shift the IQ by more than 3 to 5 points above or below the value it would have had under normal environmental conditions.

3. The nature or hereditary component in intelligence causes greater variation than does environment. When nature and nurture are operative, shifts in IQ as great as 20 IQ points are observed with shifts in the cultural level of the home and neighborhood.

4. Variation in the personality traits measured in this study other than that of intelligence appears to be accounted for less by variation in heredity than by variation in environment.

6

Behavior Genetics:

Selective Breeding

It is apparent that statistical studies of family resemblance—even those dealing with such special groups as twins and foster children have failed to provide clear-cut data on the role of heredity in behavior development. As a group, these studies share the weaknesses of all **ex post facto** experimental designs, in which the experimenter has no control over the conditions to which subjects are exposed. The experimenter, for example, does not choose children for adoption nor does he choose the homes to which they are assigned. When dealing with human subjects, these decisions obviously must be based on the welfare of the individual rather than the objectives of the experiment. For these reasons, animal research permits the use of better controlled experimental designs and the introduction of more extreme environmental variations than is possible with human subjects. The results of some of these animal studies are cited in the two papers presented in Chapter 7.

A more direct approach to behavior genetics is provided by animal experiments on selective breeding. Since the pioneer work of Mendel in the nineteenth century, geneticists have employed selective breeding with many forms of animal and plant life and have thereby accumulated a vast amount of knowledge regarding the inheritance of physical traits. The application of selective breeding techniques to behavior genetics is more recent and much more limited.

A classic experiment on selective breeding for a behavioral characteristic was conducted by Tryon and first reported in the 1940 Yearbook of the National Society for the Study of Education. The strains of "maze-bright" and "maze-dull" rats originally bred by Tryon are still providing subjects for behavior research today. One fact established both by Tryon and by other investigators is that the strains cannot be said to differ in "general intelligence" or in general learning ability, since the maze-dull rats equal or excel the maze-bright rats in other types of learning tasks. Apparently their differences are more narrowly limited to the behavioral functions for which they were initially selected. Insofar as heredity underlies these behavioral differences, moreover, it must operate through organic factors. Some of these organic differences have been tentatively identified, but the search continues today.

Robert Choate Tryon

Genetic Differences in Maze-Learning Ability in Rats*

The experimental geneticist is inclined to be somewhat skeptical of conclusions from nature-nurture studies on human beings. The complex breeding system deriving from the adventitious circumstances of "young love" and the wide differences in environments into which the progeny of such matings are born and reared present such a complex matrix of determiners of "mental" differences that it would appear hopeless to endeavor to separate out the relative effects of those termed "nature" and those termed "nurture." Furthermore, the indubitable tendency in the uncontrolled human environment for different genotypes to seek out different environments, and conversely, for different environments to

*R. C. Tryon. Genetic differences in maze-learning ability in rats. *39th Yearb., Nat. Soc. Stud. Educ.*, 1940, Part I, 111–119. Reprinted by permission of the publisher.

select special genotypes, and all this to an unknown degree, creates a correlation between nature and nurture that confounds any analyst who has neither an hereditary nor an environmental axe to grind. And on top of it all, to make the confusion worse, are the ambiguous psychological omnibus tests of mental ability, about the psychological validity of which the most able psychologists cannot agree.

After several centuries of the type of groping called "natural history," the biologist in his role as experimental geneticist has discovered that the only way to get definite answers to the nature-nurture question in plants and animals is to establish a pure strain experimentally by means of a controlled selective breeding schedule and then experimentally to vary systematically the milieu for different samples of the strain. The logic is, indeed, very simple: In a given species, (1) hold heredity constant by choosing a pure strain, then study the effects of different environment on it, and (2) hold the environment constant, then vary heredity by studying the development of different pure strains in it, and (3) compare the relative effects of the two types of variations that are, respectively, nature and nurture. Though the logic is simple, its experimental execution is arduous, often requiring many years of work even when investigating only one character in one species.

As the psychologist cannot, of course, perform such experiments on human beings, he must turn to animals. During the last three decades, the animal psychologist has developed techniques for the reliable and valid measurement of individual differences in numerous psychological characters of animals, especially of rats. The securing of definite answers to the question of the relative effects of nature and nurture on psychological characters is thus made possible. An experimental genetics focused on animal *behavior* and ultimately based on studies of numerous species of animals varying in phylogenetic complexity should give us the answers we wish. . . .

The attempts of the writer to design and execute such a psychological genetics experiment are outlined below. The essential aims have been to establish under environmental control a maze-bright and a maze-dull strain of rats, to determine the nature of the genetic determiners at work, to discover the constancy of this psychological difference throughout a large range of the rats' life span, and to find important biological and psychological correlates of the differences in this maze ability. Finally, the effects of systematic environmental changes on each strain are to be investigated. Though the work has now been in progress eleven years, it is in many respects still preliminary. Findings are complete with respect to some of the objectives but not to others. A brief summary is presented below under the various types of analyses.

Proof of the Inheritance of Individual Differences in Maze Ability

An experiment was begun in 1927 that had as its purpose the establishment by selective breeding of a pure line of maze-bright and a pure line of maze-dull rats. Each animal was run nineteen trials through a seventeen-blind T maze. His score was the total number of entrances into blind alleys. The breeding schedule consisted in mating together the brightest rats within each of the brightest litters, the dullest within each of the dullest. Rigorous environmental controls were effected (1) by instituting standard procedure of animal care and of breeding, (2) by using an automatic mechanical device for delivering the animals into the maze without handling, and (3) by employing an electric recorder for the scoring of each rat's maze run. These controls have remained constant for eleven years. Selective breeding has been continued for eighteen generations. As success in establishing strains of bright and dull animals is crucial to

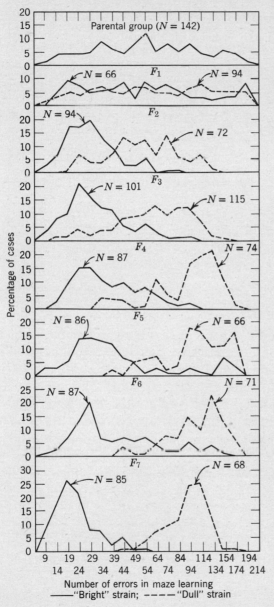

FIG. 1   Effects of selective breeding on maze learning. Along the bottom is the scale of brightness as evidenced by the total number of blind-alley entrances made in 19 trials. All the distributions use this common scale. For instance, a bright animal who made from 10 to 14 errors would fall under the scale step, the upper limit of which is marked 14, a dull who made from 195 to 214 errors would fall under 214, etc. The first generation of rats, marked "Parental group," is shown at the top. The total number of these rats was 142, and the percentage of them lying at each point on the scale is indicated in the distribution. The brightest of these were bred together, and then the dullest, giving the two F_1 groups, as shown. The selective breeding effects are shown down to the F_7, where progeny of B_6 (bright F_6) are markedly different from the progeny of D_6 (dull F_6).

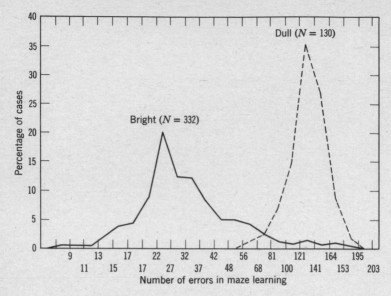

FIG. 2   Bright and dull strains of the fifteenth to eighteenth generations.

the proposed project, I present in Figure 1 the basic data showing the effects of selective breeding through the F_7 generation. For brevity, I have not presented all the later generations, but to show the latest results, I have given in Figure 2 the results in the F_{15}, F_{16}, F_{17}, F_{18} generations. In this figure the distributions of the two strains are shown for these later generations combined. There appears to be a law of diminishing returns, for after the F_7 negligible effects of selective breeding are noted. The results for all generations will be depicted in final form in terms of the improved normalized scale.

The Genetic Basis of Differences in Maze-Learning Ability

What is the genetic factor basis of differences in learning ability? How many factors must be postulated and what is the nature of their interaction? Geneticists propose a multiple cumulative-factor theory as the genetic explanation of the plant and animal characters that have statistical frequencies similar to those of maze-learning. One crucial experimental test of this theory is the cross between the pure lines at the two extremes of the scale. The F_1 progeny of such a cross should show a homogeneous median performance. The next generation progeny of the F_1 should vary widely over the whole scale. Figure 3 shows the actual results of such a test on our behavior trait. The F_2 progeny

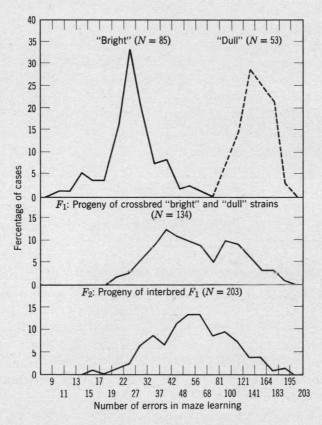

FIG. 3 F_1 and F_2 of bright × dull.

of the F_1 do *not* vary more than the F_1. Because the going theory was not verified, I repeated this crucial type of cross several years after the first attempt, but the results were the same. Figure 3 combines the findings of both series of experiments.

We need to develop and verify a factor hypothesis consistent with the facts of Figures 1, 2, and 3, and with the results of certain back-cross experiments. One method is that of expressing a given hypothesis concretely in terms of a dice-pattern. A random parental population is then set up in which the score of each fictitious individual is determined by a dice throw. These "individuals" are then "bred" according to the actual breeding schedule of the rat experiment and the theoretical results compared for fit with the experimental findings. The hypothesis that gives the best fit and that is most consistent with genetic theory will be the one finally chosen. I have performed several such artificial experiments, and from these it appears that the most promising hypothesis investigated to date is one that postulates multiple factors, some dominant for bright performance, some (but fewer) dominant for dull, and some cumulative. The effects of linkage and crossing-over, and of reciprocal crossing—that is, bright male $\times$ dull female vs. dull male $\times$ bright female—must be investigated.

Biological Correlates of Brightness and Dullness

Large groups of bright and dull animals have been carefully measured in respect to brain size and weight, body weight, and fertility. Significant differences have been discovered. The bright animals show physical superiority throughout, except in the one particular of fertility. Because of the intensive inbreeding that has occurred during the process of selective breeding, the evaluation of these findings is to some extent equivocal.

The Constancy of Differences in Ability

The extent to which brightness and dullness persist throughout the lives of the animals was investigated. One hundred and seven animals were measured in maze ability when they were young; then an interval of seven months, amounting to about two-thirds of a rat's life span, was permitted to elapse before remeasurement. The correlation between the early and late measurements was .80, indicating a high degree of constancy. For different subgroups that experienced different degrees of environmental variation during the intervening period between measurements, the correlation was the same—a result suggesting that environment as varied in these experiments plays a negligible role in this ability.

Psychological Nature of Brightness and Dullness

A variety of experiments were conducted that aimed to provide some insight into the psychological nature of the differences between the bright and dull groups.

Evidence from Ratings of Emotional Characteristics. Using reliable, objective rating scales, carefully standardized on a large group of pre-experimental animals, three judges independently rated 234 bright, dull, and stock animals on their hiding, avoidance, and escape reactions to controlled handling by the experimenter, and on their reactions to novel inanimate objects in the maze situation. The results show clearly that the bright animals are most adjusted "emotionally" in the maze-learning situation, whereas in response to handling they are "neurotic." Exactly the reverse is the case for dulls.

Evidence from a Cluster Analysis. In addition to the measures of emotionality, this same group of 234 animals was measured on eleven different aspects of efficiency at different stages of learning the maze; for example, efficiency as measured by errors, speed (rate) of running, hesitation time at choice-points. The significant result from the analysis appears to be that the hereditary difference in maze ability, which was itself discovered by selection on the basis of errors only, is reflected in all the measures of efficiency as well as in those of emotionality.

Evidence from Experiments on the Sensory Nature of Ability Differences. Are bright animals superior to dull because of superiority in *sense acuity,* or does their superiority reside in a capacity for *abstracting* the spatial relations of the complex maze path? On the sense acuity hypothesis, one would assume that during the 19 trials in the maze the bright animals had learned to follow visual, auditory, kinesthetic, tactual, and olfactory cues by virtue of genetic superiority in their senses. Five experiments were conducted to investigate this hypothesis. In each experiment about 70 bright and 70 dull animals were subjects. Stated briefly, the technique was that of experimentally disrupting cues of the various sense modalities on the trials following the nineteenth. In every experiment the bright animals showed relatively negligible disturbance; many showed no disturbance at all as a consequence of cue disruption. These results fail to support the sense theory, but rather support the view that bright animals are superior to dull in a capacity to generalize the spatial pattern.

Evidence from an Analysis of the "Qualitative" Behavior of Bright and Dull Animals in the Maze Situation. To investigate further the differences between bright and dull animals in the nonsensory determinants of their maze behavior, I analyzed the frequency pattern of errors made in the 17 blind alleys of the maze by 500 bright and 500 dull animals. As the error patterns of the two types of animals were quite different, especially in the later stages of learning, I attempted to deduce the existence of a number of psychological gradients of a nonsensory spatial character that theoretically determined the behavior of brights and dulls. As the postulation of such gradients constituted being "wise after the event," I then attempted to predict the pattern of errors made by 150 animals in a quite different twenty-blind maze. The correlation between the predicted error pattern and the actual error frequencies was .70, and with minor changes in the weights of the gradients, the correlation was .92. The hypothesis of nonsensory gradients is therefore supported.

Evidence from the Study of the Behavior of Maze-Bright and Maze-Dull Animals in Other Problem-Solving Situations. To what degree does hereditary brightness and dullness represent a *general* capacity to learn? In one experiment 150 animals were run through another maze. In another study, conducted by Krechevsky, bright and dull groups were studied in a brightness discrimination box. At the present time Searle is engaged in a program of observing the performance of bright and dull animals in a number of tasks requiring discrimination of distance, angles, and brightness. From the work done and under way, and from published data of other workers showing the relation between maze-learning and other types of learning, the evidence clearly supports the view that maze-learning is specific. The doctrine of alleged "general ability" supported by many psychologists has not been substantiated in rats.

A significant contribution to behavior genetics is to be found in the research conducted by Hirsch. In collaboration with Tryon, Hirsch developed techniques for obtaining reliable individual measures of behavior among such organisms as the fruit fly, Drosophila. It thus became possible to capitalize on the mass of available genetic knowledge regarding the morphology of Drosophila, as well as on such other advantages as the brief time span between generations and the abundance of progeny. Using these techniques in later research, Hirsch has succeeded in producing strains of fruit flies that are positively or negatively geotactic, respectively, as well as others that are positively or negatively phototactic. In the former experiment, one selectively bred strain tends to fly upward, the other downward when released in a vertical maze. In the latter experiment, one tends to fly toward a source of light, the other away from it. The possibilities opened up by this type of research may be visualized when we consider that all these strain differentiations were accomplished in a few months, in contrast to the eleven years required for Tryon's original rat-breeding experiment.

Jerry Hirsch and Robert Choate Tryon

Mass Screening and Reliable Individual Measurement in the Experimental Behavior Genetics of Lower Organisms*

At our present stage of ignorance about how genes determine behavior, we might well concentrate on experimental studies of lower organisms. Their reactions may be thought of as the emergent behavior which developed through evolution into the complex behaviors of higher organisms. Knowledge gained from such studies may provide conceptual models leading to an understanding of how hereditary and stimulus components interact in determining higher forms of behavior.

For this purpose the use of lower organisms offers distinct advantages. There is a brief time span between generations, permitting E to perform in a short time period the various crossings essential to fundamental genetic studies. Each gen-

*J. Hirsch and R. C. Tryon. Mass screening and reliable individual measurement in the experimental behavior genetics of lower organisms. *Psychol. Bull.*, 1956, **53**, 402–410. (Pp. 402–407.) Reprinted by permission of the authors and the American Psychological Association.

eration produces abundant progeny, enabling E to recover the extreme behavior types required in selective breeding experiments. And further, the genetics of their morphology is better understood than is that of higher forms. The fruit fly, *Drosophila*, has all of these advantages.

First, however, reliable techniques for measuring individual differences (hereafter referred to as *ID*s) in behavior must be developed. Reliability coefficients *must* be calculated, and they must be *high*. The problem reduces to the question: How can we observe the behavior of large numbers of very small Ss and at the same time reliably measure the performance of each S?

This paper presents a method which accomplishes both these objectives. We call it the method of "*mass screening with reliable individual measurement*." As an illustration of the method, we will show that in the mass observation of a particular behavior of *Drosophila*, reliability coefficients of about .9 can be secured in an experimental test period of four minutes. During this time 15 sample observations of 15 sec. each were made. Each individual was observed as a member of a group of other flies. The method shows that *Drosophila* *ID*s can be measured as reliably as human *ID*s. Indeed, we know of no experiment on men covering 15 brief observations that yields a reliability as high as .9.

Genetics has up to the present concerned itself with physical characteristics rather than with behavior. The reliability of individual measurement is not so obviously important in the study of morphological characteristics; usually the characteristic is either present or absent, or present in only a small number of forms, and its presence or absence is immediately obvious, (e.g., eye color, notched wing, bar eyes, etc.). Individual differences in behavior, on the other hand, are not so easily recognized: such recognition requires special methods. . . .

The next section of this paper presents a method for reliably measuring *ID*s in behavior by means of *mass screen-*

ing, a procedure that achieves the objective of reliably *classifying every individual's behavior without handling or observing each small organism individually*. The method is completely general and easily applicable to the study of any behavior, both unconditioned and conditioned.

This objective is illustrated by the results of an experiment that employed the mass screening technique in the study of the geotropic reactions of *Drosophila melanogaster*. A series of 15 successive mass screenings, for example, produced 16 test tubes, each containing a different geotropic class of *Drosophila*. The flies in the tubes 0 to 15 represent different degrees of the negative geotropism. That is, the flies are differentiated on this final composite 16-point scale based on 15 prior mass screenings in which the individuals were not separately handled. The reliability coefficient of this final scale score is determinable and, in principle, it can be increased to any desired value by further mass screenings.

Conceptualization and Definition of the Behavior. The behavior chosen was the unconditioned disposition to go in the direction opposite to gravity. This negative geotropism is operationally defined as an upward movement of the fly whenever it is placed in any situation permitting travel upward, other external stimuli which might induce vertical movement being controlled.

Standard Test Sample Procedure. The test situation consists of two test tubes, a lower one standing upright in a rack, the other inverted over the mouth of the lower one. Since the flies are also phototropic, the light source was placed at right angles to the vertical. A group of flies are placed in the lower tube, shaken to the bottom, and then allowed to ascend. At the end of an arbitrary "cutting point" time of 15 sec., a card is inserted between the lower and the upper tubes. The upper tube is scored and labeled "1," and lower tube "0."

Thus the standard sample observation in this case is like a dichotomous test item, the top tube scored "pass" and the lower one "fail.'" A cutoff point of 15 sec. was found empirically to divide the group of flies into two approximately equal pass and fail subgroups, a division which avoids skewness in the distribution of final composite X_t scores.

It should be emphasized that dichotomous scoring is *not* a necessary restriction of the method. The standard procedure could have been devised to provide more classes. The pass–fail break was chosen for experimental convenience.

This standard test procedure, though satisfying the operational definition of geotropism, might not elicit uniquely a systematic reaction to gravity. Since the test tube situation permits only movement upward it may be that, if there is an *activity* differential among the Ss, the flies that are upwardly mobile may be very active flies. Only additional experiments which control activity can resolve the matter. Thus, we use the term "geotropism" here only in an operational sense, recognizing that the *ID*s observed in this situation might later be shown to be significantly influenced by additional components.

Choice of an Unselected Sample. Since the range and reliability of *ID*s is partly a function of the heterogeneity of the Ss, a stock of unselected *Drosophila* with a history of random mating was chosen.

Mass Screening. A random sample of 106 flies was screened and scored by the following procedure.

First composite score, $X_{t_1} = X_1$. The results of the first observation are shown in Figure 1, which reproduces part of the score sheet actually used. Under X_1 and f_1 it can be seen that 54 flies ascended to the upper tube, earned a "pass" and thus received a score of $X_1 = 1$. There are 52 flies that remained in the lower tube, earned a "fail" and received a score of $X_1 = 0$. The scores, X_{t_1}, of this trial take the values of 1 and 0.

Second composite score, $X_{t_2} = X_{t_1} + X_2$. The 54 flies with $X_{t_1} = 1$ were put through the standard procedure a second time for Trial 2. The 46 flies that ascended earn a

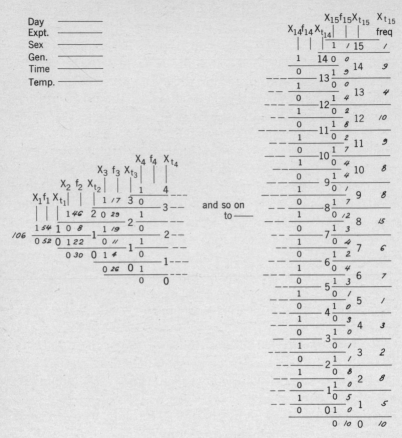

Fig. 1   Mass screening score form.

tube score, $X_2 = 1$, and a composite score $X_{t2} = 2$; the 8 remaining down have $X_2 = 0$ and $X_{t2} = 1$, as shown. In similar fashion the flies with $X_{t1} = 0$ divide into 22 earning $X_2 = 1$, $X_{t2} = 1$ and 30 earning $X_2 = 0$, $X_{t2} = 0$.

Third composite score, $X_{t3} = X_{t2} + X_3$. The standard procedure is repeated for each of the three X_{t2} classes resulting from Trial 2.

Note, even though there are four X_2 tubes of flies at the end of Trial 2, there are only three X_{t2} classes. The two subgroups with 8 and 22 flies have been combined in one tube because both received the same score, $X_{t2} = 1$, i.e., the same composite score is the cumulative sum of all previous scores irrespective of the order in which the individual "passes" and "fails" were obtained.

Additional composite scores, X_{t4}, X_{t5}, ... The procedure is continued by taking further sample observations; at the end of each one, subgroups having the same X_t score are combined for the next observation. Figure 1 shows the results schematically up through X_{t15}.

The reason for the "experimental convenience" of dichotomous classes in the standard procedure should now be apparent; with more than two classes the number of subgroups becomes unmanageable.

Analysis

The distribution of X_t *scores.* One of the objectives of experimental behavior genetics is reliable differentiation between individuals and subsequent genetic validation of differences by means of selective breeding. Since, for a given behavior, it is assumed that there is a range of ability and that the Ss in a population are distributed over the range, it follows that any methods which tend to pile up the final scores in a few extreme categories should be eschewed in favor of others which distribute the scores more widely. The individuals whose behavior is under observation will be used for breeding, hence it is important to differentiate them clearly on the behavioral scale. Failure to do this prevents the discovery of any genotypic differences that might exist.

The E can usually control the form of the distribution of total X_t scores. In our illustrative experiment this control was accomplished through selection of the time interval in which the response can be performed, i.e., the proportions p of "passes" and q of "fails" vary as a function of the amount of time allowed in the test tube. In examples from several experiments it may be shown that when $p > .5$, the X_t distribution is negatively skewed and when $p < .5$, X_t is positively skewed. Either type of skewness is undesirable because cases pile up in the extreme categories where, for the purposes of selective breeding, the finest differentiations are needed. . . .

Reliability of X_t scores. It is important that the composite X_t score be reliable if E is to use the differentiations between individuals as the basis for further experimental work on selective breeding, conditioning, or the investigation of the generality of behavior X. The reliability coefficient, r_{tt}, cannot be computed by the split-half method in the mass screening method because combining into a single group all Ss with the same composite X_t score loses the specific sample score history of each individual. The coefficient can be estimated accurately, however, from the variances of the composite X_t score and of the individual test sample scores. . . .

The authors go on to show that in this situation a reliability coefficient can be computed by the techniques commonly known as Kuder-Richardson formulas 20 and 21. The former requires a record of the proportion of individuals who "pass" and the proportion who "fail" in each trial, as well as the variance of total scores. When only total scores are available (as in the multiple-unit maze described in the next selection), reliability can be computed with the shorter formula 21, which requires only mean and variance of total scores. In Hirsch and Tryon's investigation, reliability of total scores, computed with formula 20, was .87. The authors also propose the use of the error of measurement to decide when to terminate selective breeding, explaining that this point is reached when the standard deviation of total scores is no greater than the error of measurement.

Since the publication of the original paper by Hirsch and Tryon in 1956, several improvements and refinements have been introduced in the experimental procedure. The following article illustrates the multiple-unit vertical maze that replaced the crude test-tube technique described in the first paper. It also reports the experimental development of two strains of fruit flies, one positively geotactic and one negatively geotactic.

Jerry Hirsch and Loise Erlenmeyer-Kimling

Sign of Taxis as a Property of the Genotype*

In previous behavior genetic studies of *Drosophila melano-gaster*, it was assumed that certain tactic orientations were normal, and individual differences were measured as deviations from the assumed normal orientation. Furthermore, these assumptions were often incorporated into the methods of observation and analysis, effectively guaranteeing that the results would accord with the preconception of the normal. In the study of geotaxis, individuals were scored on the strength of their negative geotaxis. The alternatives on every trial were those of responding or not responding, that is, ascending the walls of a test tube or failing to do so. In studies of phototaxis, individual and population differences were measured in terms of the strength of positive phototaxis. The alternatives in these studies were effectively those of approaching a light source or not. . . .

The present study places no restrictions on the sign of the taxis. Apparatus has been developed which affords objective and automatic measurement of both positive and negative geotactic behavior in populations under a single set of stimulus conditions as well as reliable mass screening measurements of individual differences in the expression of each. The observations have been made in a 15-trial modification of the multiple unit classification maze (Fig. 1), which has

*J. Hirsch and Loise Erlenmeyer-Kimling. Sign of taxis as a property of the genotype. *Science*, 1961, **134**, 835–836. (Pp. 835–836.) Copyright 1961 by the American Association for the Advancement of Science. Reprinted by permission of the authors and the publisher.

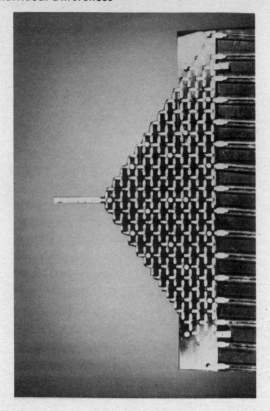

FIG. 1   Photograph of a 15-unit vertically placed maze. Large groups of flies are introduced into the vial at left and collected from vials at right. The flies are attracted by food in the vials at right and by a fluorescent light in a vertical position at the right. Small, trap-like funnels discourage backward movement in the maze.

been described elsewhere.[1] The alternatives at each choice point in the maze require diametrically opposite responses, namely, going against the pull of gravity by climbing up (negative geotaxis) or going toward the pull of gravity by climbing down (positive geotaxis).

[1] J. Hirsch. Studies in experimental behavior genetics: II. Individual differences in geotaxis as a function of chromosome variations in synthesized *Drosophila* populations. *J. comp. physiol. Psychol.*, 1959, **52**, 304–308.

With the maze, geotaxis has been studied in an unselected wild-type population of *Drosophila melanogaster*. . . . The middle ogive in Fig. 2 shows that observation of the performance in the maze of large numbers of individuals from the unselected population reveals a response distribution which contains a spectrum of geotactic scores. The expression of geotaxis in this population ranges from a score of —7.5, which represents the extreme of negative geotaxis, through 0, a score indicating a neutral response to gravity, to +7.5, the extreme of positive geotaxis. The distribution is slightly skewed; 47 per cent receive positive scores and 53 per cent negative scores.

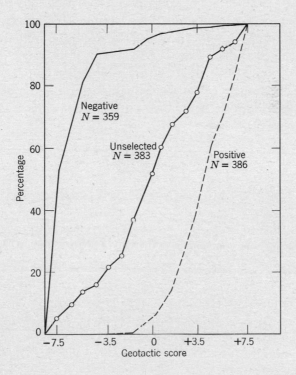

Fig. 2 Cumulated percentage of animals (males and females) receiving various geotactic scores in the maze in the unselected foundation population (middle ogive) and in the two selected strains (outer ogives).

With a system of assortative mating, two-way selection pressure is applied. The maximum separation so far obtained was reached at the 48th generation of selection and is shown by the outer ogives in Fig. 2. The curve near the ordinate shows that 96 per cent of the individuals in the strain selected for negative geotaxis receive a negative score in the maze, with 50 per cent receiving the extreme negative score of −7.5. The curve farthest from the ordinate shows that 95 per cent of the individuals in the other strain receive positive scores in the maze, with 16 per cent receiving the extreme positive score of +7.5.

These experiments show that, when the conditions of observation permit, the members of a population may display a spectrum of geotactic reactions. Some individuals give a negative response, others a positive response, and there are varying degrees in the extent to which individuals respond positively or negatively to gravity. Furthermore, it is possible to breed races of animals which perform in diametrically opposite fashion to the same physically specified stimulus conditions.

7

Behavior Genetics:
Theoretical Orientation

What is the present status of the heredity-environment problem in psychology? At the turn of the century, Pearson, Thorndike, and other students of individual differences reacted against a naive environmentalism that regarded the mind as a blank tablet upon which experience writes. But in its place they substituted an equally naive hereditarianism, which permeated psychological thought for nearly half a century. Gradually, psychologists came to recognize that the relationship between heredity and environment is much more complex than these early views indicated, and they approached the problem with a growing theoretical sophistication. The next article, by Hebb, illustrates this shift in theoretical orientation. It also brings together the findings of much intervening research, particularly that dealing with animal behavior.

Donald Olding Hebb

Heredity and Environment in Mammalian Behaviour*

A persistent theme in the study of behavior, one that has dominated psychological thought since Locke and Leibnitz at least, has been the question: What is inborn, what acquired? Is the mind *tabula rasa?* If there are no innate ideas, is there not some framework prior to all experience into which experience is received and by which it must be shaped? Is intelligence inherited, or in what proportion? And so with schizophrenia, visual form and depth, maternal behavior, gregariousness, pugnacity, even spinal reflexes—there is no aspect of behavior with which this debate has not been concerned at one time or another.

So far as I can now see, even to ask the question, in the form in which it is usually asked, is a sympton of confusion.

In view of what is to follow, it should be said here that my bias is on the nativistic side. If a choice had to be made, I would support—as I have in fact supported—Hobhouse and Köhler against Thorndike (*sic*) and Holt, Lashley against Watson, Kallman against Alexander, as a corrective against the common overemphasis by psychologists and psychiatrists on experience and learning in behavior. This is what I would be inclined still to do, if I had to choose sides; but the fact is that we have no such choice.

We cannot dichotomize mammalian behavior into learned and unlearned, and parcel out these acts and propensities to

*D. O. Hebb. Heredity and environment in mammalian behaviour. *Brit. J. Anim. Behav.*, 1953, 1, 43–47. (Pp. 43–47.) Reprinted by permission of the publisher.

the nativist, those to the empiricist. My first example is from Dennis:[1] "Rage . . . is unlearned in this sense, that when the child has developed a purposive sequence of behavior which can be interfered with, he will exhibit 'rage' on the first occasion on which this interference occurs." The behavior is unlearned; but it is not possible without the learning required for the development of purposive behavior. Again, the first time a chimpanzee baby of a certain age sees a stranger approach he is terrified. The reaction is strongest on the first occasion, it does not have to be practiced, and we must say that the shyness is not learned: but it is definitely a product of learning, in part, for it does not occur until the chimpanzee has learned to recognize his usual caretakers. The shyness or fear of strangers appears at about four months of age, or six months in the human baby. The chimpanzee reared in darkness to an age at which the fear is normally at its peak is not disturbed by his first sight of a stranger, but is disturbed by it as soon as he has had sufficient opportunity to learn to recognize those who care for him daily.

Fear of strangers, therefore, or a temper tantrum is not learned and yet is fully dependent on other learning. Do we then postulate three categories of behavior, (1) unlearned, (2) unlearned but dependent on learning, (3) learned? Perhaps instead we had better re-examine the conception of unlearned versus learned behavior.

The two examples given are not isolated phenomena. The neurotic disturbances in dog, cat, sheep, or goat described first by Pavlov, and studied further by Gantt, Liddell, and Masserman, depend on a conflict between learned modes of response and yet the breakdown itself is clearly not learned. Insight in the chimpanzee, as Köhler showed, is the occur-

---

[1] W. Dennis. Infant reaction to restraint: An evaluation of Watson's theory. *Trans. N.Y. Acad. Sci.*, Series 2, 1940, **2**, 202–218.

Note: Additional references in support of points made throughout the article are cited by Hebb. Many of these have been deleted in this reproduction for the sake of brevity—Ed.

rence of an unlearned solution to a problem; but Birch[2] has shown that other experience must precede. I shall not multiply examples, but can refer you here to the finding that mammalian perceptions in general appear to depend, not on formal training, it is true, but on a prolonged period of patterned sensory stimulation. A paper of my own is on record to the contrary,[3] a clear case of a biased failure to observe, since the same paper included data whose significance I did not see until certain physiological considerations had suggested another point of view. All that a mammal does is fundamentally dependent on his perception, past or present, and this means that there is no behavior, beyond the level of the reflex, that is not essentially dependent on learning.

It is equally clear that no behavior can be independent of an animal's heredity: this is so obvious, logically, that it need not be spelled out. Our conclusion then is that all behavior is dependent both on heredity and on environment, and all non-reflex behavior at least involves the special effects of environmental stimulation that we call learning.

Assuming that this is conceded, however, the question may still be asked, to what extent a given piece of behavior is dependent on one of these influences. Is it fifty per cent environment, fifty per cent heredity, or ninety to ten, or what are the proportions? This is exactly like asking how much of the area of a field is due to its length, how much to its width. The only reasonable answer is that the two proportions are one hundred per cent environment, one hundred per cent heredity. They are not additive; any bit of behavior whatever is *fully* dependent on each. What proportion of an animal's behavior would be left if there had not been, since the moment of fertilization, the highly specialized environment necessary for the growth of the embryo; or what basis

[2] H. G. Birch. The relation of previous experience to insightful problem-solving. *J. comp. Psychol.*, 1945, **38**, 367–383.
[3] D. O. Hebb. The innate organization of visual activity: I. Perception of figures by rats reared in total darkness. *J. genet. Psychol.*, 1937, **51**, 101–126.

is there for thinking of this environment as not causal, but only permissive, in determining the direction of embryonic growth? The newborn mammal is "caused" by a uterine environment acting on a fertilized ovum. Contrariwise, without the fertilized ovum and its special properties no behavior can result; learned behavior, further, can never be thought of as something apart from the heredity that made possible a particular kind of sensory structure and nervous system.

The last alternative is to ask how much of the *variance* of behavior is determined by heredity, how much by the environment. This is a meaningful and useful question, capable of an intelligent answer, but the limits of meaning of the answer must be recognized. If for example by inbreeding we produce a strain of dogs in which heredity is constant and all the variance of behavior can be attributed to environment, we have not in any way reduced the importance of heredity for the behavior in question. In other words, such as "analysis of variance" cannot be translated into a statement of causal relations for the individual animal. This is seen best if we classify one of our hypothetical inbred dogs in two ways: (*a*) as above, treat the animal statistically as one of a group with common heredity but different environments, and (*b*) as one of a group reared precisely as that one animal was, but with varying heredities (this latter set of conditions might be achieved, including a common uterine environment, by mating a group of inbred bitches to males of diverse breeds). If the proportionate variance is regarded as an estimate of the relative importance of heredity and environment for the individual animal's behavior, then we should have to conclude (*a*) that environment is the only important determinant, and (*b*) that heredity is the only important determinant, for the same dog's behavior. If again, eighty per cent of the variance of neuroticism in a particular district of London is due to variations of heredity, this does not make environment less important than heredity for the behavior in question. It may mean only that the relevant environmental influences are much the same throughout that district, and it does not preclude finding another sample of human beings with more similar heredity and less similar experiences, such that the degree of neuroticism varies with environment rather than heredity.

Analysis of variance, in the present sense, is an excellent tool for studying the interaction of heredity and environment, but entirely misleading if it is interpreted as isolating things that are inherited and things that are acquired. We are on solid ground if we think consistently of all behavior as "caused by" or fully dependent on both environment and heredity, and cast our research in the form of asking how they interact: for each given heredity, asking over what range behavior can vary, and how it can be manipulated by control of the environment (not only the postnatal environment); or what different heredities will permit survival in each given environment, and how behavior is correlated with them. To misuse another term of the statisticians, what we want is an analysis of covariance rather than analysis of one variable while forgetting the other.

Here the significance of the theoretical analysis by Haldane is plain. We cannot generalize freely from one small part of either continuum, hereditary or environmental. The heredity that is "good" in one part of the environmental range may be poor in another, as in Haldane's example of the beef-producing qualities of Aberdeen Angus and Galloway cattle in favorable and unfavorable environments. In the parallel case of man's intelligence and mental health, the heredity that gives best results in an optimal environment may give the worst in a poor one. We can say nothing about such possibilities (obviously of first significance for ideas about eugenics) on the basis of data obtained in a naturalistic study, with a limited sample of heredities and a limited range of environmental variation. The necessary experiments being impossible with man, we clearly need systematic animal studies in which for any given species the widest range of genetic variation is studied over the widest sample of feasible environments, from which for the mental health problem, we must cautiously extrapolate to man.

In all this, of course, we are really dealing with the question of instinct. I am considerably indebted in my discussion to a recent address by Professor Frank Beach, entitled "The Descent of Instinct," in which he recants his earlier view that instinct is a scientifically useful conception. Whether his conclusions are accepted or not, some of his points must be reckoned with.

Much of Beach's emphasis is on the consistently negative definition of instinct or instinctive behavior: instinctive behavior is what is not learned, or not determined by the environment, and so on. There must be great doubt about the unity of the factors that are identified only by exclusion. There is also a common tendency to identify unlearned with genetically determined behavior, and Beach points out that the chemical environment of the mammalian embryo, and nutritive influences on the invertebrate larva, are factors in behavior which do not fall either under the heading of learning or under that of genetic determinants. (One might cite here the significance of the "royal jelly" in the development of the queen bee, or the fact that the temperature at which the fruit-fly larva is kept determines bodily characteristics such as the number of legs, a feature which of course must affect behavior). If thus "instinctive" is to be equated with "unlearned," it cannot also be equated with "genetic." Very often when behavior is attributed to purely genetic determinants no real experimental control of environmental influence has been made; and very often learning is excluded simply on the ground that no obvious opportunity for it was observed by the experimenter.

Let us look at this last point more closely. The crucial but implicit assumption has always been made in the study of instinct that we know what learning is and how it operates. The notion is that learning, if relevant to the instinctive act, is the practice of that act or a closely related one—at the very least, observation of the act by another animal. If therefore there has been no opportunity for such observation, and no practice, and the act is performed effectively when the proper circumstances come along, we say that the behavior is unlearned and thus instinctive. But, as I have already tried to show, to say that behavior is unlearned does not mean that it is independent of learning.

For our present purposes, I shall use "learning" to refer to a stable unidirectional change of neural function, resulting from sensory stimulation (including the stimulation that results from response). There is a great deal that we do not know about learning, and we cannot assume that we know what conditions determine it. The occurrence of learning may be far from obvious. There is a great deal of visual learning, in the sense of my definition, in the period when the young mammal first opens its eyes on the world, though nothing but physical growth seems to be going on, and the fact of learning can only be discovered by comparing the normal infant with one reared without pattern vision. The experiment of Nissen, Chow, and Semmes[4] makes the same point concerning somesthetic learning, in the period when the baby seems only to be thrashing about aimlessly. This experiment is very important as showing that the importance of early learning demonstrated by Senden[5] and Riesen[6] is not restricted to visual function. What Nissen, Chow, and Semmes did was to raise an infant chimpanzee with cardboard mailing-tubes over hands and feet, thus preventing normal tactual explora-

[4] H. W. Nissen, K. L. Chow, and Josephine Semmes. Effects of restricted opportunity for tactual, kinesthetic, and manipulative experience on the behavior of a chimpanzee. *Amer. J. Psychol.*, 1951, **64**, 485–507.
[5] M. v. Senden. *Raum- und Gestaltauffassung bei operierten Blindgeborenen vor und nach der Operation.* Leipzig: Barth, 1932.
[6] A. H. Riesen. The development of visual perception in man and chimpanzee. *Science*, 1947, **106**, 107–108; Arrested vision. *Scient. Amer.*, 1950, **183**, 16–19; Postpartum development of behavior. *Chicago med. Sch. Quart.*, 1951, **13**, 17–24.

tion of the environment and of the chimpanzee's own body. Subsequently, somesthetic learning and localization of tactual stimulation of various points on the body were defective. The conditions of rearing could hardly produce any failure of development in primary sensory equipment of the skin, so it appears that the more or less random tactual experience of the normally reared infant is essential to the development of somesthetic perception.

Such early visual and somesthetic learning must modify all subsequent behavior; and there are strong indications that this does not apply only to "higher" behavior but to instinctive and even to reflexive responses as well. The supposedly instinctive grooming of the chimpanzee was not found in Nissen, Chow, and Semmes' animal, and responses to pain stimuli, usually considered reflexive, were atypical. The preliminary experiments of Riess and of Birch[7] on the relation of early experience to maternal behavior in rats, Lorenz's studies of imprinting in birds, and Thorpe's studies of early environmental influences on the subsequent behavior of both birds and insects, all imply that the behavior that ordinarily is "species-predictable," and independent of special experience, is not independent of the experience that is ordinarily inevitable for all members of the species. It has appeared to me in the past that instinctive behavior, especially in nonmammals, is correlated closely with unvarying genetic factors and not with the varying environment. But is this true? Is the environment so completely variable? It seems to me now that certain essentials of the environment are actually constant—just as constant as the animal's heredity; and therefore that we have no logical basis for giving the one correlation, that with heredity, any greater emphasis than the other correlation, with environment.

I propose consequently that we must study both variables

[7] Cited by F. A. Beach. Instinctive behavior: Reproductive activities, in S. S. Stevens (Ed.), *Handbook of experimental psychology*. New York: John Wiley, 1951. (P. 424.)

together, in the nonmammalian world as well as the mammalian. My difficulty with the ethological program as laid out by Tinbergen, in terms of first studying the innate before studying learning, is that it is logically impossible. "Innate behavior is behavior that has not been changed by learning processes,"[8] and we must know when and where learning occurs before we can say what this behavior is; just as the "learning theorist" must know what growth processes do to behavior before he can certainly say what learning does in the growing infant. Evidently we cannot separate the two tasks; they must be carried out together.

I would not suggest for a moment that the problems in this area are unreal; I do suggest that they have been poorly stated, inasmuch as we cannot dichotomize behavior into learned and unlearned, environmentally determined and hereditarily determined. I urge that there are not two kinds of control of behavior, and that the term "instinct," implying a mechanism or neural process independent of environmental factors, and distinct from the neural processes into which learning enters, is a completely misleading term and should be abandoned. "Instinctive behavior" may be nearly as misleading, but it might be kept as a convenient designation for species-predictable behavior, as long as it is thought of, not as determined by an invariant heredity alone, but also by an environment that is equally invariant in most or all important matters. Instinctive behavior therefore is not valid as an analytical conception, though it may be useful as a rough descriptive term.

However, it is not enough to make destructive criticism alone, especially in a field where it is clear that important theoretical issues are involved. However well or ill-conceived the term instinct may be, or how well-framed the traditional question of environmental or hereditary control of behavior, there is something here that we must deal with theoretically

---

[8] N. Tinbergen. *The study of instinct.* Oxford: Clarendon Press, 1951.

and about which we must be able to make positive state ments.

In distinguishing hereditary from environmental influence, therefore, I conclude that it is reasonable and intelligible to say that a difference in behavior from a group norm, or between two individuals, is caused by a difference of heredity, or a difference of environment; but not that the deviant behavior is caused by heredity or environment alone. The fact that we speak English *instead* of French is determined by environment alone; but speaking English is not caused by environment independent of heredity, for no environment can make a dog or cat (or chimpanzee) speak either language, English or French. Making the reference to a difference or deviation really implies: *With environment held constant,* heredity has such and such effects (or vice versa, with heredity constant); it does not say that the behavior is due to heredity alone. If this is correct, we can also quite accurately speak of the variance due to environment or heredity; variance again being a reference to deviations. We will, I believe, not only pay a proper respect to logic but also plan our experiments better if we speak and think of the effect that environmental influence has on a given heredity, or, in dealing with the differences between heredities, specify the environment in which they are manifested. The behavior one can actually observe and experiment with is an inextricable tangle of the two influences, and one of them is nothing without the other.

In the preceding article, Hebb notes that psychologists may have been asking the wrong questions about heredity and environment —questions that are meaningless and unanswerable. This point is further explored in the following article by Anastasi, who proposes that a more relevant question is "How?" That is, what are the specific etiological mechanisms whereby hereditary and environmental conditions influence behavior? In the effort to seek answers to this question, Anastasi proposes a continuum of indirectness along which hereditary influences can be ordered. Environmental influences of an organic nature can be similarly ordered. Behavioral or experiential influences, on the other hand, can be arranged along a continuum of breadth. Cultural differentials may affect behavior development through either organic or experiential mechanisms.

Anne Anastasi

Heredity, Environment, and the Question "How?"*

Two or three decades ago, the so-called heredity-environment question was the center of lively controversy. Today, on the other hand, many psychologists look upon it as a dead issue. It is now generally conceded that both hereditary and environmental factors enter into all behavior. The reacting organism is a product of its genes and its past environment, while present environment provides the immediate stimulus for current behavior. To be sure, it can be argued that, although a given trait may result from the combined influence of hereditary and environmental factors, a specific difference in this trait between individuals or between groups may be traceable to either hereditary or environmental factors alone. The design of most traditional investigations undertaken to identify such factors, however, has been such as to yield inconclusive answers. The same set of data has frequently led to opposite conclusions in the hands of psychologists with different orientations.

Nor have efforts to determine the proportional contribution

* Anne Anastasi. Heredity, environment, and the question "How?" *Psychol. Rev.*, 1958, 65, 197–208. (Pp. 197–208.) Reprinted by permission of the American Psychological Association.

of hereditary and environmental factors to observed individual differences in given traits met with any greater success. Apart from difficulties in controlling conditions, such investigations have usually been based upon the implicit assumption that hereditary and environmental factors combine in an additive fashion. Both geneticists and psychologists have repeatedly demonstrated, however, that a more tenable hypothesis is that of interaction. In other words, the nature and extent of the influence of each type of factor depend upon the contribution of the other. Thus the proportional contribution of heredity to the variance of a given trait, rather than being a constant, will vary under different environmental conditions. Similarly, under different hereditary conditions, the relative contribution of environment will differ. Studies designed to estimate the proportional contribution of heredity and environment, however, have rarely included measures of such interaction. The only possible conclusion from such research would thus seem to be that both heredity and environment contribute to all behavior traits and that the extent of their respective contributions cannot be specified for any trait. Small wonder that some psychologists regard the heredity-environment question as unworthy of further consideration!

But is this really all we can find out about the operation of heredity and environment in the etiology of behavior? Perhaps we have simply been asking the wrong questions. The traditional questions about heredity and environment may be intrinsically unanswerable. Psychologists began by asking *which* type of factor, hereditary or environmental, is responsible for individual differences in a given trait. Later, they tried to discover *how much* of the variance was attributable to heredity and how much to environment. It is the primary contention of this paper that a more fruitful approach is to be found in the question *"How?"* There is still much to be learned about the specific *modus operandi* of hereditary and environmental factors in the development of behavioral differences. And there are several current lines of research which offer promising techniques for answering the question "How?"

Variety of Interaction Mechanisms

Hereditary Factors

If we examine some of the specific ways in which hereditary factors may influence behavior, we cannot fail but be impressed by their wide diversity. At one extreme, we find such conditions as phenylpyruvic amentia and amaurotic idiocy. In these cases, certain essential physical prerequisites for normal intellectual development are lacking as a result of hereditary metabolic disorders. . . .

A somewhat different situation is illustrated by hereditary deafness, which may lead to intellectual retardation through interference with normal social interaction, language development, and schooling. In such a case, however, the hereditary handicap can be offset by appropriate adaptations of training procedures. . . .

A third example is provided by inherited susceptibility to certain physical diseases, with consequent protracted ill health. If environmental conditions are such that illness does in fact develop, a number of different behavioral effects may follow. Intellectually, the individual may be handicapped by his inability to attend school regularly. On the other hand, depending upon age of onset, home conditions, parental status, and similar factors, poor health may have the effect of concentrating the individual's energies upon intellectual pursuits. The curtailment of participation in athletics and social functions may serve to strengthen interest in reading and other sedentary activities. Concomitant circumstances would also determine the influence of such illness upon personality development. And it is well known that the latter effects could run the gamut from a deepening of human sympathy to psychiatric breakdown.

Finally, heredity may influence behavior through the mechanism of social stereotypes. A wide variety of inherited physical characteristics have served as the visible cues for identifying such stereotypes. These cues thus lead to behavioral restrictions or opportunities and—at a more subtle level—to social attitudes and expectancies. The individual's own self concept tends gradually to reflect such expectancies. All of these influences eventually leave their mark upon his abilities and inabilities, his emotional reactions, goals, ambitions, and outlook on life.

The geneticist Dobzhansky[9] illustrates this type of mechanism by means of a dramatic hypothetical situation. He points out that, if there were a culture in which the carriers of blood group AB were considered aristocrats and those of blood group O laborers, then the blood group genes would become important hereditary determiners of behavior. Obviously the association between blood group and behavior would be specific to that culture. But such specificity is an essential property of the causal mechanism under consideration.

More realistic examples are not hard to find. The most familiar instances occur in connection with constitutional types, sex, and race. Sex and skin pigmentation obviously depend upon heredity. General body build is strongly influenced by hereditary components, although also susceptible to environmental modification. That all these physical characteristics may exert a pronounced effect upon behavior within a given culture is well known. It is equally apparent, of course, that in different cultures the behavioral correlates of such hereditary physical traits may be quite unlike. A specific physical cue may be completely unrelated to individual

[9] T. Dobzhansky. The genetic nature of differences among men, in S. Persons (Ed.), *Evolutionary thought in America*. New Haven: Yale University Press, 1950. Pp. 86–155.

differences in psychological traits in one culture, while closely correlated with them in another. Or it may be associated with totally dissimilar behavior characteristics in two different cultures.

It might be objected that some of the illustrations which have been cited do not properly exemplify the operation of hereditary mechanisms in behavior development, since hereditary factors enter only indirectly into the behavior in question. Closer examination, however, shows this distinction to be untenable. First it may be noted that the influence of heredity upon behavior is always indirect. No psychological trait is ever inherited as such. All we can ever say directly from behavioral observations is that a given trait shows evidence of being influenced by certain "inheritable unknowns." This merely defines a problem for genetic research; it does not provide a causal explanation. Unlike the blood groups, which are close to the level of primary gene products, psychological traits are related to genes by highly indirect and devious routes. Even the mental deficiency associated with phenylketonuria is several steps removed from the chemically defective genes that represent its hereditary basis. Moreover, hereditary influences cannot be dichotomized into the more direct and the less direct. Rather do they represent a whole "continuum of indirectness," along which are found all degrees of remoteness of causal links. The examples already cited illustrate a few of the points on this continuum.

It should be noted that as we proceed along the continuum of indirectness, the range of variation of possible outcomes of hereditary factors expands rapidly. At each step in the causal chain, there is fresh opportunity for interaction with other hereditary factors as well as with environmental factors. And since each interaction in turn determines the direction of subsequent interactions, there is an ever-widening network of possible outcomes. If we visualize a simple sequential grid with only two alternatives at each point, it is obvious that there are two possible outcomes in the one-stage situation, four outcomes at the second stage, eight at the third, and so on in geometric progression. The actual situation is undoubtedly much more complex, since there will usually be more than two alternatives at any one point.

In the case of the blood groups, the relation to specific genes is so close that no other concomitant hereditary or environmental conditions can alter the outcome. If the organism survives at all, it will have the blood group determined by its genes. Among psychological traits, on the other hand, some variation in outcome is always possible as a result of concurrent circumstances. Even in cases of phenylketonuria, intellectual development will exhibit some relationship with the type of care and training available to the individual. That behavioral outcomes show progressive diversification as we proceed along the continuum of indirectness is brought out by the other examples which were cited. Chronic illness *can* lead to scholarly renown or to intellectual immaturity; a mesomorphic physique *can* be a contributing factor in juvenile delinquency or in the attainment of a college presidency! Published data on Sheldon somatotypes provide some support for both of the latter outcomes. . . .

A large portion of the continuum of hereditary influences which we have described coincides with the domain of somatopsychological relations, as defined by Barker et al.[10] Under this heading, Barker includes "variations in physique that affect the psychological situation of a person by influencing the effectiveness of his body as a tool for actions or by serving as a stimulus to himself or others." Relatively direct neurological influences on behavior, which have been the traditional concern of physiological psychology, are excluded from this definition, Barker being primarily concerned with what he calls the "social psychology of physique." Of the examples cited in the present paper, deafness, severe

[10] R. G. Barker, Beatrice A. Wright, L. Myerson, and Mollie R. Gonick. Adjustment to physical handicap and illness: A survey of the social psychology of physique and disability. *Soc. Sci. Res. Coun. Bull.*, 1953, No. 55.

illness, and the physical characteristics associated with social stereotypes would meet the specifications of somatopsychological factors.

The somatic factors to which Barker refers, however, are not limited to those of hereditary origin. Bodily conditions attributable to environmental causes operate in the same sorts of somatopsychological relations as those traceable to heredity. In fact, heredity-environment distinctions play a minor part in Barker's approach.

Environmental Factors: Organic

Turning now to an analysis of the role of environmental factors in behavior, we find the same etiological mechanisms which were observed in the case of hereditary factors. First, however, we must differentiate between two classes of environmental influences: (a) those producing organic effects which may in turn influence behavior and (b) those serving as direct stimuli for psychological reactions. The former may be illustrated by food intake or by exposure to bacterial infection; the latter, by tribal initiation ceremonies or by a course in algebra. There are no completely satisfactory names by which to designate these two classes of influences. In an earlier paper,[11] the terms "structural" and "functional" were employed. However, "organic" and "behavioral" have the advantage of greater familiarity in this context and may be less open to misinterpretation. Accordingly, these terms will be used in the present paper.

Like hereditary factors, environmental influences of an organic nature can also be ordered along a continuum of indirectness with regard to their relation to behavior. This continuum closely parallels that of hereditary factors. One end is typified by such conditions as mental deficiency resulting from cerebral birth injury or from prenatal nutri-

[11] Anne Anastasi, and J. P. Foley, Jr. A proposed reorientation in the heredity-environment controversy. *Psychol. Rev.*, 1948, **55**, 239–249.

tional inadequacies. A more indirect etiological mechanism is illustrated by severe motor disorder—as in certain cases of cerebral palsy—*without* accompanying injury to higher neurological centers. In such instances, intellectual retardation may occur as an indirect result of the motor handicap, through the curtailment of educational and social activities. Obviously this causal mechanism corresponds closely to that of hereditary deafness cited earlier in the paper.

Finally, we may consider an environmental parallel to the previously discussed social stereotypes which were mediated by hereditary physical cues. Let us suppose that a young woman with mousy brown hair becomes transformed into a dazzling golden blonde through environmental techniques currently available in our culture. It is highly probable that this metamorphosis will alter, not only the reactions of her associates toward her, but also her own self concept and subsequent behavior. The effects could range all the way from a rise in social poise to a drop in clerical accuracy! . . .

Environmental Factors: Behavioral

The second major class of environmental factors—the behavioral as contrasted with the organic—are by definition direct influences. The immediate effect of such environmental factors is always a behavioral change. To be sure, some of the initial behavioral effects may themselves indirectly affect the individual's later behavior. But this relationship can perhaps be best conceptualized in terms of breadth and permanence of effects. Thus it could be said that we are now dealing, not with a continuum of indirectness, as in the case of hereditary and organic-environmental factors, but rather with a continuum of breadth.

Social class membership may serve as an illustration of a relatively broad, pervasive, and enduring environmental factor. Its influence upon behavior development may operate through many channels. Thus social level may determine the range and nature of intellectual stimulation provided by home and community through books, music, art, play activities, and the like. Even more far-reaching may be the effects upon interests and motivation, as illustrated by the drive to perform abstract intellectual tasks, to surpass others in competitive situations, to succeed in school, or to gain social approval. Emotional and social traits may likewise be influenced by the nature of interpersonal relations characterizing homes at different socioeconomic levels. Somewhat more restricted in scope than social class, although still exerting a relatively broad influence, is amount of formal schooling which the individual is able to obtain.

A factor which may be wide or narrow in its effects, depending upon concomitant circumstances, is language handicap. Thus the bilingualism of an adult who moves to a foreign country with inadequate mastery of the new language represents a relatively limited handicap which can be readily overcome in most cases. At most, the difficulty is one of communication. On the other hand, some kinds of bilingualism in childhood may exert a retarding influence upon intellectual development and may under certain conditions affect personality development adversely. A common pattern in the homes of immigrants is that the child speaks one language at home and another in school, so that his knowledge of each language is limited to certain types of situations. Inadequate facility with the language of the school interferes with the acquisition of basic concepts, intellectual skills, and information. The frustration engendered by scholastic difficulties may in turn lead to discouragement and general dislike of school. Such reactions can be found, for example, among a number of Puerto Rican children in New York City schools. In the case of certain groups, moreover, the child's foreign language background may be perceived by himself and his associates as a symbol of minority group status and may thereby augment any emotional maladjustment arising from such status.

A highly restricted environmental influence is to be found in the opportunity to acquire specific items of information occurring in a particular intelligence test. The fact that such opportunities may vary with culture, social class, or individual experiential background is at the basis of the test user's concern with the problem of coaching and with "culture-free" or "culture-fair" tests. If the advantage or disadvantage which such experiential differences confer upon certain individuals is strictly confined to performance on the given test, it will obviously reduce the validity of the test and should be eliminated.

In this connection, however, it is essential to know the breadth of the environmental influence in question. A fallacy inherent in many attempts to develop culture-fair tests is that the breadth of cultural differentials is not taken into account. Failure to consider breadth of effect likewise characterizes certain discussions of coaching. If, in coaching a student for a college admission test, we can improve his knowledge of verbal concepts and his reading comprehension, he will be better equipped to succeed in college courses. His performance level will thus be raised, not only on the test, but also on the criterion which the test is intended to predict. To try to devise a test which is not susceptible to such coaching would merely reduce the effectiveness of the test. Similarly, efforts to rule out cultural differentials from test items so as to make them equally "fair" to subjects in different social classes or in different cultures may merely limit the usefulness of the test, since the same cultural differentials may operate within the broader area of behavior which the test is designed to sample.

Methodological Approaches

The examples considered so far should suffice to highlight the wide variety of ways in which hereditary and environmental factors may interact in the course of behavior development. There is clearly a need for identifying explicitly the etiological mechanism whereby any given hereditary or environmental condition ultimately leads to a behavioral characteristic—in other words, the "how" of heredity and environment. Accordingly, we may now take a quick look at some promising methodological approaches to the question "how."

Within the past decade, an increasing number of studies have been designed to trace the connection between specific factors in the hereditary backgrounds or in the reactional biographies of individuals and their observed behavioral characteristics. There has been a definite shift away from the predominantly descriptive and correlational approach of the earlier decades toward more deliberate attempts to verify explanatory hypotheses. Similarly, the cataloguing of group differences in psychological traits has been giving way gradually to research on *changes* in group characteristics following altered conditions.

Among recent methodological developments, we have chosen seven as being particularly relevant to the analysis of etiological mechanisms. The first represents an extension of selective breeding investigations to permit the identification of specific hereditary conditions underlying the observed behavioral differences. When early selective breeding investigations such as those of Tryon on rats indicated that "maze learning ability" was inherited, we were still a long way from knowing what was actually being transmitted by the genes. It was obviously not "maze learning ability" as such. Twenty—or even ten—years ago, some psychologists would have suggested that it was probably general intelligence. And a few might even have drawn a parallel with the inheritance of human intelligence.

But today investigators have been asking: Just what makes one group of rats learn mazes more quickly than the other? Is it differences in motivation, emotionality, speed of running,

general activity level? If so, are these behavioral characteristics in turn dependent upon group differences in glandular
development, body weight, brain size, biochemical factors,
or some other organic conditions? A number of recent and
ongoing investigations indicate that attempts are being made
to trace, at least part of the way, the steps whereby certain
chemical properties of the genes may ultimately lead to specified behavior characteristics. . . .

A second line of attack is the exploration of possible relationships between behavioral characteristics and physiological variables which may in turn be traceable to hereditary
factors. Research on EEG, autonomic balance, metabolic
processes, and biochemical factors illustrates this approach.
A lucid demonstration of the process of tracing a psychological condition to genetic factors is provided by the identification and subsequent investigation of phenylpyruvic
amentia. In this case, the causal chain from defective gene,
through metabolic disorder and consequent cerebral mal-
functioning, to feeblemindedness and other overt symptoms
can be described step by step. Also relevant are the recent
researches on neurological and biochemical correlates of
schizophrenia. Owing to inadequate methodological controls,
however, most of the findings of the latter studies must be
regarded as tentative.

Prenatal environmental factors provide a third avenue of
fruitful investigation. Especially noteworthy is the recent
work of Pasamanick and his associates,[12] which demonstrated
a tie-up between socioeconomic level, complications of pregnancy and parturition, and psychological disorders of the
offspring. In a series of studies on large samples of whites
and Negroes in Baltimore, these investigators showed that
various prenatal and paranatal disorders are significantly related to the occurrence of mental defect and psychiatric dis-

[12] B. Pasamanick, Hilda Knobloch, and A. M. Lilienfeld. Socioeconomic
status and some precursors of neuropsychiatric disorder. *Amer. J. Ortho-
psychiat.*, 1956, **26**, 594–601.

orders in the child. An important source of such irregularities in the process of childbearing and birth is to be found in deficiencies of maternal diet and in other conditions associated with low socioeconomic status. An analysis of the data did in fact reveal a much higher frequency of all such medical complications in lower than in higher socioeconomic levels, and a higher frequency among Negroes than among whites.

Direct evidence of the influence of prenatal nutritional factors upon subsequent intellectual development is to be found in a recent, well controlled experiment by Harrell et al.[13] The subjects were pregnant women in low-income groups, whose normal diets were generally quite deficient. A dietary supplement was administered to some of these women during pregnancy and lactation, while an equated control group received placebos. When tested at the ages of three and four years, the offspring of the experimental group obtained a significantly higher mean IQ than did the offspring of the controls.

Mention should also be made of animal experiments on the effects of such factors as prenatal radiation and neonatal asphyxia upon cerebral anomalies as well as upon subsequent behavior development. These experimental studies merge imperceptibly into the fourth approach to be considered, namely, the investigation of the influence of early experience upon the eventual behavioral characteristics of animals. Research in this area has been accumulating at a rapid rate. In 1954, Beach and Jaynes[14] surveyed this literature for the *Psychological Bulletin*, listing over 130 references. Several new studies have appeared since that date. The variety of factors covered ranges from the type and quantity of available food to the extent of contact with human culture. A large

[13] Ruth F. Harrell, Ella Woodyard, and A. I. Gates. *The effect of mothers' diets on the intelligence of the offspring.* New York: Teachers College, Columbia University, Bureau of Publications, 1955.
[14] F. A. Beach and J. Jaynes. Effects of early experience upon the behavior of animals. *Psychol. Bull.,* 1954, **51,** 239–263.

number of experiments have been concerned with various forms of sensory deprivation and with diminished opportunities for motor exercise. Effects have been observed in many kinds of animals and in almost all aspects of behavior, including perceptual responses, motor activity, learning, emotionality, and social reactions. . . .

The human counterpart of these animal studies may be found in the comparative investigation of child-rearing practices in different cultures and sub-cultures. This represents the fifth approach in our list. An outstanding example of such a study is that by Whiting and Child.[15] Utilizing data on 75 primitive societies from the Cross-Cultural Files of the Yale Institute of Human Relations, these investigators set out to test a number of hypotheses regarding the relationships between child-rearing practices and personality development. This analysis was followed up by field observations in five cultures, the results of which have not yet been reported.

Within our own culture, similar surveys have been concerned with the diverse psychological environments provided by different social classes. Of particular interest are the study by Williams and Scott[16] on the association between socioeconomic level, permissiveness, and motor development among Negro children, and the exploratory research by Milner[17] on the relationship between reading readiness in first-grade children and patterns of parent-child interaction. Milner found that upon school entrance the lower-class child seems to lack chiefly two advantages enjoyed by the middle-class child. The first is described as "a warm positive family atmosphere or adult-relationship pattern which is more and

[15] J. W. M. Whiting and I. L. Child. *Child training and personality: A cross-cultural study*. New Haven: Yale University Press, 1953.
[16] Judith R. Williams and R. B. Scott. Growth and development of Negro infants: IV. Motor development and its relationship to child rearing practices in two groups of Negro infants. *Child Developm.*, 1953, **24**, 103–121.
[17] Esther A. Milner. A study of the relationships between reading readiness in grade one school children and patterns of parent-child interaction. *Child Develpm.*, 1951, **22**, 95–112.

more being recognized as a motivational prerequisite of any kind of adult-controlled learning." The lower-class children in Milner's study perceived adults as predominantly hostile. The second advantage is an extensive opportunity to interact verbally with adults in the family. The latter point is illustrated by parental attitudes toward mealtime conversation, lower-class parents tending to inhibit and discourage such conversation, while middle-class parents encourage it. . . .

A sixth major approach involves research on the previously cited somatopsychological relationships. To date, little direct information is available on the precise operation of this class of factors in psychological development. The multiplicity of ways in which physical traits—whether hereditary or environmental in origin—may influence behavior thus offers a relatively unexplored field for future study.

The seventh and final approach to be considered represents an adaptation of traditional twin studies. From the standpoint of the question "How?" there is need for closer coordination between the usual data on twin resemblance and observations of the family interactions of twins. Available data already suggest, for example, that closeness of contact and extent of environmental similarity are greater in the case of monozygotic than in the case of dizygotic twins. Information on the social reactions of twins toward each other and the specialization of roles is likewise of interest. Especially useful would be longitudinal studies of twins, beginning in early infancy and following the subjects through school age. The operation of differential environmental pressures, the development of specialized roles, and other environmental influences could thus be more clearly identified and correlated with intellectual and personality changes in the growing twins. . . .

Summary

The heredity-environment problem is still very much alive.
Its viability is assured by the gradual replacement of the
questions, "Which one?" and "How much?" by the more basic
and appropriate question, "How?" Hereditary influences—
as well as environmental factors of an organic nature—vary
along a "continuum of indirectness." The more indirect their
connection with behavior, the wider will be the range of
variation of possible outcomes. One extreme of the continuum of indirectness may be illustrated by brain damage
leading to mental deficiency; the other extreme, by physical
characteristics associated with social stereotypes. Examples
of factors falling at intermediate points include deafness,
physical diseases, and motor disorders. Those environmental
factors which act directly upon behavior can be ordered
along a continuum of breadth or permanence of effect, as
exemplified by social class membership, amount of formal
schooling, language handicap, and familiarity with specific
test items.

Several current lines of research offer promising techniques
for exploring the *modus operandi* of hereditary and environmental factors. Outstanding among them are investigations
of: (a) hereditary conditions which underlie behavioral differences between selectively bred groups of animals; (b)
relations between physiological variables and individual differences in behavior, especially in the case of pathological
deviations; (c) role of prenatal physiological factors in behavior development; (d) influence of early experience upon
eventual behavioral characteristics; (e) cultural differences
in child-rearing practices in relation to intellectual and emotional development; (f) mechanisms of somatopsychological
relationships; and (g) psychological development of twins
from infancy to maturity, together with observations of their

social environment. Such approaches are extremely varied with regard to subjects employed, nature of psychological functions studied, and specific experimental procedures followed. But it is just such heterogeneity of methodology that is demanded by the wide diversity of ways in which hereditary and environmental factors interact in behavior development.

8

Cultural Deprivation:

Cross-Sectional Approaches

In the preceding chapter it was noted that the causes of individual differences may be found in organic factors (of either hereditary or environmental origin) and in experiential factors. It was further suggested that the question "how" is of prime importance in investigating the contribution of all these factors to behavior development. Research on cultural deprivation, considered in this chapter, illustrates some of the ways in which psychologists have been exploring the question "how" in reference to experiential factors.

Only recently has the term "cultural deprivation" been widely adopted to describe certain types of human environments. Nevertheless we can trace to the first quarter of this century the growing awareness among psychologists that deficiencies in home environment, schooling, and other areas of early experience affect intellectual development. Many lines of research have helped to shape the current concept of cultural deprivation and have provided evidence of the behavioral effects of such deprivation.

Comparative psychological studies of groups differing in sex, race, or socioeconomic level led some investigators to consider the influence of culturally determined differences in the experiential backgrounds of these groups on their subsequent psychological development. Of particular interest were a few studies of extreme cultural deprivation, as found in certain isolated mountain communities, gypsy camps, and canal boats. These two types of studies, both utilizing cross-sectional approaches, will be illustrated in this chapter.

188   Individual Differences

Longitudinal studies, which permit a more direct analysis of causal relations, will be reserved for Chapter 9. These include longitudinal investigations of both populations and individuals. In the former, comparable samples of the same population are examined after an interval of several years during which cultural conditions may have changed. Longitudinal studies of individuals permit the identification of intellectual changes occurring after different amounts of intervening education. From still another angle, children from culturally deprived environments have been given special training under experimentally controlled conditions, in the effort to discover the extent to which their intellectual functioning would thereby be altered. This type of research also suggests the part played by cultural deprivation in producing mental retardation of the simple, nonorganic variety; and it opens up the possibility of reducing the incidence of such retardation through specially developed experiential programs.

The first paper in this chapter is concerned with the interpretation of IQ differences among national and racial minorities in the United States. Shortly after the development of the original Binet-Simon scales, attempts were made to compare the intelligence of different national and racial groups through these instruments. With the advent of group tests during the First World War, similar investigations were undertaken on a much larger scale with both adults and children. In a book that aroused a storm of controversy, Brigham[1] analyzed the intelligence test scores obtained by foreign-born men in the United States Army of the First World War, classified according to country of birth. This was followed by several studies of school children, classified according to parental country of birth, as well as of Negro and American Indian children. In accordance with the strongly hereditarian orientation of the time, the resulting differences in scores were attributed largely to genetic differences among the nations or races.

One of the earliest investigators to question this interpretation and to examine cultural differences among these groups was Ada H. Arlitt. In a 1921 article entitled—mildly enough—"On the need for caution in establishing race norms," Arlitt reported evidence that

[1] C. C. Brigham. *A study of American intelligence.* Princeton, N. J.: Princeton University Press, 1923. Brigham later retracted the conclusions reached in this study, because of methodological limitations (C. C. Brigham. Intelligence tests of immigrant groups. *Psychol. Rev.*, 1930, **37**, 158–165.)

socioeconomic level may account for some of the deficiencies in intelligence test performance found among racial and national minorities. Today psychologists recognize that even the small residual "racial" differences found by Arlitt cannot be unequivocally attributed to genetic factors. Although Arlitt equated paternal occupation in terms of broad categories, it cannot be assumed that cultural differences among the Negro, Italian, and native white groups studied were thereby eliminated. It is likely, for example, that more Negroes and Italians than native whites fell near the bottom of each of the broad occupational categories employed. Even if specific occupations had been matched, moreover, the homes of Negroes, Italians, and native whites may still have differed in income level and other cultural characteristics. Another important uncontrolled factor is that of social stereotypes. The attitudes and expectations encountered by minority group members tend to influence their own self concept and their motivation for school achievement and for upward social mobility—conditions that will in turn be reflected in their intelligence test performance.

Ada Hart Arlitt

On the Need for Caution in Establishing Race Norms*

In recent years there has been a tendency to establish race norms on the basis of mental tests given to representatives of various races who have emigrated to the United States. The results of tests made of groups of children of foreign-born parents have been stated and comparisons made with the distribution of intelligence in groups of children of American-born parents. So far as we have been able to ascertain except

*Ada H. Arlitt. On the need for caution in establishing race norms. *J. appl. Psychol.*, 1921, 5, 179–183. (Pp. 179–183.) Reprinted by permission of the American Psychological Association.

in the case of Negro children[2] no attempt has been made to check up the influence of factors, other than that of race, which might quite as well account for the differences which it has been assumed were traceable to race alone. Particularly is this true in regard to the part played by social status. Much has been written about the effect of social status on the median intelligence in any group of American children, little or nothing has been said as to how much this may account for the low or high median score or median intelligence quotient in groups of children of other races. For instance Terman[3] speaking of the influence of race on Intelligence Quotient cites the median I.Q. for Italian children as being 84 or 16 points below that usually given for American children.

It was with a view to determining the relative influence of the two factors, race and social status, that this investigation was begun. The tests used were the Stanford Revision of the Binet tests. . . . The children, 343 in all, were taken from the primary grades in a single school district. Of these, 191 were children of native-born white parents, 87 were Italians, and 71 were Negroes. All of the Italians spoke English without difficulty.

The native-born white children were divided on the basis of social status into five groups with reference to the occupation of the father. The separation into groups by occupation followed Taussig's division into the five non-competing groups, i.e., (1) Professional classes; (2) Semi-professional and higher business; (3) Skilled; (4) Semi-skilled; (5) Unskilled. The home conditions followed closely the division by occupation. The last two groups, children of unskilled and semi-skilled workers, contained too few children to be treated separately. They were therefore combined. As a matter of convenience these children will be called throughout the

[2] Dagney Sunne. A comparative study of white and Negro children. *J. appl. Psychol.*, 1917, **1**, 71–83.

[3] L. M. Terman. *Intelligence of school children*. Boston: Houghton Mifflin, 1919. (P. 56.)

"Inferior Group," the children whose parents fall into the skilled class will be called "Average," those of the semi-professional and higher business class "Superior" and those of the professional class "Very Superior." . . .

The outstanding characteristics of each group can best be seen from Table 1. Over 40% of the Inferior social status

TABLE 1. *The Effect of Social Status on the Distribution of Intelligence Quotients*

Social Status	50–59.9	60–69.9	70–79.9	80–89.9	90–109.9	110–119.9	120–129.9	130–139.9	Above 140	Total
Very superior	0	0	1	·0	6	4	6	3	4	24
Superior	0	0	0	0	12	17	14	4	1	48
Average	0	1	3	2	41	16	10	2	1	76
Inferior	1	3	5	9	23	1	0	1	0	43

group have I.Q.'s below 90 and only 4.6% have I.Q.'s above 110. There are only two children of very superior mentality in this group. In the Average group 50% are of average mentality and over 25% are above average i.e., have I.Q.'s above 110. The curve for the Superior group shows it to be as much better than the Average group as that was superior to the Inferior social status group. The median I.Q. is 118.7 or 10.2 points above that of the Average group. Seventy-five per cent of these children have I.Q.'s above 110 and none have I.Q.'s below 90. A curve for the Very Superior group would have two modes, one at 90–110 the other at 120–129. Seventy per cent of these children have I.Q.'s above 110 and of these, 76% have I.Q.'s above 120. The difference between the Superior and Very Superior social status group lies not in the proportion of the children who reach 110 or above but in the fact that a larger proportion of those whose I.Q.'s pass 110 reach 120 or above.

It is interesting to note that very few children of superior mentality were found in the Inferior social status group and that only one child of inferior mentality was found in the Superior and Very Superior social status groups.

The median I.Q.'s for the four groups were respectively 92, 107, 118.7, and 125.9 or a difference of 33.9 points between children of Inferior and Very Superior social status of the same race and attending the same grades in the same school.

We are well aware, as has been stated, that previous writers have emphasized the part played by social status. It is here cited chiefly because the variation due to social status is wider than that usually reported and serves to demonstrate all the more clearly the part that this factor may play in determining the distribution of intelligence in any non-selected group.

The effect of social status on the native-born white group having been determined, the total group was divided on the basis of race alone. It is a significant fact that there were too few children in the Italian and Negro groups of even average social status to enable us to study the combined effect of race and social status in these groups.

The median I.Q. for the native white group was 106.5, for the Italian group 85, and for the Negro group 83.4. The native-born white group had a median I.Q. 21.5 points above that of the Italian and 23.1 points above that of the Negro group. This disparity is great and if it had been due to race alone would have demonstrated beyond a doubt the superiority of the native white group, but 37% of the native white group came from families of Superior and Very Superior social status whereas 93% of the Negro and 90% of the Italian group came from families of Inferior and Very Inferior social status.

The Italian and Negro children were then compared with the group of native-born white children of Inferior and Very Inferior social status (Table 2). The median I.Q. for the native white group was then 92 or 8.6 point above that of the Negro and 7 points above that of the Italian group.

This difference is not due to a larger proportion of children of superior or very superior mentality in the native white

TABLE 2. *The Effect of Race on the Distribution of Intelligence Quotients*

Race	50–59.9	60–69.9	70–79.9	80–89.9	90–109.9	110–119.9	120–129.9	130–139.9	Above 140	Total
Native born white	1	3	5	9	23	1	0	1	0	43
Italian	3	11	19	17	26	4	1	0	0	81
Negro	1	7	16	20	25	1	1	0	0	71

group. There are five such children in the Italian group, two in the Negro, and one in the native-born white group. It is due to the proportion of children in the Negro and Italian groups whose I.Q.'s are below 80. In the native-born white group 20.9% have I.Q.'s below 80, in the Negro group 33.8% have I.Q.'s below 80, and in the Italian group 41.2% fall below 80. As all of these children live in the same section of the same community and attend the same grades in the same schools this difference both as to the median I.Q. and as to proportion of dull children seems to be racial. But the difference in median I.Q. which is due to race alone is in this case at most only 8.6 points whereas the difference between children of the same race but of Inferior and Very Superior social status may amount to 33.9 points. It is apparent that such differences as we have between the Negro and Italian children and between these and children of native-born white parents are not nearly so striking as the difference between children of the same race but of different social status. Of the two factors social status seems to play the more important part. To such an extent is this true that it would seem to indicate that there is more likeness between children of the same social status but different race than between children of the same race but of different social status.

A more extreme degree of cultural deprivation than that studied by Arlitt was investigated in England by Gordon.[4] In a report prepared as part of his official duties as Inspector of Schools, Gordon analyzed the Stanford-Binet IQ's of children whose schooling was deficient. Among them were children of gypsies and children whose families lived and worked on canal boats. Both groups were educated in special schools maintained for them. The canal-boat children attended school only a few days at a time, while the boats were tied up for loading and unloading cargo. Their homes also provided little intellectual stimulation. Many of the parents were illiterate and each family led a relatively isolated existence. These children obtained a mean IQ of 70. When different ages were compared, however, the youngest children had IQ's close to normal, and IQ declined with age even among siblings in the same family. This relationship was expressed by a correlation of —.76 between IQ and chronological age in the entire group. Among the gypsy children, whose school attendance was somewhat better and whose home environments were less deficient than those of the canal-boat children, the mean IQ was 75 and the correlation between IQ and chronological age —.43.

Both the low mean IQ and the age decrement have been confirmed in studies of other culturally deprived groups in depressed rural areas and in urban slums. These findings are illustrated in the following American investigation, conducted by Sherman and Key in the Blue Ridge Mountains during the early 1930's. One explanation proposed for the age decrement is that the simple intellectual needs of the young child can be satisfied as well in a culturally deprived environment as in a culturally enriched environment. As the child grows older, however, the differential effects of poor home environment and deficient schooling become increasingly manifested. A further explanation may be found in the changing nature of the functions covered by intelligence tests at different ages. The increasing emphasis upon verbal and other abstract functions at older ages may present a progressively greater handicap to children whose environments do not encourage the development of these abilities.

[4] H. Gordon. Mental and scholastic tests among retarded children. Educ. Pamphlet No. 44, Board of Educ., London, 1923.

Mandel Sherman and Cora Beale Key

The Intelligence of Isolated Mountain Children*

This report of the results of intelligence tests made of mountain children is part of a larger study begun in the summer of 1929 to determine the cultural influences which affect intellectual, emotional, and personality development and the influences determining the attitudes of mountain people living in relative degrees of isolation.

The communities studied were four hollows located approximately 100 miles west of Washington, D. C., in the Blue Ridge Mountains and a small village at the base of the Blue Ridge about the same distance from Washington to the southwest. Of great significance is the ancestry of these people. The hollows were settled in the pre-colonial period by English and Scotch–Irish immigrants. When German immigrants were given most of the land in the Shenandoah valley surrounding these mountain ranges the English and Scotch–Irish people were forced up the mountainside. The topography of this region is such that the settlers were forced further within the mountains, settling in hollows surrounded by mountain ranges. There they built their log and mud cabins many of which still remain and are inhabited. Each of the hollows selected for study—Colvin, Needles, Oakton, and Rigby—are close to each other but are separated by comparatively high mountain ranges. Of these hol-

*M. Sherman and Cora B. Key. The intelligence of isolated mountain children. *Child Develpm.*, 1932, 3, 279–290. (Pp. 279–281, 283–284, 287, 289.) Reprinted by permission of the authors and the Society for Research in Child Development.

lows, Colvin is at the lowest level in social development. This hollow is small, consisting of a small number of families living in scattered, mud-plastered log huts. There is no road, except for a trail, to the outside world. One small log and mud cabin is rented by the county school board for a school. There is no general meeting place and the church meetings which have been held in the past have been discontinued except for a very occasional revival meeting. With three exceptions, the adults are illiterate. They are descendants of the original settlers who married relatives and mixed very little with the people outside of the hollows. . . .

Needles Hollow, adjacent to Colvin Hollow, is next in the scale of social development. It is reached by a rocky road from a small hamlet at the base of the mountains. Its patches of ground, from two to five acres on the average, surrounding the cabins, approach the status of small farms. It is a more socialized community and many of the adults are literate. The children have had good school advantages compared to Colvin Hollow.

Oakton Hollow, next higher in the social scale, is separated from Colvin Hollow by a high mountain. The road to the valley is passable for old Fords and wagons most of the year. The Hollow boasts of a combined general store and post-office and many of the inhabitants receive mail and an occasional magazine. There exists a greater social consciousness than in Colvin or Needles Hollows. Oakton Hollow has had about four months of school each year for some time. The people are fairly prosperous although they have but little surplus farm products to sell in the valley.

Rigby Hollow, culturally further developed, can be reached from the valley much more easily than any of the other three hollows. The present school was established by missionaries about nine years ago and has been conducting regular school terms. Church and Sunday School services are held regularly. The farms are larger than those of the other hollows and there nearly always is a surplus which is sold in the valley. School terms have been about seven months each year for the past eight years and approximately 75 per cent of the inhabitants are literate.

For purposes of comparison a small farm and sawmill town, Briarsville, was chosen. It is located at the base of the mountains to the south of the hollows. The town has a hard surfaced road connecting it with the principal cities of Virginia. The school building is a modern structure with four classrooms, three of which are used regularly. The school board employs three well-trained teachers. The town has a good general store, telephones, and receives newspapers.

The comparison of the intelligence test results of the mountain children with those of the children of Briarsville is especially significant in view of the origin of many of the residents of this town. Many of the inhabitants migrated from the mountains in the past to obtain work on the adjacent farms and in the sawmill. At first socially isolated from the "first" families of this town, the children now mingle freely. It was thought that a comparison of intelligence test results of the mountain children with those of Briarsville would be much more significant than with children of an average town or city.

Intelligence tests were given to more than half of the children of the four mountain hollows and Briarsville. Not every child was tested, for some of the younger children could not be taken to the place where the tests were given, and a few of the others refused to cooperate. Nine tests were used: the Stanford-Binet; The National Intelligence Test, Scale B, Form 2; Pintner-Cunningham Primary Mental Test. For performance tests the following were employed: Manikin, Seguin Form Board, Mare and Foal, Healy Puzzle "A," and Knox Cube Test from the Pintner-Paterson scale of performance tests, and Goodenough's Drawing of a Man.

A representative sample of the school population thus was tested. A total of 386 tests were given to the children in the mountain communities and 198 in Briarsville. . . . Table 1

TABLE 1. *Average Intelligence Quotients according to Various Tests*

Tests	Mountain Communities			Briarsville		
	Number of Cases	Average	S.D.	Number of Cases	Average	S.D.
Stanford-Binet	32	61.5	11.2			
National	24	61.2	17.5	50	96.1	15.2
Pintner-Cunningham	42	75.9	17.1	31	87.6	13.0
Four performance tests:						
Year Scale	54	83.9	24.8	10	118.6	17.1
Med. M.A. Scale	54	79.1	23.8	10	95.6	16.3
Drawing of a man	63	72.3	17.9	67	76.3	17.0

shows the average intelligence quotient of the children in the four mountain communities and Briarsville. . . . The average intelligence quotient of the Briarsville children was higher than that of the mountain children in every test, and had a smaller standard deviation. The results give further evidence of the effect of systematic training upon intelligence test ratings, a factor often slighted in comparative studies of intelligence test scores.

The dependence of the intelligence quotients on the kind of test used is shown in a comparison of the average I.Q.'s of the mountain children on the different tests used. The highest average intelligence quotients are found in the tests presumably most independent of language and of school training, and lowest in those utilizing language ability.

When we examine the results of the tests in Briarsville, on the other hand, we find that while the highest average I.Q. was obtained in the performance tests, the next highest was on the National Intelligence Test—a test dependent upon language ability. This may be additional evidence that systematic and consistent training in a community of a comparatively high order of social organization is a stimulus to the development of the kind of intelligence we ordinarily measure by tests.

These mountain children are slow and cautious with a slow tempo of response. The way in which the environment influences a child's method of responding probably has not been studied sufficiently in intelligence test results. In scoring the results it was found that the children rated highest in those tests in which the tempo of the directions and the responses was slowest. It is not surprising to find that the children rated highest on tests which took into account least the factor of speed. The children in these mountains live in an environment which does not put a premium on speed and the problem of evaluation of their test scores thus is complicated further. . . .

Table 2 gives the average intelligence quotients on various tests according to increasing chronological age. It shows a decrease in intelligence quotients with increase in chronological age for every test except the National, applied to the mountain children. The decrease in the intelligence quotients in some of the tests is as great from the 6th to the 10th year as from the 10th to the 16th year. In some cases the decline in intelligence for children over 10 is greater than for children between 6 and 10. An intelligence test is an indirect measure. An estimate of intelligence is based on the information the child has been able to obtain. In the mountain environment increments of information become less large with increases in age, and the seven-year-old has relatively more chance to gather information and to learn by experience than the twelve-year-old in the same environment. . . .

[Further analysis revealed that] the per cent of cases below average intelligence increases with the decrease in the cultural level of the community. In Colvin Hollow, socially lowest in the group, the per cent of cases below average intelligence is considerably greater than in any of the other communities. Briarsville, the highest community culturally, had the smallest per cent of cases below average with one exception. . . .

TABLE 2. Average Intelligence Quotient on Five Tests according to Increasing Chronological Age

Chrono-logical Age	Number of Cases*		Pintner–Cunningham		National Intelligence		Drawing of a Man		Performance Scale			
									Year Scale		Med. M.A. Scale	
	Moun-tains	Briars-ville	Moun-tains	Briars-ville	Moun-tains-	Briars-ville	Moun-tains	Briars-ville	Moun-tains	Briars-ville	Moun-tains	Briars-ville
6–8	12–13	8	84	94			80	93	91		89	
8–10	15–23	4–22	70	91		117	66	82	84	119	76	93
10–12	5–16	5–20	53	76	66	101	71	69	86	108	70	87
12–14	7–12	16			67	91	69	73	83		83	
14–16	8–15	14			52	87	49	70	75		73	

*The figures indicating the number of cases do not mean that every test was given to the numbers indicated. The minimum and maximum number of children given a test at the respective chronological ages is shown.

Summary

The results of the intelligence tests of mountain children living in varying degrees of isolation appear to corroborate the belief of many psychologists that the expression of intelligence, as measured by standardized tests, depends in a large measure upon the opportunities to gather information and upon the requirements made upon the individual by his environment. Since the ancestry of the children of all the hollows came from the same stock the claim cannot be made that some of these mountain people are "degenerate" and therefore their children are expected to be retarded intellectually, a claim too often advanced for the supposed inferiority of isolated mountain children. Furthermore, as has been shown in this paper, the young children of the various hollows do not differ greatly in intelligence, whereas great differences are found between the older children of the different hollows. The only plausible explanation of the increasing difference with increasing age is that children develop only as the environment demands development.

9

Cultural Deprivation:

Longitudinal Approaches

What happens to the intellectual level of children in culturally deprived areas when cultural conditions improve? This was the question
raised by Wheeler in the study reported below. Having tested a
group of mountain children similar to those studied by Sherman and
Key (see Chapter 8), Wheeler returned to the same communities ten
years later. In the interval, the area had undergone conspicuous improvements in its socioeconomic level, transportation facilities, and
educational system. These changes were reflected in significant rises
in both the intelligence test performance and the school progress of
its children.

Lester Rosin Wheeler

A Comparative Study of the Intelligence of East Tennessee Mountain Children*

Certain trends in the investigations of the intelligence of rural and mountain children raise questions of vital importance to education. Does the deviation of these children from the normal distribution indicate that they are inherently inferior? Are they by training and experience made less capable of dealing with intelligence tests than children in other environments? To what extent do intelligence ratings vary as a result of improving environmental conditions? Is the decrease in IQ with an increase in chronological age due to defects in the process of maturation of intelligence, or to the increasing influence of poor cultural conditions? . . .

Intelligence of Mountain Children

In 1930 we made a study of the intelligence of East Tennessee Mountain children. The Dearborn IA and IIC Intelligence Tests were given to 1147 children in Grades I–VIII from 21 mountain schools, and the Illinois Intelligence Test was given to 564 of these cases in Grades III–VIII. The median IQ was 82 on the Dearborn and 78 on the Illinois Test. The IQ on the Dearborn Test was 95 at age six, and de-

* L. R. Wheeler. A comparative study of the intelligence of East Tennessee mountain children. *J. educ. Psychol.*, 1942, **33**, 321–334. (Pp. 321–324, 329, 332–333.) Reprinted by permission of the copyright holder.

creased to 74 at age sixteen. A marked school retardation was evident, from one-and-a-half years in the first grade to over two years in the eighth grade. The conclusions reached were: (1) The results of both tests were materially affected by environmental factors, (2) the mountain children were not as far below normal intelligence as the tests indicated, and (3) with proper environmental changes the mountain children might test near a normal group. It was noted that,

The growing educational opportunities in the mountains are materially changing the isolated sections. The State is providing modern and adequate schools in the very heart of the mountains, and is sending well-trained teachers, many of whom are holding or working toward college degrees, into those schools to teach the mountain children. . . . Educational opportunities of the mountains have advanced with the improvement of roads, thus enabling consolidation of schools in a number of sections. As this is only a recent development, it will be interesting to note the influence of better schools on the results of later intelligence test data on the same groups of children.[1]

Ten years have elapsed since this initial study was made, and we have retested the same mountain areas. The data for this second investigation were gathered during the Spring and Fall of 1940. Obviously we could not retest the same children, but we have repeated the same test on children in the same areas and largely from the same families; 91 per cent of the families represented in this study have been life-residents of the area, 8 per cent have moved into the areas since 1930 from adjacent Appalachian Mountain sections, leaving only one per cent shifting into the mountains from undetermined areas. The overlapping of a majority of the family names in the two studies agrees with this general trend, and the data indicate that any major changes found in the results of the intelligence tests are due to other factors than population shift.

[1] L. R. Wheeler. The intelligence of East Tennessee mountain children. *J. educ. Psychol.*, 1932, 23, 351–370. (P. 354.)

Some Environmental Changes in the Mountain Area

During the past decade there have been many changes in the economic, social, and cultural life of these mountain people. The State has completed an excellent road system which gives every community access to progressive areas outside of the mountains, and has developed transportation facilities for schools and industry. Our data show about 60 per cent of the families in one county and 40 per cent in another had one or more members working in industrial plants. In 1930 neither State nor county provided transportation; in 1940, 2316 children were transported daily to and from school. This probably accounts for much of the 17 per cent increase in enrollment in 1940, and for the 32 per cent higher average daily attendance. Basing the allotment of State money to county schools on the basis of average daily attendance now stimulates the teachers and community to keep the children in school. Hot lunches are served regularly in all the larger schools.

There has been a general shift from the one-room to larger schools, a reorganization made possible by improved roads. An improvement is also indicated in the types of school buildings. Many schools now have adequate playgrounds and fairly well equipped gymnasiums. A circulating library, maintained by the State and counties, makes available around 14,000 volumes for these schools, and free textbooks are furnished for the first three grades. While a decade ago the average training of the teachers was less than two years of college work, today it is about three years. A majority of the teachers are either college graduates or receiving training-in-service from accredited teacher-training colleges. New teachers employed are required to have four years of college training. Well-trained, progressive college graduates have displaced the politically appointed county superintendents of a decade ago. An excellent supervisory program is provided for the area with well-trained county supervisors and a State regional supervisor who assist in coördinating instruction. Schools have been improved by the innovation of a State rating system based on points for improved instruction, additional books and materials, provision for health facilities, and general equipment.

During the past ten years the rapid growth of industry in the area enables the families to supplement its agricultural livelihood with ready cash through employment in the rayon, lumber, pottery, and other industrial plants. Farming methods have materially changed; pasture lands now replace many of the corn fields on the rough mountain slopes, and stock raising and dairy farming is proving profitable. Small but modern frame houses located on or near the main highways have replaced many of the log cabins and small rough-board houses. There has been unusual development in the area, and the improvement in roads, schools, agriculture, and the economic life of the communities has materially changed the general environment of these people. . . .

The average mountain child is eight months younger for his grade than ten years ago. . . . The differences in chronological age range from three months in Grade I to fifteen months in Grade V. There is a consistent difference in favor of the 1940 group in each grade and a significant difference in most of the grades, substantiating other investigations which indicate that age-grade retardation decreases with improvement in instruction and general educational opportunities. There seems to be a tendency for the older children to leave the elementary school earlier than they did ten years ago, probably due to better opportunities for high-school attendance and industrial employment. . . .

The median IQ for the 1930 group, $82 \pm .40$, has increased over ten points to $93 \pm .25$ in 1940. This gain is further shown by a study of the percentage of overlapping: 74

per cent or about three-fourths of the 1930 cases are below the 1940 median. In 1930 the median IQ classified the children as a dull group, while in 1940 the group is within the normal classification. . . .

Summary

1. There is a general agreement among investigators that urban children rate higher on intelligence tests than rural or mountain children.

2. The majority of studies indicate a decrease in IQ with an increase in chronological age.

3. There are diverse opinions concerning the factors which cause rural–urban differences and the decline in IQ.

4. During the Spring and Fall of 1940, intelligence tests were given to 3252 children in 40 mountain schools of East Tennessee, and the results are compared with a similar study made ten years ago.

5. During the decade there has been definite improvement in the economic, social, and educational status of this mountain area.

6. Today the average mountain child is about eight months younger chronologically and nine months older mentally for his grade than the average child of ten years ago.

7. The difference between the chronological and mental age of the average mountain child is now about one-third as great as it was a decade ago.

8. The 1940 group of mountain children is mentally superior to the 1930 group at all ages and all grades, as measured by the same tests.

9. The average mountain child has gained ten points in IQ, or nearly one point a year during the past ten years.

10. The average mountain child's IQ decreases about two points each year from age six to sixteen. This is about the same rate of decline as was found ten years ago.

11. Over-ageness, or age-grade retardation, among mountain children appears to be the predominating cause of the decline in IQ with increase in chronological age.

12. The results of this investigation give further light on the findings of the 1930 study, and indicate that intelligence, as measured by these tests, may be improved with an improvement in educational and general environmental conditions.

Wheeler's study may be characterized as a longitudinal study of a population, since comparable samples of the same population were examined after a lapse of several years. Other investigators have followed this approach on a larger scale, with more broadly defined populations and longer time intervals. An outstanding example is provided by the Scottish Surveys.[2] In 1932, a group test of intelligence was administered to nearly all 11-year-olds in Scotland. The identical test was repeated in 1947, an attempt again being made to include all Scottish children who were then aged 11. The two samples comprised 87,498 and 70,805 children, respectively, representing 87 and 88 per cent of the total estimated number of 11-year-olds in Scotland on the two occasions. Mean scores showed a small but statistically significant improvement over the 15-year interval.

This rise in mean score was of particular interest since it contradicted a predicted decline in intelligence based on the negative correlations generally reported between intelligence and family size. Such correlations are of the order of $-.30$. Since children from larger families thus tend to have lower IQ's than those from smaller families, it has been argued that each successive generation should show a slight loss in intellectual level. Further analyses of the data, however, indicate that the problem is far more complex than was originally supposed and that such predicted declines are highly questionable.[3]

[2] Scottish Council for Research in Education. *The trend of Scottish intelligence.* London: University of London Press, 1949.
[3] For a discussion of methodological problems and pertinent findings, see Anne Anastasi. Intelligence and family size. *Psychol. Bull.*, 1956, **53**, 187–209.

Similar studies conducted elsewhere have also failed to substantiate the anticipated decline in intelligence. It is noteworthy that a survey of the intelligence test performance of American high school students over a 20-year period suggested that this, too, had improved, despite the marked increase in proportion of students enrolled in high school.[4] Since a larger proportion of the total population was attending high school at the end than at the beginning of this 20-year period, a decrease in mean score would be expected in the high school group unless the total population had improved sufficiently to counteract such a drop. The results indicate that the latter must actually have occurred.

Chief among the cultural factors that may account for the consistently observed rise in mean intelligence test scores is the general improvement in available educational facilities and in other opportunities for intellectual development. Improved quality of instruction, lengthening of school term (particularly in rural areas), development of mass media of communication, and advances in public health and nutrition may all have played a part. The rising educational level of the general population also means that children are reared by parents who have themselves received more schooling than had the preceding generation. Increasing familiarity with psychological tests is another possible contributing factor, but there is some evidence in the Scottish Surveys that its effect is not large.

Although most of the data on intellectual changes of populations have been obtained with children, an opportunity for comparing the performance of large adult samples over an interval of 25 years was provided by the army drafts of the First and Second World Wars. The mean educational level of the United States Army draftees was 8 grades in the First World War and 10 grades in the Second World War. Thus a difference in amount of schooling received by the two samples is now added to the more general cultural differences affecting the child samples of other surveys. The following analysis of the army data by Tuddenham reveals that these experiential changes were in fact accompanied by a pronounced rise in tested intelligence.

[4] F. H. Finch. Enrollment increases and changes in mental level. *Appl. Psychol. Monogr.*, 1946, No. 10.

Read Duncan Tuddenham

Soldier Intelligence in World Wars I and II*

Cattell,[5] Lentz,[6] Maller,[7] and others, arguing from the observation that family size is inversely related to test performance, education, and socioeconomic level, have contended that the mean IQ of the population is declining at the rate of three or four points per generation. In contrast, data collected by the Personnel Research Section, AGO, during the closing months of World War II indicate at least for that fraction of the population selected for military service, that performance on a group test of the kind usually described as measuring "general learning ability" or "verbal intelligence" has markedly increased from World War I to World War II. The study here reported was a by-product of another research and is not so unequivocal as one should like. Nevertheless it offers direct evidence on a problem hitherto attacked only indirectly, and suggests that the future may not be as black as the eugenicists would have us believe.

In the course of establishing the score equivalence between certain Army tests and several commercial ones, the Wells

* R. D. Tuddenham. Soldier intelligence in World Wars I and II. *Amer. Psychologist*, 1948, **3**, 54–56. Reprinted by permission of the author and the American Psychological Association.

5 R. B. Cattell. Effects of human fertility trends upon the distribution of intelligence and culture. 39th *Yearb., Nat. Soc. Stud. Educ.*, 1940, 221–233.
6 T. F. Lentz, Jr. Relation of IQ to size of family. *J. educ. Psychol.*, 1927, **18**, 486–496.
7 J. B. Maller. Vital indices and their relation to psychological and social factors. *Hum. Biol.*, 1933, **5**, 94–121.

Revision (Form 5) of Army Alpha Examination was administered to a representative sample of the World War II draft. The population consisted of 768 white enlisted men selected on the basis of Army General Classification Test (AGCT) scores, as recorded on their qualification cards, to yield a distribution by Army Grade like that for all inductees entering during 1943. The distribution desired and that obtained are compared in Table 1. Since the correspondence

TABLE 1.

Army Grade	Army Standard Score	Inductees Entering in 1943	Experimental Sample
I	130 and above	6.4%	6.4%
II	110–129	28.6	28.8
III	90–109	31.1	30.7
IV	60–89	28.5	28.8
V	below 60	5.4	5.3

was very close, the 768 men without further selection were administered the Wells Revision (Form 5) of Army Alpha Examination.

The correlation between Wells Alpha and AGCT was .90, indicating a very large degree of community in the functions measured. The AGCT yielded a mean Army Standard Score of 98.3 and a standard deviation of 22.7. The mean raw score on Wells Alpha was 101.2 and the standard deviation was 46.0. Centile norms for the two tests are presented in Table 2.

The comparison of the intelligence test performance of soldiers in World War I and World War II is complicated by the fact that for the purposes of the major study it was necessary to test the World War II group with the commercially available Wells Revision, Form 5 of the Alpha Examination instead of the original Alpha used in World War I. However, there is general agreement that the two versions yield very similar score distributions, especially in the upper quartile.

TABLE 2. Centile Equivalents of Scores on AGCT and on Wells Alpha
Examination, Form 5, for a Sample of 768 White Enlisted Men

Centile	AGCT Standard Score	Alpha Raw Score	Centile	AGCT Standard Score	Alpha Raw Score
99	145	194	50	100	104
95	132	175	45	97	97
90	126	160	40	94	90
85	122	150	35	91	82
80	118	143	30	87	74
75	115	136	25	83	66
70	112	130	20	78	58
65	109	122	15	73	50
60	106	116	10	67	38
55	103	110	5	59	23
			1	42	3

Bingham[8] states: "The Wells Revision . . . make(s) the
examination more suitable for use in schools and industries
while preserving the irreplaceable norms. Scores which fall in
the upper quartile of the distribution are directly comparable
with the original Alpha scores." The published norms on
Wells Alpha for the "general adult population" agree closely
with norms obtained on the original Alpha for literate white
soldiers of World War I. Lorge[9] has published data indicating that the Wells Alpha yields larger raw scores than
does the original form, but that the difference is not greater
than five percentile points.

If it is conceded that scores on the Wells revision correspond closely to scores on the original Alpha Examination,
it is difficult to escape the conclusion that soldiers of World

[8] W. V. Bingham. Aptitudes and aptitude testing. New York: Harper, 1937.
(P. 330.)
[9] I. Lorge. A table of percentile equivalents for eight intelligence tests frequently used with adults. J. appl. Psychol., 1936, 19, 392–395.

War II were markedly superior to their fathers in the functions measured by this test.

As may be seen in Table 3, the differences between the two groups are very large throughout the range, and are as conspicuous above the seventy-fifth centile, where the equiv-

TABLE 3. *A Comparison of Performance on Alpha Examinations of 48,102 White Enlisted Soldiers of World War I and a Representative Sample of 768 White Enlisted Soldiers of World War II*

Centile	World War I Original Alpha Raw Score	World War II Wells Alpha, Form 5 Raw Score	Centile	World War I Original Alpha Raw Score	World War I Wells Alpha, Form 5 Raw Score
99	166	194	50	62	104
95	137	175	45	57	97
90	120	160	40	52	90
85	108	150	35	48	82
80	98	143	30	44	74
75	91	136	25	39	66
70	84	130	20	35	58
65	78	122	15	30	50
60	72	116	10	25	38
55	67	110	5	18	23
			1	8	3

alence of raw scores on Army Alpha and Wells Alpha is best established, as they are below this point. For the principal literate white sample of World War I reported in the *Memoirs*,[10] the median raw score is 62. This is in close agreement with a median of 61 for Wells Alpha as cited in the published norms. However, a raw score of 62 reaches only the 22nd centile of the World War II distribution. Conversely, a raw score of 104, the median for the World War II group, falls at the 83rd centile of the World War I population. Such differences are, of course, highly significant.

[10] R. M. Yerkes (Ed.). Psychological examining in the United States Army. *Mem. nat. Acad. Sci.*, 1921, 15.

No satisfactory answer can be given to the fundamental question of whether a similar difference exists between the national population of 1917–18 and 1940–45 from which the troops were drawn. Indeed, the members of the armed forces constitute by far the largest and most representative sample of the general population ever subjected to psychometric procedures. Considering the greater size of the Army in World War II, it seems likely that the draft population during the recent conflict was more nearly representative of the general population than was the case in World War I. However, the size and direction of selective differences between the armies and the populations from which they were drawn can only be guessed at.

Considering only the Army samples here reported, many factors can be adduced to account for the superiority of the World War II group. Only a few can be mentioned here.

1. For soldiers in World War I objective tests were wholly unfamiliar. Most soldiers in World War II had had considerable experience with them in schools, industry, etc. Previous practice on AGCT probably served to raise the Alpha scores of the men here reported. However, practice effects on AGCT produce an average gain of only about five points in taking a second form of the same test and would be even smaller in taking a different test, as in this instance. It seems unlikely that greater familiarity with objective tests can account for a very large part of the superiority of the World War II sample.

2. Numerous investigators have reported that as a nation we are increasing in height, in weight, and in longevity. The indirect influence of improvements in public health and nutrition may have operated to increase test performance, though to an unknown degree.

3. The Army of World War II was definitely superior to that of World War I in amount of education. Since amount of schooling is correlated with test performance, it seems likely that educational differences contribute heavily to the supe-

rior test performance of the World War II group. In the present study, the number of years of education completed by each of the 768 enlisted men was recorded from his qualification card. The mean was 10.0 years; the S.D was 3.0 years. The correlations between years of education and test score were .74 and .75 for AGCT and Wells Alpha, respectively. Comparable statistics for the principal literate white sample of World War I soldiers have been computed from the *Memoirs*.[11] The correlation between Alpha and years of education completed was .63. The mean education was 8.0 years; the S.D. was 2.6 years. As a rough device for estimating the amount of difference in Alpha performance attributable to educational differences, the columns of Table 281

TABLE 4.

Decile	World War I Unweighted Raw Score	World War I Weighted Raw Score	World War II Raw Score
90	120	144	160
80	98	125	143
70	84	110	130
60	72	97	116
50	62	85	104
40	52	73	90
30	44	61	74
20	35	49	58
10	25	34	38

(*Memoirs*) were reweighted to conform to the distribution with respect to education of the World War II sample. Decile values were then computed from the reweighted table, with the result shown in Table 4. Weighting of the World War I findings to make the population comparable in education to

[11] R. M. Yerkes. (Ed.) Psychological examining in the United States Army. *Mem. nat. Acad. Sci.*, 1921, **15**. (Table 281, p. 748.)

the World War II sample removes over half of the obtained difference in test scores between the two groups. If additional allowance is made for the progressive increase in the length of the school year and for improvements in school facilities and in the professional preparation of teachers, it is evident that the superior test performance of the World War II group *can* be accounted for largely in terms of education.

While the data presented in this study offer no proof, the writer is inclined to interpret them as indicating that the present population is superior in mental test performance to the population of a generation ago, and that a large proportion of this superiority is a consequence of more and better education for more people.

The *magnitude* of the improvement in test performance from World War I to World War II cannot be established on the basis of existing data, nor is it possible to estimate it very precisely even for Army populations. The major potential source of error in the present study is the use of two different measuring instruments, Army Alpha and Wells Alpha, in comparing the World War I and World War II groups; but a comparison which involved only Army Alpha would not eliminate difficulties of interpretation. Various items of the original version have grown obsolete and cannot be assumed to have remained constant in difficulty. Yet omitting such items, or replacing them with new material would alter the instrument and introduce, though perhaps in lesser degree, the same source of error which may be operative in the investigation reported here.

The findings of the present study, despite their limitations, cast doubts on Cattell's contention that the national IQ is dropping at a rapid rate. His references to IQ changes seem to imply a belief that the population is declining with respect to intelligence as measured by psychological tests. The present study indicates a change in the opposite direction, though one cannot rule out the possibility of a decline in the purely native component of intellectual performance were it possible to measure it. On one point the writer would be in complete agreement with Cattell, viz., that changes in the population, as well as the obsolescence of test content, make it desirable that test norms be subjected to periodic revision.

Several investigations have been more specifically concerned with the relation between the intelligence test performance of individual adults and the amount of schooling completed by each. In Tuddenham's article, reference was made to correlations in the .60's and .70's found between these two variables in the army samples of both World Wars. Such correlations may of course result from progressive selection of the brighter individuals in the educational system, as well as from the effects of education upon intellectual development.

Longitudinal investigations involving the retesting of the same persons after periods of 10 to 30 years have provided a more direct approach to this problem. Follow-up studies of New York City elementary school graduates,[12] midwestern college students,[13] and Swedish school children agree in finding that individuals who continue their education longer show larger gains in intelligence test scores than do those with less intervening education. The most extensive of these studies, conducted in Sweden by Husén, is summarized in the next selection. Note also the author's comprehensive discussion of methodological problems encountered in longitudinal studies.

[12] I. Lorge. Schooling makes a difference. *Teach. Coll. Rec.*, 1945, **16**, 483–492.
[13] W. A. Owens, Jr. Age and mental abilities: A longitudinal study. *Genet. Psychol. Monogr.*, 1953, **48**, 3–54.

Torsten Husén

The Influence of Schooling upon IQ*

The influence of schooling on the results of conventional intelligence tests is one of the most debated problems in educational psychology, and from a methodological point of view one of the most difficult to answer. A very large number of relevant variables have to be dealt with, and, as a rule, only a few of these are under control. Moreover, the problem of sampling and the regression effect further complicate the interpretation of the results obtained. . . .

Methodological Problems

When it is desired to investigate the effect of theoretical schooling on the intelligence quotient, the latter being defined by conventional group tests, it should be endeavoured, from the outset, to obtain a clear idea as to the extent that the schooling variable can be studied separately. This is of the greatest importance for the interpretation of the interindividual differences or group differences that arise. The possibility of attaining the ideal conditions for investigation, as given below, vary from case to case, depending upon the comprehensiveness of the data available for the investigator.

1. The use of a control and an experimental group is highly desirable, not to say necessary. If it is desired to study the influence of schooling on ability, it is preferable to employ

* T. Husén. The influence of schooling upon IQ. *Theoria*, 1951, **17**, 61–88. (Pp. 61, 63–73, 75–76.) Reprinted by permission of the author and the publisher.

two groups that are equivalent to commence with. One of these groups does not display any variations with regard to theoretical schooling received (control group), while the other has continued, after primary school, to a varying extent, to receive schooling (experimental group).

2. Naturally, the equivalence ought primarily to refer to the test variable which defines the IQ; but if possible, it should also embrace such social variables as parents' income, socio-economic group, education, occupation, etc. The ideal would be to match at random each control individual with an experimental individual, so that both individuals who constitute a pair would be similar as to all relevant variables. This matching should take place *a priori*, because if it is done *a posteriori*, there is a risk of the factor which has caused an individual to become an experimental or a control individual, being correlated with the variable whose effect it is desired to study. If . . . we desire to study the effect of nursery school teaching on intellectual development, and if, with this purpose in mind, a number of children are tested both before and after they have received this teaching, and should these test results be then compared with the corresponding results for a group of children who have not attended a nursery school, the differences obtained will be very difficult to interpret. It may very easily be the case that more well-to-do parents who are better educated and more socially ambitious send their children to a greater extent to the nursery schools. The superiority displayed by children who have had a pre-school training, when compared with those who have not, may, to no small extent, depend on the stimulation that the home environment is able to give from an intellectual point of view. The experimental and control groups, matched *a priori*, constitute, as has already been pointed out, an ideal that is as a rule unattainable.

3. Generally, the experimental group is already given in the form that some subjects have begun, or are about to begin, a certain course of training. This does not prevent one,

however, from trying to make the two groups equivalent with regard to those variables that can be controlled. But here one is met with the difficulty that is due to the limited scope of the material. If we have, let us say, a group of 400 individuals, and wish to control this with reference to age, parents' income, and the subjects' schooling, there is considerable risk of obtaining such small subgroups that large group differences are required in order for these to be statistically significant. A way out, which has been used in this investigation, is to attempt to control one variable at a time. If it is desired, as in our case, to determine the influence of schooling on IQ, and the experimental and control groups are not equivalent from a social point of view, it is possible to compare the mean effect that every variable has in itself, when excluding the influence of the other variables.

4. The question of sampling is of the greatest importance. In longitudinal studies, we often obtain a positive selection, because that part of the material which is worst off intellectually and socially is more difficult to control as regards public registration. If, for example, a follow-up is undertaken for 300 children and, after a number of years only 125 of these can be traced, naturally these 125 should not be compared with the original data for the 300, but with the corresponding data for the 125 remaining subjects. . . .

5. One of the most important factors in longitudinal studies, when the same group is tested either twice or several times, is the so-called regression effect, the influence of which, with regard to the effect of training of ability, was first pointed out by McNemar.[14] The regression effect implies that individuals obtaining extreme scores tend, when retested, to regress towards the average. If we test a number of persons, and select all who have an IQ over 130, and then retest them with the same test, we shall find that the new mean is 5–10 units lower. In the same way, we should have

[14] Q. McNemar. A critical examination of the University of Iowa studies of environmental influences upon the IQ. *Psychol. Bull.*, 1940, **37**, 63–92.

obtained a mean that was 5–10 units higher, if we had chosen subjects with an IQ under 70. The reason for this phenomenon is the insufficient measuring accuracy of the test, its lack of ideal reliability. Random errors influence the individual scores. The regression effect is reversible. If we select all the subjects who attain an IQ of over 130 at the second testing, we shall find that their mean for the first testing was 5–10 units lower.

One must bear in mind that the regression effect, under certain conditions, can act as a contributory factor with regard to the appearance of group differences. If two groups, which are drawn from two different populations, are compared, and the two "mother populations" differ as regards the variable that the group comparison is concerned with, then the regression effect takes place. We shall have occasion to return to this problem later in connection with the group comparisons that our investigation gives rise to.

A condition under which the regression effect makes its influence felt may now be mentioned. If we examine the influence that secondary schooling has on the IQ at various levels of ability, it will be found that it "raises" the IQ on lower levels, and "lowers" it on higher levels. The phenomenon has, at times, been erroneously interpreted as if schooling exerted a "levelling" effect. But, since the extreme test scores, as has already been pointed out, tend on retesting to regress towards the mean, the changes described above may be expected to occur. As a rule, they are interrelated with systematic changes of other kinds.

6. The magnitude of the deviations that take place between two applications on different occasions, with the same or comparable tests and with regard to the same subjects, depends on three factors, viz.:

(a) the length of the interval,
(b) the subject's age at the first testing,
(c) the reliability of the test. . . .

7. If possible, the same test should be employed for both test and retest. In principle, this is possible when carrying out follow-up studies of children within a limited interval or of adults within any interval. But if, as in our case, the same persons are tested at respectively 10 and 20 years of age, scales with a different content must be employed (the test items will have to vary); this does not imply, however, that there need be a difference in the structure of the scales. Both the test scales employed in this case happened to have the same structure in the following respects. They were both

(a) group test scales,
(b) segregated (divided) scales with 4 subtests,
(c) time-limited scales, and
(d) scales where 3 subtests were mainly verbal and 1 was a non-verbal test.

It was not possible to use a scale that had been administered in Malmö in 1938 at the induction of the conscripts, because, for one reason, the distribution of the scores obtained would have been positively skewed without any possibilities of differentiation in the better half of the subjects tested, where the majority of those who have had secondary education are to be found.

In what follows, we shall give an account of an investigation on the influence of schooling upon changes in IQ. In 1938 the whole school population, 1,549 children, in the third grade of the primary schools in Malmö, a Swedish city with about 140,000 inhabitants, was given an intelligence group test. The mean age of the subjects was 9.65 years. Ten years later, in 1948, the male part of the population was retested at the induction into military service. Complete test data and social data from 1938 was available for 722 boys, born in 1928. On the later occasion we succeeded in identifying 95 per cent of the original population. Complete test data and school records were available for 85 per cent or 613 subjects. The identified group could be shown to be a representative sample of the whole population in terms of the initial test scores. . . .

The 1938 test was given shortly before any differentiation in school training had started. The 1948 test was given when the differentiation was practically finished. The subjects were grouped in five categories according to the highest school grade completed, as shown in Table 1. . . .

TABLE 1. IQ Change in Relation to Intervening Schooling
(adapted from Husén, pp. 69, 71)

Schooling Completed	Grade Equivalent	Number of Cases	Mean IQ Change	Percentage of Cases with IQ Gains
Primary	7	431	−1.2	46
Junior secondary without certificate	7–10	28	+2.1	54
Junior secondary with certificate	9 or 10	73	+3.0	63
Senior secondary with matriculation	11–13	66	+7.2	77
Matriculation	12 or 13	15	+11.0	87

It appears that a distinct raising of IQ takes place, the higher the level of schooling that is attained. A significant deviation from 0 only takes place with regard to the three highest groups. As will be seen, the increase is not linear, but grows rapidly above the secondary school stage with leaving certificate.

We then come to the principal question: whether the existing mean IQ differences may be attributed entirely or partly to the differences in schooling between the various groups. Since recruitment to secondary schooling is considerably greater from the higher social and income groups than from the lower, there is good reason to ask whether these social variables that are correlated with schooling have not, to a quite appreciable extent, affected the mean differences observed. As has been stated in fuller detail in another connection, there is a mean increase of about 3 units in the IQ in the highest income groups. Of the four social groups, it is only group I that shows a significant mean increase of about 7.5 units. The most "pure" of the social variables is income. Since the latter does not at all give rise to mean differences of the same magnitude as are due to schooling, it is justifiable to attribute to the latter the principal role in producing the differences shown in Table 1. The mean increase in IQ manifested by social group I can be mainly attributed to the fact that about 80 per cent of its members received secondary schooling (the majority, about 60 per cent received senior secondary schooling).

A conclusion which may be drawn as a result of the analysis of the connections of the different variables with the IQ differences is that schooling, at any rate as regards the three lower social groups, has incomparably the greatest significance for the systematic changes in IQ between 10 and 20 years of age.

One may well ask why the increase in IQ is considerably greater in the senior secondary school and matriculation groups than in the junior secondary school group. Three reasons for this may be discussed: (1) A certain selection of ability, as regards facility for intellectual training, has taken place on transition from junior secondary school to senior secondary school. (2) A decrease due to lack of training, which might appear in the junior secondary school group without leaving certificate, on account of the interval between completion of schooling and test administration. (3) A gain due to training in the senior secondary school group, because of more prolonged intellectual training.

Since our junior secondary school group with leaving certificate only contains those subjects who left school on passing this examination, we do not know what the distribution of the IQ differences was like for *all* who passed this examination. In the transition from junior secondary school to senior secondary school, the manifested ability (defined by school reports, test scores, etc.), as well as social factors are of importance. . . . In our material, there is no significant difference in terms of the 1938 test between the group with the junior secondary school leaving certificate, on the one hand, and the two highest groups of schooling, on the other. No selection of ability of any importance seems to have taken place. It is difficult to determine whether those who are more susceptible to training have been selected in this way.

The second explanation of the big increase in IQ in the senior-secondary-school group, viz., loss due to lack of training as regards the junior secondary school group with leaving certificate, is more difficult to verify. . . . Here it is a question of a comparison between those who left school after finishing the primary school and those who continued their schooling until 18 years of age. In our case, there are two groups that have received further schooling; one of these was tested about 3 years after leaving school, the other while still attending school or shortly after leaving school. But practically speaking, all the members of the secondary school with leaving certificate have vocations that afford opportunities for verbal and numerical training, and consequently the loss due to lack of training after leaving school must be much less than for those who take up purely manual work.

The third explanation: the gain due to training which is dependent on prolonged theoretical training, may hypothetically be looked upon as the most important. . . .

To sum up, it may be said that there is reason to suppose that theoretical schooling, subsequent to leaving the primary school, considerably increases the intellectual level which is measured with group tests of a conventional type. On an average, the increase lies between 0 and 10 IQ units, according to the scope of the schooling. On an average, the increase amounts for all who have received some form of further schooling to 4.84 units. The senior secondary schooling raises the level, on an average, by 7–10 units.

A still more direct procedure for investigating the effects of education on intellectual development is the experimental administration of specially developed educational programs. The upsurge of interest in cultural deprivation since midcentury has led to the initiation of several experimental programs designed to improve the intellectual skills and learning ability of children from culturally deprived backgrounds. Interest has centered particularly on the preschool ages, when cultural deficiencies of home environment might be counteracted in preparing the child for admission to the first grade.

The growing recognition that many cases of simple, nonorganic mental retardation may arise from cultural deprivation in early life has given added impetus to this type of research. The project described below by Kirk is typical of this approach. Essentially it provides intensive training to small groups of mentally retarded preschool children, whose subsequent progress is compared with that of control groups not exposed to the experimental program.

Samuel Alexander Kirk

Early Education of the Mentally Retarded: An Experimental Study*

The educable mentally retarded child has been a misfit in the schools because his slow learning ability does not allow him to keep up with the requirements of the regular classes. His intellectual level does not warrant institutionalization, yet his inability to cope with the curriculum of the elementary school makes his lot and that of his teachers a trying one.

Earlier, many such children were sent to institutions to be educated and then returned to the community. Because of

* S. A. Kirk. Early education of the mentally retarded: An experimental study. Urbana, Ill.: University Illinois Press, 1958. (Pp. 1–2, 203–208.) Reprinted by permission of the publisher.

overcrowding, however, institutions gradually restricted their space to those who were more markedly mentally deficient. At the turn of the century special classes for these educable mentally retarded children were organized in the public schools.

The usual practice of schools is to admit these children into the first grade at the age of six with other six-year-olds. Because of their intellectual deficit they do not learn as do other first-graders. In some school systems, if a mentally retarded child is found in the kindergarten or first grade, the parents are asked to keep him at home for a year or so until he has matured sufficiently to cope with the program. Sometimes he is allowed to fail for several years before he is examined and found to be mentally handicapped. In some communities such a child is excluded from school as mentally defective, and institutionalization is recommended. In some communities, where special classes have been organized, the practice is to be sure that the child has failed in the regular grades before placing him in a special class. Each school has to decide what policy will best fit the needs of all concerned.

None of these various practices with educable mentally retarded children has been entirely satisfactory. Keeping the child at home until he has matured sufficiently to attend the regular grades is based on the assumption that maturation is the only factor to be considered. If, however, a lack of training in the home has retarded the child's development, keeping him at home only accentuates the effects of such factors.

Allowing the child to fail in school for the first two or three years is likewise considered unsatisfactory. Such an experience for children during their formative years may produce inhibitions and poor attitudes toward learning when they do become ready for instruction; it may produce a distaste for school in general. School failure at this age level is considered a deterrent to good personality development.

— — —

Can intensive educational programs at the preschool level accelerate the rate of development of young mentally retarded children? If such acceleration of rate does occur, will this accelerated rate continue after the preschool period? These are the general questions of the present investigation.

It is contended by some that educational provisions for mentally retarded children are based on the premise that skills, habits, and general adjustments can be developed only within the limits of inherent potentialities. It is not generally claimed that educational provisions will accelerate a rate of development, or that education will change a mentally retarded child to one who can function at a normal or average level. Another point of view is represented by those who believe that intelligence is not always a static condition of the organism, fixed by inheritance, but that it may be depressed by adverse conditions or accelerated by training and beneficial changes in environment. These opposing contentions relate to the nature–nurture controversy—a controversy which is not yet resolved.

The purpose of this experiment is to provide factual data for or against the general contention that special educational provisions at a young age can alter the rate of development of mentally retarded children. Since the literature on this issue gives contradictory evidence, attempts have been made in the present experiment to isolate certain variables within the child and within the environment which may help to clarify some factors which might account for acceleration or depression in rate of development. These variables are found in the *nature* of the child, as well as in the physical, social, or psychological *nurture* provided by the environment.

Organization of the Study

In the present study, 81 mentally retarded children between the ages of three and six were identified and studied over a period of from three to five years. Twenty-eight of these children formed the *Community Experimental Group*. This group attended a preschool in the community and was followed up with tests and observations for from one to four years after leaving the preschool. A second group (15 children who had been committed earlier to an institution for mental defectives) was enrolled in an institution preschool and followed up after discharge from this preschool, either to the institution school or to the community. This group constituted the *Institution Experimental Group*. The members of a third group (26 children in communities) were identified as mentally retarded, similar to the Community Experimental Group, but did not attend a preschool. They were tested at the same intervals as those in the Community Experimental Group and followed up after they entered the regular school at the age of six. This group was called the *Community Contrast Group*. A fourth group (12 children) was identified in a different institution and formed the *Institution Contrast Group*. This group did not attend a preschool but was followed up after admission to the institution school after the age of six.

The children in all four groups, with a few exceptions, ranged between three and six years of age and had IQ's between 45 and 80. They were thoroughly examined at the beginning of the experiment, during the preschool period, before discharge from the preschool, and at regular follow-up intervals. Some of the children were followed up for as long as five years.

Analysis of Data

The analysis of the data of the experiment was made by two methods: (1) case studies of the experimental children, and (2) statistical comparisons of the two experimental and two contrast groups. It is well known that in experiments of this kind the statistical approach alone is limiting and narrow. Processes of change and growth are too complex for adequate interpretation with available statistical procedures. Clinical judgments of the dynamics of growth and the synthesis of studies require a non-statistical approach. On the other hand, statistical methods are of inestimable value whenever the data lend themselves to statistical analysis.

For the case studies, each child in the experimental groups was classified, according to his level of mental and social development, into one of the following seven categories: (0) uneducable, (1) questionable educability, (2) low educable, (3) high educable, (4) borderline, (5) low average, and (6) average. These levels represented varying degrees of mental and social development at the time of the assessment. The uneducable child, for example, was generally one whose IQ was below 45. An average child was one whose IQ was 95 or above. Generally there was a 10-point IQ difference between each level. These categories were not wholly dependent on the IQ but represented a composite picture of various factors of development. They established arbitrary but significant and distinguishable changes in a child's development, upwards or downwards from his initial rate of development.

For the statistical treatment, the results of various objective tests and ratings were analyzed and comparisons were made between the experimental and the contrast groups.

The analysis of the case studies and the statistical results have been presented in previous sections. This section will summarize the major findings and discuss their implications for both theory and practice.

The Over-All Results

The over-all effects of preschool education on the development of young mentally retarded children were positive. In general, preschool education has some favorable effects in modifying the developmental picture of mentally retarded children, for, on the whole, the preschool experimental groups showed increased rates of growth following educational opportunities at a young age. This conclusion is justified from two points of view.

In the first place, when the case studies were analyzed it was found that, of the 43 children who received preschool education, 30 children, or 70 per cent, showed an acceleration in rates of growth during the preschool and retained that level during the follow-up period. These 30 children raised their classification from one to three levels. If, on the other hand, rates of growth were irrevocably fixed by inheritance or by the condition of the organism, we would expect that, of the 43 children in the two experimental groups, all would remain in their original level of rate of growth. Instead, 30 of the 43 increased their level.

In the second place, when objective tests were evaluated, the over-all IQ and SQ [Social Quotient on the Vineland Scale] increases of the experimental groups beyond those of the contrast groups on the Binet, Kuhlmann, and Vineland scales were all significant at less than the 5 per cent level.

These results, though affirmative, do not tell the whole story. They do not tell us what kind of children, and under what circumstances these children, made the most progress. They do not tell us why some children did not make progress.

Organic Versus Non Organic Etiologies

In dealing with problems of human welfare, it is important to discover in what children, and under what circumstances, changes in rate of growth can occur. It is also of importance to study the children who did not change in rate of growth. One of the findings that appeared significant was the difference between the group of children whose mental retardation seemed to be associated with a definitive diagnosis of organic defect and those whose retardation appeared to be associated

with a non-organic condition or an environmental one. . . .
[The data] indicate that it is much more difficult to displace
the rate of growth of children with biological defects by the
educational procedures used in this experiment, than it is to
displace the rate of growth of children not so diagnosed.

Various pieces of evidence point to this conclusion:

1. Of the 14 organic cases in the study, 7 in the community
and 7 in the institution, only 7, or 50 per cent, accelerated
their rate of growth. Of the 29 children with no definitive
diagnoses of organic etiology, 23, or 79 per cent, made progress of one or more levels in growth.

2. In addition, the magnitude of change for the non-
organic group was significantly greater than for the organic
group.

3. A third piece of evidence is related to the incidence of
parole from the institution group. Five of the 8 children
diagnosed as non-organic made sufficient change in rate of
growth to be paroled from the institution to the community.
Only 1 of the 7 organic cases was paroled.

These results should not lead to the conclusion that the
rate of growth of mentally retarded children whose mental
retardation is attributable to organic etiology will not be
accelerated by additional stimulation through education at
the preschool level. One-half of the organic cases did show
such acceleration. There are probably other factors which
account for progress or lack of progress in addition to the
organic pathology. Individual case studies point to such possibilities.

In the first place, there was definite evidence that the
illness of a child during infancy, together with the organic
disabilities, tended to produce environmental deprivations,
even though the parents were adequate and accepting of the
child. The retardation in these cases could be ascribed to the
organic etiology as well as to the somatopsychological effects
of the disability. In these cases of organic etiology, where the
depressing effects could be counteracted or compensated

for, acceleration of rate of growth was possible. In other cases labelled as organic, the home factors also were depressing. In the latter cases, the children were both organically impaired and culturally deprived.

Although the evidence is not conclusive, it would appear that we have three, rather than two, categories: children who are organically impaired, children who are culturally deprived, and children who are both culturally deprived and organically impaired. Change of rate of growth under optimum educational and home conditions would appear to be most effective with the culturally deprived and with the organically impaired and culturally deprived, and least effective with those with organic pathologies uncomplicated by somatopsychological or environmental factors.

Another consideration to be given to the development of organically impaired children is the type of education offered. The present experiment provided the children with educational opportunities in a group setting. A few of the children received individual tutoring for specific psychological defects, and showed improvement and acceleration in rate of growth. It is possible that another type of educational program, especially of a tutorial nature on specific psychological disabilities, would net more positive results for some of the brain-damaged children. . . .

The Influence of Home Environment

A portion of the data within the total experiment throws some light on the role of the home in the development of the children. [One part of the study] describes children who were placed in foster homes and attended the preschool, while [another part] describes a group of children who attended the preschool and compares their subsequent development with that of their siblings who did not attend the preschool. Two conclusions were suggested by these results:

Within limits, the greater the changes that are made in the environment, the greater are the changes in the rate of growth. All four of the children who were removed from inadequate homes and placed in foster homes while attending the community preschool increased their rate of development. One changed from the high educable classification, 3, to the average level, 6. Another child gained two levels and each of the other two changed one level. Although only four foster home cases are included in the study, the consistency and degree of progress suggests the above conclusion.

Children living in psycho-socially deprived homes who do not attend preschool tend either to remain at the same rate of development or to drop to a lower level. On the other hand, a majority of the children from the same homes who attended preschool received compensation for their inadequate home environment sufficient to accelerate the rate of development. There were 12 children who were studied during and after preschool experience whose progress was compared to 14 siblings who did not attend preschool. Thus it was possible to hold the home factor constant and to compare the 12 children who attended preschool with the 14 siblings and twins who did not attend. The results of this comparison show statistically significant differences in rate of growth in favor of the children who attended preschool.

A study of these families and their influence on the development of children should be of some concern to those interested in cultural etiologies of mental retardation. It should make us reconsider the belief that "a poor home or a poor mother is better than no home or no mother." Social agencies and courts request removal of children from their own homes only when physical neglect or moral abuse can be proved, or when the parents voluntarily give up the children. Mental abuse is not easy to identify, and such evidence is difficult to prove in court. The case study data suggest that if children in homes such as those [under consideration] are not assisted, either by special preschool education or by removal from the homes, there is a chance of their becoming mentally retarded.

The studies of sibling and twin controls living in the same homes and the case study results on foster home children have major implications for child welfare agencies. Prevention of some cases of mental retardation may result from early detection of neglected children and a "total push" program for their development. The two procedures available are foster home placement and/or an intensive preschool program for these children. Attempts to change the attitudes of parents, their child-rearing practices, and other factors in the home through sporadic interviews will not be sufficient to change the course of development of the children. It is necessary for society to consider more intensive changes of environment for children in psycho-socially deprived homes.

The term "psycho-social" has been used here to emphasize the psychological climate of the home as well as the socioeconomic level. [Our] family case studies . . . present some evidence that there are differences in families of the same socioeconomic level. In some families, where the training was consistent and the parents cooperative and interested in the children, the preschool children accelerated their rate of growth. Although the siblings who did not attend the preschool did not, generally, change their rate of growth, they at least retained their original rate of development and did not drop in rate of growth as they grew older. Where the home environment was restrictive and the families uncooperative, it was more difficult to change the rate of growth of the children who attended the preschool, and those siblings who were not enrolled tended to drop in rate of growth as they grew older. These case studies indicate that opportunity for preschool education was not the only factor operating in changing the growth rate of the children, but that the home environment was also a major consideration. Although an attempt was made to point out the specific parental attitudes and behavior which appeared to account for growth or lack of growth in children of specific families, no clear-cut generalizations were possible. Answers to questions about the specific factors operating in a family, or the constellations of such factors, besides the current theoretical speculations must await more intensive empirical research.

10

Nature of Genius:
Early Exploration

Like research on individual differences as a whole, the investigation of the intellectually gifted first focused on their identification and hereditary antecedents. Only recently has interest in the fostering and development of talent come to the fore, as the role of experiential factors in all intellectual development came to be recognized.

Research on giftedness and genius is widely diversified with regard to conceptual definition, methodology, and nature of the population studied.[1] Some investigators have identified their population in terms of eminence, others in terms of IQ on a traditional intelligence test, and still others in terms of creativity. Some have studied children, others living adults who have made highly creative contributions to their respective fields, and still others eminent men long dead whose achievements could be evaluated by the judgment of posterity. Methodology has included statistical surveys of published data, detailed analyses of individual biographies, intensive clinical case studies, lifetime longitudinal investigations, and the administration of standardized psychological tests of many kinds. Experimentation with training procedures and working conditions that stimulate creativity,

[1] For surveys of different approaches to research on genius and creativity, see Anne Anastasi. *Differential psychology.* (3rd ed.) New York: Macmillan, 1958 (Ch. 13); S. E. Golann, Psychological study of creativity. *Psychol. Bull.,* 1963, **60,** 548–565; C. W. Taylor and F. Barron (Eds.). *Scientific creativity: Its recognition and development.* New York: John Wiley, 1963.

although of recent origin, has been undertaken with subjects ranging from preschool children to research scientists. Theoretical orientation of the investigators has ranged from pathological theories that link genius with insanity, through psychoanalytic viewpoints with their emphasis on unconscious processes, to psychometric and factor-analytic approaches.

The publication of Galton's "Hereditary Genius" in 1869 initiated a series of statistical surveys of the families of eminent men. All these studies agree in showing that eminence tends to "run in families." Eminent persons have far more relatives who have themselves achieved eminence (often in the same or closely related fields) than would be expected by chance. To conclude from such findings that genius is hereditary is, of course, an unwarranted leap beyond the established facts. The same interpretive cautions are applicable to these data as to all data on family resemblances. These cautions were discussed in Chapter 5.

In the following excerpts, Galton clearly establishes his strongly hereditarian orientation, as well as his thorough-going statistical approach to the identification of genius. He defines degrees of eminence in terms of their frequency of occurrence in the general population, using normal curve frequencies for this purpose. The "equal grades" of ability that he describes correspond essentially to what are now known as normalized standard scores. A picturesque note is introduced by Galton's belief that such numbers as 4,000 and a million are too large for his readers to grasp and hence require special aids —which he provides with characteristic charm. To modern readers accustomed to speaking glibly of billion-dollar budgets, Galton's "visual aids" should prove enlightening!

To test his hypothesis regarding hereditary genius, Galton analyzed the pedigrees of 977 eminent men, distributed through 300 families. In order to facilitate the tracing of family histories and the location of descendants and other relatives, he limited his study to eminent men who were either English or well known in England. Data on eminence as well as on family relationships were obtained from biographical directories and were supplemented by direct inquiry among relatives and acquaintances of the men themselves. Within each family, the most eminent man was taken as a point of reference, or index case, and all kinships were expressed in relation to him. Following the name of each index case, Galton listed all eminent relatives, together with the nature of their kinship to the index case. From these data, he computed the number of eminent relatives per 100 families, as explained and tabulated in the next selection.

Although only tangential to the study proper, Galton's observations about the superior health and physique of eminent men are of considerable interest. His comments represent one of the earliest attempts to dispel the popular compensatory notion that eminent men as well as gifted children are weak, puny, and sickly. Galton's views on this matter have been amply corroborated by later research, particularly that on gifted children.

Francis Galton

Hereditary Genius: An Inquiry into Its Laws and Consequences*

The idea of investigating the subject of hereditary genius occurred to me during the course of a purely ethnological inquiry, into the mental peculiarities of different races; when the fact, that characteristics cling to families, was so frequently forced on my notice as to induce me to pay especial attention to that branch of the subject. I began by thinking over the dispositions and achievements of my contemporaries at school, at college, and in after life, and was surprised to find how frequently ability seemed to go by descent. Then I made a cursory examination into the kindred of about four hundred illustrious men of all periods of history, and the results were such, in my own opinion, as completely to establish the theory that genius was hereditary, under limitations that required to be investigated. . . .

* F. Galton. *Hereditary genius: An inquiry into its laws and consequences.* London: Macmillan, 1869. (Pp. v–vi, 1, 6, 10–12, 26, 34–35, 37–38, 316–321, 331–332.)

The theory of hereditary genius, though usually scouted, has been advocated by a few writers in past as well as in modern times. But I may claim to be the first to treat the subject in a statistical manner, to arrive at numerical results, and to introduce the "law of deviation from an average" into discussions on heredity. . . . I propose to show in this book that a man's natural abilities are derived by inheritance, under exactly the same limitations as are the form and physical features of the whole organic world. . . . The arguments by which I endeavour to prove that genius is hereditary, consist in showing how large is the number of instances in which men who are more or less illustrious have eminent kinsfolk. . . .

When I speak of an eminent man, I mean one who has achieved a position that is attained by only 250 persons in each million of men, or by one person in each 4,000. 4,000 is a very large number—difficult for persons to realize who are not accustomed to deal with great assemblages. On the most brilliant of starlight nights there are never so many as 4,000 stars visible to the naked eye at the same time; yet we feel it to be an extraordinary distinction to a star to be accounted as the brightest in the sky. This, be it remembered, is my narrowest area of selection. I propose to introduce no name whatever into my lists of kinsmen (unless it be marked off from the rest by brackets) that is less distinguished.

The mass of those with whom I deal are far more rigidly selected—many are as one in a million, and not a few as one of many millions. I use the term "illustrious" when speaking of these. They are men whom the whole intelligent part of the nation mourns when they die; who have, or deserve to have, a public funeral; and who rank in future ages as historical characters.

Permit me to add a word upon the meaning of a million, being a number so enormous as to be difficult to conceive. It is well to have a standard by which to realize it. Mine will be understood by many Londoners; it is as follows: One summer day I passed the afternoon in Bushey Park to see the magnificent spectacle of its avenue of horse-chestnut trees, a mile long, in full flower. As the hours passed by, it occurred to me to try to count the number of spikes of flowers facing the drive on one side of the long avenue—I mean all the spikes that were visible in full sunshine on one side of the road. Accordingly, I fixed upon a tree of average bulk and flower, and drew imaginary lines—first halving the tree, then quartering, and so on, until I arrived at a subdivision that was not too large to allow of my counting the spikes of flowers it included. I did this with three different trees, and arrived at pretty much the same result: as well as I recollect, the three estimates were as nine, ten, and eleven. Then I counted the trees in the avenue, and, multiplying all together, I found the spikes to be just about 100,000 in number. Ever since then, whenever a million is mentioned, I recall the long perspective of the avenue of Bushey Park, with its stately chestnuts clothed from top to bottom with spikes of flowers, bright in the sunshine, and I imagine a similarly continuous floral band, of ten miles in length. . . .

The method I shall employ . . . is an application of the very curious theoretical law of "deviation from an average." First, I will explain the law, and then I will show that the production of natural intellectual gifts comes justly within its scope. The law is an exceedingly general one. M. Quetelet, the Astronomer-Royal of Belgium, and the greatest authority on vital and social statistics, has largely used it in his inquiries. He has also constructed numerical tables, by which the necessary calculations can be easily made, whenever it is desired to have recourse to the law. . . .

It will, I trust, be clearly understood that the numbers of men in the several classes in my table depend on no uncertain hypothesis. They are determined by the assured law of deviations from an average. It is an absolute fact that if we pick out of each million the one man who is naturally the ablest, and also the one man who is the most stupid, and divide the

TABLE 1. Classification of Men According to Their Natural Gifts

Grades of natural ability, separated by equal intervals		Number of men comprised in the several grades of natural ability, whether in respect to their general powers, or to special aptitudes	
Below average	Above average	Proportionate, viz., one in	In each million of the same age
a	A	4	256,791
b	B	6	161,279
c	C	16	63,563
d	D	64	15,696
e	E	413	2,423
f	F	4,300	233
g	G	79,000	14
x (all grades below g)	X (all grades above G)	1,000,000	1

remaining 999,998 men into fourteen classes, the average ability in each being separated from that of his neighbours by *equal grades,* then the numbers in each of those classes will, on the average of many millions, be as is stated in the table. The table may be applied to special, just as truly as to general ability. It would be true for every examination that brought out natural gifts, whether held in painting, in music, or in statesmanship. The proportions between the different classes would be identical in all these cases, although the classes would be made up of different individuals, according as the examination differed in its purport. . . .

Is reputation a fair test of natural ability? It is the only one I can employ—am I justified in using it? How much of a man's success is due to his opportunities, how much to his natural power of intellect? . . . By reputation, I mean the opinion of contemporaries, revised by posterity—the favourable result of a critical analysis of each man's character, by many biographers. . . .

By natural ability, I mean those qualities of intellect and

disposition, which urge and qualify a man to perform acts that lead to reputation. I do not mean capacity without zeal, nor zeal without capacity, nor even a combination of both of them, without an adequate power of doing a great deal of very laborious work. But I mean a nature which, when left to itself, will, urged by an inherent stimulus, climb the path that leads to eminence, and has strength to reach the summit— one which, if hindered or thwarted, will fret and strive until the hindrance is overcome, and it is again free to follow its labour-loving instinct. It is almost a contradiction in terms, to doubt that such men will generally become eminent. On the other hand, there is plenty of evidence in this volume to show that few have won high reputations without possessing these peculiar gifts. It follows that the men who achieve eminence, and those who are naturally capable, are, to a large extent, identical. . . .

Let us now bring our scattered results side to side, for the purpose of comparison. . . . In comparing the results obtained from the different groups of eminent men, it will be our most convenient course to compare . . . the number of eminent kinsmen in various degrees on the supposition that the number of families in the group to which it refers is 100. All the entries [in Table 2] have therefore the same common measure, they are all *percentages*, and admit of direct intercomparison. I hope I have made myself quite clear: lest there should remain any misapprehension, it is better to give an example. Thus, the families of Divines are only 25 in number, and in those 25 families there are 7 eminent fathers, 9 brothers, and 10 sons; now in order to raise these numbers to percentages, 7, 9, and 10 must be multiplied by the number of times that 25 goes into 100, namely by 4. They will then become 28, 36, and 40, . . . [as can be seen in Table 2].

The general uniformity in the distribution of ability among the kinsmen in the different groups, is strikingly manifest. The eminent sons are almost invariably more numerous than the eminent brothers, and these are a trifle more numerous

TABLE 2. Number of Eminent Relatives in Each Degree of Kinship to the Most Eminent Man of the Family (per 100 Families)

Occupational Group	Judges	Statesmen	Commanders	Literary	Scientific	Poets	Artists	Divines	All Groups Combined
Number of families, each containing more than one eminent man	85	39	27	33	43	20	28	25	300
Total number of eminent men in all families	262	130	89	119	148	57	97	75	977
Father	26	33	47	48	26	20	32	28	31
Brother	35	39	50	42	47	40	50	36	41
Son	36	49	31	51	60	45	89	40	48
Grandfather	15	28	16	24	14	5	7	20	17
Uncle	18	18	8	24	16	5	14	40	18
Nephew	19	18	35	24	23	50	18	4	22
Grandson	19	10	12	9	14	5	18	16	14
Great-grandfather	2	8	8	3	0	0	0	4	3
Great-uncle	4	5	8	6	5	5	7	4	5
First-cousin	11	21	20	18	16	0	1	8	13
Great-nephew	17	5	8	6	16	10	0	0	10
Great-grandson	6	0	0	3	7	0	0	0	3
All more remote	14	37	44	15	23	5	18	16	31

than the eminent fathers. On proceeding further down the table, we come to a sudden dropping off of the numbers at the second grade of kinship, namely, at the grandfathers, uncles, nephews, and grandsons. . . . On reaching the third grade of kinship, another abrupt dropping off in numbers is again met with, but the first cousins are found to occupy a decidedly better position than other relations within the third grade. . . .

In contrasting the . . . different groups, the first notable peculiarity that catches the eye is the small number of the sons of Commanders; they being 31, while the average of all the groups is 48. There is nothing anomalous in this irregularity. I have already shown, when speaking of the commanders, that they usually begin their active careers in youth, and therefore, if married at all, they are mostly away from their wives on military service. It is also worth while to point out a few particular cases where exceptional circumstances stood in the way of the Commanders leaving male issue, because the total number of those included in my lists is so small, being only 32, as to make them of appreciable importance in affecting the results. Thus, Alexander the Great was continually engaged in distant wars, and died in early manhood: he had one posthumous son, but that son was murdered for political reasons when still a boy. Julius Caesar, an exceedingly profligate man, left one illegitimate son, by Cleopatra, but that son was also murdered for political reasons when still a boy. Nelson married a widow who had no children by her former husband, and therefore was probably more or less infertile by nature. Napoleon I was entirely separated from Marie Louise after she had borne him one son.

Though the great Commanders have but few immediate descendants, yet the number of their eminent grandsons is as great as any other group's. I ascribe this to the superiority of their breed, which ensures eminence to an unusually large proportion of their kinsmen.

The next exceptional entry in the table is the number of eminent fathers of the great scientific men as compared with that of their sons, there being only 26 of the former to 60 of the latter, whereas the average of all the groups gives 31 and 48. I have already attempted to account for this by showing, first, that scientific men owe much to the training and to the blood of their mothers; and, secondly, that the first in the family who has scientific gifts is not nearly so likely to achieve eminence, as the descendant who is taught to follow science as a profession, and not to waste his powers on profitless speculations.

The next peculiarity in the table is the small number of eminent fathers in the group of Poets. This group is too small to make me attach much importance to the deviation; it may be mere accident.

The Artists are not a much larger group than the Poets, consisting as they do of only 28 families, but the number of their eminent sons is enormous and quite exceptional. It is 89, whereas the average of all the groups is only 48. The remarks I made about the descendant of a great scientific man prospering in science, more than his ancestor, are eminently true as regards Artists, for the fairly-gifted son of a great painter or musician is far more likely to become a professional celebrity than another man who has equal natural ability, but is not especially educated for professional life. The large number of artists' sons who have become eminent testifies to the strongly hereditary character of their peculiar ability. . . .

I have now done with the exceptional cases; it will be observed that they are mere minor variations in the law expressed by the general average of all the groups, for, if we say that to every 10 illustrious men, *who have any eminent relations at all,* we find 3 or 4 eminent fathers, 4 or 5 eminent brothers, and 5 or 6 eminent sons, we shall be right in 17 instances out of 24; and in the 7 cases we are wrong, the error will consist of less than 1 unit in 2 cases (the fathers of the commanders and men of literature), of 1 unit in 4 cases (the fathers of poets, and the sons of judges, commanders, the divines), and of more than 1 unit in the sole case of the sons of artists.

The deviations from the average are naturally greater in the second and third grades of kinship, because the numbers of instances in the several groups are generally small; but as the proportions in the large subdivision of the 85 Judges correspond with extreme closeness to those of the general average, we are perfectly justified in accepting the latter with confidence. . . .

There is a prevalent belief . . . that men of genius are un-healthy, puny beings—all brain and no muscle—weak-sighted, and generally of poor constitutions. I think most of my readers would be surprised at the stature and physical frames of the heroes of history, who fill my pages, if they could be assembled together in a hall. I would undertake to pick out of any group of them even out of that of the Divines . . . an "eleven" who should compete in any physical feats whatever, against similar selections from groups of twice or thrice their numbers, taken at haphazard from equally well-fed classes. In the notes I made, previous to writing this book, I had begun to make memoranda of the physical gifts of my heroes, and regret now that I did not continue the plan, but there is even almost enough printed in the Appendices to warrant my assertion. I do not deny that many men of ex-traordinary mental gifts have had wretched constitutions, but deny them to be an essential or even the usual accom-paniment. University facts are as good as any others to serve as examples, so I will mention that both high wranglers and high classics have been frequently the first oarsmen of their years. The Hon. George Denman, who was senior classic in 1842, was the stroke of the University crew. Sir William Thompson, the second wrangler in 1845, won the sculls. In the very first boat-race between the two Universities, three men who afterwards became bishops rowed in one of the

contending boats, and another rowed in the other. It is
the second and third-rate students who are usually weakly.
A collection of living magnates in various branches of intellectual achievement is always a feast to my eyes; being, as they are, such massive, vigorous, capable-looking
animals. . . .

In 1921, Lewis M. Terman launched a psychometric and longitudinal
study of gifted children that is continuing today, having outlived its
original investigator. In the words of the present project administrator,[2] "We can be grateful for the courage and vision of the man
who finally broke the barrier of the limited lifetime alloted to any one
researcher, and got under way a study of man that will encompass
the span of the subjects' lives, not just those of the researchers. . . .
On actuarial grounds, there is considerable likelihood that the last
of Terman's Gifted Children will not have yielded his last report to
the files before the year 2010!"
    Beginning with a group of about 1500 California school children
with Stanford-Binet IQ's of 140 or higher, Terman and his co-workers
have so far followed the development of their subjects to midlife, including in their study the spouses and children of their original "gifted
children." This project unquestionably provides the largest body of
data on the backgrounds and personal characteristics of children with
high IQ's, as well as on their subsequent accomplishments in school,
on the job, and in society at large.
    While it is undoubtedly true that intellectually gifted children as a
group are also superior in physical and personality development and
that as adults they turn out very well indeed, the findings of Terman's
study may be somewhat overoptimistic because of certain methodological features. One is a matter of sampling. As a first step in the
selection of subjects, teachers were asked to nominate children they
believed to be of superior intelligence. These nominees were subsequently screened further through group tests and individually ad-

[2] *Foreword* by Robert M. Sears to: L. M. Terman and Melita H. Oden. *The
gifted group at mid-life: Thirty-five years' follow-up of the superior child.*
Stanford, Calif.: Stanford University Press, 1959. (P. ix.)

ministered Stanford-Binet tests. A check conducted in one school suggested that about 10 per cent of the children with IQ's of 140 or higher were lost to the study through this nominating procedure. It is likely that this 10 per cent included a large proportion of children with emotional and educational problems. A second condition making for unduly favorable outcomes is participation in the study itself. Not only the knowledge that one is a "gifted child," but also the continuing and close association with the project staff and the availability of counseling services from this staff, may have contributed to an appreciable degree to the subsequent success of these subjects.

Lewis Madison Terman

The Discovery and Encouragement of Exceptional Talent*

I have often been asked how I happened to become interested in mental tests and gifted children. My first introduction to the scientific problems posed by intellectual differences occurred well over a half-century ago when I was a senior in psychology at Indiana University and was asked to prepare two reports for a seminar, one on mental deficiency and one on genius. Up to that time, despite the fact that I had graduated from a normal college as a Bachelor of Pedagogy and had taught school for five years, I had never so much as heard of a mental test. The reading for those two reports opened up a new world to me, the world of Galton, Binet, and their contemporaries. The following year my MA

* L. M. Terman. The discovery and encouragement of exceptional talent. *Amer. Psychologist,* 1954, 9, 221–230. (Pp. 222–226, 228–230.) Reprinted by permission of the American Psychological Association.

thesis on leadership among children was based in part on tests used by Binet in his studies of suggestibility.[3]

Then I entered Clark University, where I spent considerable time during the first year in reading on mental tests and precocious children. Child prodigies, I soon learned, were at that time in bad repute because of the prevailing belief that they were usually psychotic or otherwise abnormal and almost sure to burn themselves out quickly or to develop postadolescent stupidity. "Early ripe, early rot" was a slogan frequently encountered. By the time I reached my last graduate year, I decided to find out for myself how precocious children differ from the mentally backward, and accordingly chose as my doctoral dissertation an experimental study of the intellectual processes of fourteen boys, seven of them picked as the brightest and seven as the dullest in a large city school.[4] These subjects I put through a great variety of intelligence tests, some of them borrowed from Binet and others, many of them new. The tests were given individually and required a total of 40 or 50 hours for each subject. The experiment contributed little or nothing to science, but it contributed a lot to my future thinking. Besides "selling" me completely on the value of mental tests as a research method, it offered an ideal escape from the kinds of laboratory work which I disliked and in which I was more than ordinarily inept. . . .

However, it was not until I got to Stanford in 1910 that I was able to pick up with mental tests where I had left off at Clark University. By that time Binet's 1905 and 1908 scales had been published, and the first thing I undertook at Stanford was a tentative revision of his 1908 scale. This, after further revisions, was published in 1916. The standardization

[3] L. M. Terman. A preliminary study in the psychology and pedagogy of leadership. *Pedag. Sem.*, 1904, **11**, 413–451.
[4] L. M. Terman. Genius and stupidity: A study of some of the intellectual processes of seven "bright" and seven "dull" boys. *Pedag. Sem.*, 1906, **13**, 307–373.

of the scale was based on tests of a thousand children whose IQ's ranged from 60 to 145. The contrast in intellectual performance between the dullest and the brightest of a given age so intensified my earlier interest in the gifted that I decided to launch an ambitious study of such children at the earliest opportunity.

My dream was realized in the spring of 1921 when I obtained a generous grant from the Commonwealth Fund of New York City for the purpose of locating a thousand subjects of IQ 140 or higher. More than that number were selected by Stanford-Binet tests from the kindergarten through the eighth grade, and a group mental test given in 95 high schools provided nearly 400 additional subjects. The latter, plus those I had located before 1921, brought the number close to 1,500. The average IQ was approximately 150, and 80 were 170 or higher.[5]

The twofold purpose of the project was, first of all, to find what traits characterize children of high IQ, and secondly, to follow them for as many years as possible to see what kind of adults they might become. This meant that it was necessary to select a group representative of high-testing children in general. With the help of four field assistants, we canvassed a school population of nearly a quarter-million in the urban and semi-urban areas of California. Two careful checks on the methods used showed that not more than 10 or 12 per cent of the children who could have qualified for the group in the schools canvassed were missed. A sample of close to 90 per cent insured that whatever traits were typical of these children would be typical of high-testing children in any comparable school population.

Time does not permit me to describe the physical measurements, medical examinations, achievement tests, character and interest tests, or the trait ratings and other supple-

[5] L. M. Terman (Ed.), et al. *Mental and physical traits of a thousand gifted children.* Vol. I. *Genetic studies of genius.* L. M. Terman (Ed.). Stanford, Calif.: Stanford University Press, 1925.

mentary information from parents and teachers. Nor can I here describe the comparative data we obtained for control groups of unselected children. The more important results, however, can be stated briefly: children of IQ 140 or higher are, in general, appreciably superior to unselected children in physique, health, and social adjustment; markedly superior in moral attitudes as measured either by character tests or by trait ratings; and vastly superior in their mastery of school subjects as shown by a three-hour battery of achievement tests. In fact, the typical child of the group had mastered the school subjects to a point about two grades beyond the one in which he was enrolled, some of them three or four grades beyond. Moreover, his ability as evidenced by achievement in the different school subjects is so general as to refute completely the traditional belief that gifted children are usually one-sided. I take some pride in the fact that not one of the major conclusions we drew in the early 1920's regarding traits that are typical of gifted children has been overthrown in the three decades since then.

Results of thirty years' follow-up of these subjects by field studies in 1927–28, 1939–40, and 1951–52, and by mail follow-up at other dates, show that the incidence of mortality, ill health, insanity, and alcoholism is in each case below that for the generality of corresponding age, that the great majority are still well adjusted socially, and that the delinquency rate is but a fraction of what it is in the general population. Two forms of our difficult Concept Mastery Test, devised especially to reach into the stratosphere of adult intelligence, have been administered to all members of the group who could be visited by the field assistants, including some 950 tested in 1939–40 and more than 1,000 in 1951–52. On both tests they scored on the average about as far above the generality of adults as they had scored above the generality of children when we selected them. Moreover, as Dr. Bayley and Mrs. Oden have shown, in the twelve-year interval between the two tests, 90 per cent increased their intellectual stature as measured by this test. "Early ripe, early rot" simply does not hold for these subjects. So far, no one has developed postadolescent stupidity!

As for schooling, close to 90 per cent entered college and 70 per cent graduated. Of those graduating, 30 per cent were awarded honors and about two-thirds remained for graduate work. The educational record would have been still better but for the fact that a majority reached college age during the great depression. In their undergraduate years 40 per cent of the men and 20 per cent of the women earned half or more of their college expenses, and the total of undergraduate and graduate expenses earned amounted to $670,000, not counting stipends from scholarships and fellowships, which amounted to $350,000.

The cooperation of the subjects is indicated by the fact that we have been able to keep track of more than 98 per cent of the original group, thanks to the rapport fostered by the incomparable field and office assistants I have had from the beginning of the study to the present. I dislike to think how differently things could have gone with helpers even a little less competent.

The achievement of the group to midlife is best illustrated by the case histories of the 800 men, since only a minority of the women have gone out for professional careers.[6] By 1950, when the men had an average age of 40 years, they had published 67 books (including 46 in the fields of science, arts, and the humanities, and 21 books of fiction). They had published more than 1,400 scientific, technical, and professional articles; over 200 short stories, novelettes, and plays; and 236 miscellaneous articles on a great variety of subjects. They had also authored more than 150 patents. The figures on publications do not include the hundreds of publications by journalists that classify as news stories, edi-

[6] L. M. Terman. Scientists and nonscientists in a group of 800 gifted men. Psychol. Monogr., 1954, 68, No. 378.

torials, or newspaper columns; nor do they include the hundreds if not thousands of radio and TV scripts.

The 800 men include 78 who have taken a PhD degree or its equivalent, 48 with a medical degree, 85 with a law degree, 74 who are teaching or have taught in a four-year college or university, 51 who have done basic research in the physical sciences or engineering, and 104 who are engineers but have done only applied research or none. Of the scientists, 47 are listed in the 1949 edition of *American Men of Science*. Nearly all of these numbers are from 10 to 20 or 30 times as large as would be found for 800 men of corresponding age picked at random in the general population, and are sufficient answer to those who belittle the significance of IQ differences.

The follow-up of these gifted subjects has proved beyond question that tests of "general intelligence," given as early as six, eight, or ten years, tell a great deal about the ability to achieve either presently or 30 years hence. Such tests do not, however, enable us to predict what direction the achievement will take, and least of all do they tell us what personality factors or ·what accidents of fortune will affect the fruition of exceptional ability. Granting that both interest patterns and special aptitudes play important roles in the making of a gifted scientist, mathematician, mechanic, artist, poet, or musical composer, I am convinced that to achieve greatly in almost any field, the special talents have to be backed up by a lot of Spearman's g, by which is meant the kind of general intelligence that requires ability to form many sharply defined concepts, to manipulate them, and to perceive subtle relationships between them; in other words, the ability to engage in abstract thinking.

The study by Catharine Cox of the childhood traits of historical geniuses gives additional evidence regarding the role of general intelligence in exceptional achievement. That study was part of our original plan to investigate superior ability by two methods of approach: (*a*) by identifying and following living gifted subjects from childhood onward; and (*b*) by proceeding in the opposite direction and tracing the mature genius back to his childhood promise. With a second grant from the Commonwealth Fund, the latter approach got under way only a year later than the former and resulted in the magnum opus by Cox entitled *The Early Mental Traits of Three Hundred Geniuses.*[7] Her subjects represented an unbiased selection from the top 510 in Cattell's objectively compiled list of the 1,000 most eminent men of history. Cox and two able assistants then scanned some 3,000 biographies in search of information that would throw light on the early mental development of these subjects. The information thus obtained filled more than 6,000 typed pages. Next, three psychologists familiar with mental age norms read the documentary evidence on all the subjects and estimated for each the IQ that presumably would be necessary to account for the intellectual behavior recorded for given chronological ages. Average of the three IQ estimates was used as the index of intelligence. In fact two IQ's were estimated for each subject, one based on the evidence to age 17, and the other on evidence to the mid-twenties. The recorded evidence on development to age 17 varied from very little to an amount that yielded about as valid an IQ as a good intelligence test would give. Examples of the latter are Goethe, John Stuart Mill, and Francis Galton. It was the documentary information on Galton, which I summarized and published in 1917,[8] that decided me to prepare plans for the kind of study that was carried out by Cox. The average of estimated IQ's for her 300 geniuses was 155, with many

[7] Catharine C. Cox. *The early mental traits of three hundred geniuses.* Vol. II. *Genetic studies of genius.* L. M. Terman (Ed.). Stanford, Calif.: Stanford University Press, 1926.

[8] L. M. Terman. The intelligence quotient of Francis Galton in childhood. *Amer. J. Psychol.,* 1917, **28**, 209–215.

going as high as 175 and several as high as 200. Estimates below 120 occurred only when there was little biographical evidence about the early years.

It is easy to scoff at these post-mortem IQ's, but as one of the three psychologists who examined the evidence and made the IQ ratings, I think the author's main conclusion is fully warranted; namely, that "the genius who achieves highest eminence is one whom intelligence tests would have identified as gifted in childhood."

Special attention was given the geniuses who had sometime or other been labeled as backward in childhood, and in every one of these cases the facts clearly contradicted the legend. One of them was Oliver Goldsmith, of whom his childhood teacher is said to have said "Never was so dull a boy." The fact is that little Oliver was writing clever verse at 7 years and at 8 was reading Ovid and Horace. Another was Sir Walter Scott, who at 7 not only read widely in poetry but was using correctly in his written prose such words as "melancholy" and "exotic." Other alleged childhood dullards included a number who disliked the usual diet of Latin and Greek but had a natural talent for science. Among these were the celebrated German chemist Justus von Liebig, the great English anatomist John Hunter, and the naturalist Alexander von Humboldt, whose name is scattered so widely over the maps of the world.

In the cases just cited one notes a tendency for the direction of later achievements to be foreshadowed by the interests and preoccupations of childhood. I have tried to determine how frequently this was true of the 100 subjects in Cox's group whose childhood was best documented. Very marked foreshadowing was noted in the case of more than half of the group, none at all in less than a fourth. Macaulay, for example, began his career as historian at the age of 6 with what he called a "Compendium of Universal History," filling a quire of paper before he lost interest in the project. Ben Franklin before the age of 17 had displayed nearly all the

traits that characterized him in middle life: scientific curiosity, religious heterodoxy, wit and buffoonery, political and
business shrewdness, and ability to write. At 11 Pascal was
so interested in mathematics that his father thought it best to
deprive him of books on this subject until he had first mastered Latin and Greek. Pascal secretly proceeded to construct
a geometry of his own and covered the ground as far as the
32nd proposition of Euclid. His father then relented. At 14
Leibnitz was writing on logic and philosophy and com-
posing what he called "An Alphabet of Human Thought."
He relates that at this age he took a walk one afternoon to
consider whether he should accept the "doctrine of substantial forms."

Similar foreshadowing is disclosed by the case histories of
my gifted subjects. A recent study of the scientists and nonscientists among our 800 gifted men[9] showed many highly
significant differences between the early interests and social
attitudes of those who became physical scientists and those
who majored in the social sciences, law, or the humanities.
Those in medical or biological sciences usually rated on such
variables somewhere between the physical scientists and the
nonscientists.

What I especially want to emphasize, however, is that both
the evidence on early mental development of historical
geniuses and that obtained by follow-up of gifted subjects
selected in childhood by mental tests point to the conclusion
that capacity to achieve far beyond the average can be detected early in life by a well-constructed ability test that is
heavily weighted with the g factor. It remains to be seen
how much the prediction of future achievement can be made
more specific as to field by getting, in addition, measures of
ability factors that are largely independent of g. It would
seem that a 20-year follow-up of the thousands of school chil-

[9] L. M. Terman. Scientists and nonscientists in a group of 800 gifted men.
Psychol. Monogr., 1954, **68**, No. 378.

dren who have been given Thurstone's test of seven "primary mental abilities" would help to provide the answer. At present the factor analysts don't agree on how many "primary" mental abilities there are, nor exactly on what they are. The experts in this field are divided into two schools. The British school, represented by Thomson, Vernon, and Burt, usually stop with the identification of at most three or four group factors in addition to *g*, while some representing the American school feed the scores of 40 or 50 kinds of tests into a hopper and manage to extract from them what they believe to be a dozen or fifteen separate factors. Members of the British school are as a rule very skeptical about the realities underlying the minor group factors. There are also American psychologists, highly skilled in psychometrics, who share this skepticism. It is to be hoped that further research will give us more information than we now have about the predictive value of the group factors. Until such information is available, the scores on group factors can contribute little to vocational guidance beyond what a good test of general intelligence will provide.

I have always stressed the importance of *early* discovery of exceptional abilities. Its importance is now highlighted by the facts Harvey Lehman has disclosed in his monumental studies of the relation between age and creative achievement.[10] The striking thing about his age curves is how early in life the period of maximum creativity is reached. In nearly all fields of science, the best work is done between ages 25 and 35, and rarely later than 40. The peak productivity for works of lesser merit is usually reached 5 to 10 years later; this is true in some twenty fields of science, in philosophy, in most kinds of musical composition, in art, and in literature of many varieties. The lesson for us from Lehman's statistics is that the youth of high achievement potential should be

[10] H. C. Lehman. *Age and achievement.* Princeton, N. J.: Princeton University Press, 1953.

well trained for his life work before too many of his most creative years have been passed.

This raises the issue of educational acceleration for the gifted. It seems that the schools are more opposed to acceleration now than they were thirty years ago. The lockstep seems to have become more and more the fashion, notwithstanding the fact that practically everyone who has investigated the subject is against it. Of my gifted group, 29 per cent managed to graduate from high school before the age of 16½ years (62 of these before 15½), but I doubt if so many would be allowed to do so now. The other 71 per cent graduated between 16½ and 18½. We have compared the accelerated with the nonaccelerated on numerous case-history variables. The two groups differed very little in childhood IQ, their health records are equally good, and as adults they are equally well adjusted socially. More of the accelerates graduated from college, and on the average nearly a year and a half earlier than the nonaccelerates; they averaged higher in college grades and more often remained for graduate work. Moreover, the accelerates on the average married .7 of a year earlier, have a trifle lower divorce rate, and score just a little higher on a test of marital happiness.[11] So far as college records of accelerates and nonaccelerates are concerned, our data closely parallel those obtained by the late Noel Keys at the University of California and those by Pressey and his associates at Ohio State University.

The Ford Fund for the Advancement of Education has awarded annually since 1951 some 400 college scholarships to gifted students who are not over 16½ years old, are a year or even two years short of high school graduation, but show good evidence of ability to do college work. Three quarters of them are between 15½ and 16½ at the time of college entrance. A dozen colleges and universities accept

[11] L. M. Terman and Melita H. Oden. *The gifted child grows up.* Vol. IV. *Genetic studies of genius.* L. M. Terman (Ed.). Stanford, Calif.: Stanford University Press, 1947.

these students and are keeping close track of their success. A summary of their records for the first year shows that they not only get higher grades than their classmates, who average about two years older, but that they are also equally well adjusted socially and participate in as many extracurricular activities.[12] The main problem the boys have is in finding girls to date who are not too old for them! Some of them have started a campaign to remedy the situation by urging that more of these scholarships be awarded to girls.

The facts I have given do not mean that all gifted children should be rushed through school just as rapidly as possible. If that were done, a majority with IQ of 140 could graduate from high school before the age of 15. I do believe, however, that such children should be promoted rapidly enough to permit college entrance by the age of 17 at latest, and that a majority would be better off to enter at 16. The exceptionally bright student who is kept with his age group finds little to challenge his intelligence and all too often develops habits of laziness that later wreck his college career. I could give you some choice examples of this in my gifted group. In the case of a college student who is preparing for a profession in science, medicine, law, or any field of advanced scholarship, graduation at 20 instead of the usual 22 means two years added to his professional career; or the two years saved could be used for additional training beyond the doctorate, if that were deemed preferable. . . .

In this address, I have twice alluded to the fact that achievement in school is influenced by many things other than the sum total of intellectual abilities. The same is true of success in life. In closing I will tell you briefly about an attempt we made a dozen years ago to identify some of the nonintellectual factors that have influenced life success among the men in my gifted group. Three judges, working

[12] *Bridging the gap between school and college.* New York: The Fund for the Advancement of Education, 1953.

independently, examined the records (to 1940) of the 730 men who were then 25 years old or older, and rated each on life success. The criterion of "success" was the extent to which a subject had made use of his superior intellectual ability, little weight being given to earned income. The 150 men rated highest for success and the 150 rated lowest were then compared on some 200 items of information obtained from childhood onward.[13] How did the two groups differ?

During the elementary school years, the A's and C's (as we call them) were almost equally successful. The average grades were about the same, and average scores on achievement tests were only a trifle higher for the A's. Early in high school the groups began to draw apart in scholarship, and by the end of high school the slump of the C's was quite marked. The slump could not be blamed on extracurricular activities, for these were almost twice as common among the A's. Nor was much of it due to difference in intelligence. Although the A's tested on the average a little higher than the C's both in 1922 and 1940, the average score made by the C's in 1940 was high enough to permit brilliant college work, in fact was equaled by only 15 per cent of our highly selected Stanford students. Of the A's, 97 per cent entered college and 90 per cent graduated; of the C's, 68 per cent entered but only 37 per cent graduated. Of those who graduated, 52 per cent of the A's but only 14 per cent of the C's graduated with honors. The A's were also more accelerated in school: on the average they were six months younger on completing the eighth grade, 10 months younger at high school graduation, and 15 months younger at graduation from college.

The difference between the educational histories of the A's and C's reflect to some degree the difference in their family backgrounds. Half of the A fathers but only 15 per cent of the C fathers were college graduates, and twice as

[13] L. M. Terman and Melita H. Oden. *The gifted child grows up*. Vol. IV. *Genetic studies of genius*. L. M. Terman (Ed.). Stanford, Calif.: Stanford University Press, 1947.

many of A siblings as of C siblings graduated. The estimated number of books in the A homes was nearly 50 per
cent greater than in the C homes. As of 1928, when the average age of the subjects was about 16 years, more than twice
as many of the C parents as of A parents had been divorced.

Interesting differences between the groups were found in
the childhood data on emotional stability, social adjustments,
and various traits of personality. Of the 25 traits on which
each child was rated by parent and teacher in 1922 (18 years
before the A and C groups were made up), the only trait on
which the C's averaged as high as the A's was general health.
The superiority of the A's was especially marked in four
volitional traits: prudence, self-confidence, perseverance,
and desire to excel. The A's also rated significantly higher in
1922 on leadership, popularity, and sensitiveness to approval
or disapproval. By 1940 the difference between the groups in
social adjustment and all-round mental stability had greatly
increased and showed itself in many ways. By that time four-
fifths of the A's had married, but only two-thirds of the C's,
and the divorce rate for those who had married was twice
as high for the C's as for the A's. Moreover, the A's made
better marriages; their wives on the average came from
better homes, were better educated, and scored higher on
intelligence tests.

But the most spectacular difference between the two
groups came from three sets of ratings, made in 1940, on a
dozen personality traits. Each man rated himself on all the
traits, was rated on them by his wife if he had a wife, and by
a parent if a parent was still living. Although the three sets
of ratings were made independently, they agreed unani-
mously on the four traits in which the A and C groups differed most widely. These were "persistence in the accom-
plishment of ends," "integration toward goals, as contrasted
with drifting," "self-confidence," and "freedom from inferiority feelings." For each trait three critical ratios were
computed showing, respectively, the reliability of the A–C

differences in average of self-ratings, ratings by wives, and ratings by parents. The average of the three critical ratios was 5.5 for perseverance, 5.6 for integration toward goals, 3.7 for self-confidence, and 3.1 for freedom from inferiority feelings. These closely parallel the traits that Cox found to be especially characteristic of the 100 leading geniuses in her group whom she rated on many aspects of personality; their three outstanding traits she defined as "persistence of motive and effort," "confidence in their abilities," and "strength or force of character."

There was one trait on which only the parents of our A and C men were asked to rate them; that trait was designated "common sense." As judged by parents, the A's are again reliably superior, the A–C difference in average rating having a critical ratio of 3.9. We are still wondering what self-ratings by the subjects and ratings of them by their wives on common sense would have shown if we had been impudent enough to ask for them!

Everything considered, there is nothing in which our A and C groups present a greater contrast than in drive to achieve and in all-round mental and social adjustment. Our data do not support the theory of Lange-Eichbaum[14] that great achievement usually stems from emotional tensions that border on the abnormal. In our gifted group, success is associated with stability rather than instability, with absence rather than with presence of disturbing conflicts—in short with well-balanced temperament and with freedom from excessive frustrations.

[14] W. Lange-Eichbaum. *The problem of genius.* New York: Macmillan, 1932.

11

Nature of Genius:

Focus on Creativity

Since about 1950, there has been a growing awareness that intelligence as measured by traditional intelligence tests is by no means synonymous with creativity. Bolstered by the need for high-level creative talent in science and engineering, research on creativity at all levels has shown a rapid upsurge. The extensive project conducted by Guilford and his associates, cited in Chapter 4, began in 1949 as a study of creativity. Describing the inception of this project, Guilford opened his Presidential address at the 1950 convention of the American Psychological Association by remarking, "I discuss the subject of creativity with considerable hesitation, for it represents an area in which psychologists, whether they be angels or not, have feared to tread."[1] Within a decade, the tread had become almost a stampede!

The principal contributions of Guilford's own research, it will be recalled, were: (1) the development of many new types of tests designed to measure different aspects of creative behavior; and (2) the use of the statistical techniques of factor analysis to identify the separate factors or aptitudes that constitute creativity. Examples of both the factors and the tests were given in Chaper 4. Although begun as a study of creativity, during the next ten years Guilford's project developed into a comprehensive reformulation of the nature

[1] J. P. Guilford. Creativity. *Amer. Psychologist*, 1950, **5**, 444–454. (P. 444.)

of intelligence as a whole. Falling chiefly under the heading of "divergent thinking," creative aptitudes were fitted into the three-dimensional model of intellect described in Guilford's 1959 paper, which was excerpted in Chapter 4. Because of the influence Guilford's project exerted on subsequent creativity research, it belongs in this chapter as much as it does in the chapter on the nature of intelligence.

Although Guilford's tests were designed for adults, other investigators modified and adapted some of his divergent thinking tests for use at younger ages. A study that has attracted wide notice, especially among educators, is that conducted by Getzels and Jackson[2] with high school students. Their procedure consisted essentially in selecting two contrasting groups of students for intensive study: one group comprised 26 students who fell in the top 20 per cent on a battery of five creativity tests but below the top 20 per cent in IQ on standard intelligence tests; the other group comprised 28 students in the top 20 per cent in IQ but below the top 20 per cent on the creativity battery. By reporting only results obtained with these artificially selected groups and omitting students who excelled in both IQ and creativity, this study tended to create a false impression of independence or even antagonism between IQ and creativity. In their effort to counteract the earlier overemphasis on IQ as measured by traditional intelligence tests, the authors swung too far in the opposite direction. Actually, a reanalysis of their own data reveals that the correlations of creativity tests with intelligence tests in the entire sample were nearly as high as those among different creativity tests.[3]

In an investigation of elementary school children, Torrance followed in part the same approach as Getzels and Jackson. His results, too, tended to exaggerate the contrast between "intelligence" (as defined by traditional intelligence tests) and creativity. Torrance's project was considerably broader in scope, however, extending over several levels, from preschool children to graduate students, and using a variety of procedures. In the next article, Torrance gives a brief overview of the varied approaches to creativity being followed at different research

[2] J. W. Getzels and P. W. Jackson. *Creativity and intelligence: Explorations with gifted students.* New York: John Wiley, 1962.
[3] R. L. Thorndike. Some methodological issues in the study of creativity. *Proc. invit. Conf. Test. Probl., Educ. Test Serv.*, 1963, 40–54.

centers in America. He then introduces his own research in progress at the Bureau of Educational Research, University of Minnesota, and reports some illustrative findings. In contrast to Terman's emphasis on the superior adjustment of gifted children, Torrance gives considerable attention to the personality problems of highly creative children and to their estrangement from peers and teachers. Of particular interest is Torrance's discussion of those educational and child-rearing practices that he regards as blocks to the development of creativity.

Ellis Paul Torrance

Current Research on the Nature of Creative Talent *

Some Major Centers of Creativity Research

Although research in this field generally has not been supported very well financially, so much is happening in the field today that it would be practically impossible to summarize the status of knowledge in the field. Many researchers are so busy conducting research and testing exciting leads that they find it extremely difficult to take the time to report their findings to professional audiences. At the moment most of the results of greatest interest to counselors are coming from seven or eight centers.

One center of this research has been the University of Southern California under the leadership of J. P. Guilford. Perhaps the most useful breakthrough from this center has been the discovery of the nature of some of man's creative thinking abilities and the development of instruments for

* E. P. Torrance. Current research on the nature of creative talent. *J. counsel. Psychol.*, 1959, 6, 309–316. (Pp. 309–316.) Reprinted by permission of the author and the publisher.

measuring them, at least in adults. More recently, Guilford has offered evidence concerning the importance of creative thinking abilities in the engineering and scientific occupations and the relatively lower importance of those thinking abilities involved in traditional measures of intelligence.

A second center is the University of Utah under the leadership of Calvin W. Taylor and Brewster Ghiselin. Much of the research at this center has been concerned with the development of criteria, the effects of organizational factors and, more recently, education. This center has also made a notable contribution through its three national invitational conferences in 1955, 1957, and 1959 and the publication of the proceedings of these conferences.[4]

A third center is the Institute of Personality Assessment and Research at the University of California at Berkeley under the leadership of Donald MacKinnon, Frank Barron, and others. This center has developed a variety of assessment devices, primarily in the area of personality. Scholars in the field are looking forward anxiously to the publication of this group's intensive studies of eminent persons in a number of occupations accepted as requiring a high degree of creativity for success.

A fourth center is The Pennsylvania State University under the leadership of Viktor Lowenfeld, head of the Department of Art Education. Long a leader in research on creativity in art education, Lowenfeld and his colleagues have recently turned their interests to the interdisciplinary aspects of creativity.[5] Through factor-analytic procedures they have discovered in the visual arts essentially the same factors as Guilford and his associates found in the scientific field.

A fifth center of creativity research of interest to counsel-

[4] Although the proceedings of these conferences are out of print, the major reports have been collected in the previously cited book by Taylor and Barron (see p. 237)—Ed.

[5] V. Lowenfeld. Current research on creativity. *Nat. educ. Assoc. J.*, 1958, **47**, 538–540.

ing psychologists is the University of Chicago. J. W. Getzels, Philip Jackson, and Morris I. Stein have provided the leadership here. An important breakthrough is marked by the discovery by Getzels and Jackson of the importance of creative thinking abilities in school achievement at the secondary level and the estrangement of the highly creative adolescent from his peers and teachers. Stein's research[6] has been concerned primarily with research chemists and should be especially useful to counselors in assisting highly creative children to achieve healthy personality development and learn to be less obnoxious without sacrificing their creativity.

A sixth center from which promising research is coming is the University of Buffalo, under the program of the Creative Education Foundation established by Alex F. Osborn. Sidney Parnes[7] is now providing the research leadership in this center and seems to be most concerned about deliberate efforts to improve the quantity and quality of the ideas produced by groups and individuals.

Some other centers from which promising research is emanating include: Ohio State University under the leadership of Ross L. Mooney and of Pepinsky and Pepinsky; Michigan State University under the sponsorship of H. H. Anderson and Elizabeth Drews; University of Illinois under the leadership of R. B. Cattell and others.

[6] M. I. Stein. A transactional approach to creativity. In C. W. Taylor and F. Barron (Eds.), *Scientific creativity: Its recognition and development.* New York: John Wiley, 1963. (Ch. 18.)
[7] S. J. Parnes and A. Meadow. Development of individual creative talent. In C. W. Taylor and F. Barron (Eds.), *Scientific creativity: Its development and recognition.* New York: John Wiley, 1963. (Ch. 25.)

The Minnesota Studies of Creativity

The Minnesota Studies in Creativity,[8] now in their second year of development, are probably unique in four major ways. First, the major study has been concerned with the development of instruments for identifying creative talent from kindergarten through graduate school. Second, there has been emphasis on the genetic development of various creative thinking abilities, peer pressures against the most highly creative members of a group, and other forces which interfere with the development and utilization of creative talent. Third, emphasis is being placed on classroom factors, evaluation procedures, and activities which influence the development of the various creative thinking abilities. Fourth, the Minnesota studies are characterized by their diversity. In addition to the studies of this writer and his colleagues in the Bureau of Educational Research, there are studies concerned with the feelings and emotions of students enrolled in courses in color and design; creativity in mathematics in the preschool and early school years; vocational success in sales work, elementary school teaching, and research work; mental breakdown; college teaching; industrial design; and counselor training.

Measurement and Identification

Thus far, several batteries of tasks for assessing the abilities involved in doing creative work have been devised and even now additional tasks are being invented and tested. Our first effort consisted of trying to adapt some of the Guilford tests so that they could be handled by children in

[8] More detailed discussion of much of this research can be found in: E. P. Torrance. *Guiding creative talent*. Englewood Cliffs, N. J.: Prentice-Hall, 1962.

the early school years. A battery consisting of five subtests (unusual uses, impossibilities, consequences, problems, improvements, and situations) was administered successfully to approximately 250 children in grades four through six and to approximately 600 college students. Measures derived therefrom were found to be related significantly to school learning as measured by the Iowa Tests of Basic Skills and the Gates Reading Tests, both before and after the effects of intelligence were partialled out. Coefficients of correlation between these measures and IQ (WISC and Stanford-Binet) are quite low, especially in the fifth and sixth grades (.12, fifth grade; .01, sixth grade; .01, another sixth grade). These measures also differentiate those highly chosen on a variety of peer and teacher nominations based on criteria of creative thinking. In an hour-long group-task requiring creative thinking, those ranking in the upper 20 per cent in their class on this nomination measure in almost every case initiated a larger number of ideas than the other subjects in the five-member groups to which they were assigned.

In one battery, children are confronted with toys such as a nurse's kit, a fire truck, and a toy dog and are asked to think of all the possible ways they can of improving them so that they would be "more fun to play with." Another task in the battery requires them to think of unusual uses of these toys other than as playthings. Other tasks were based on some of the problem situations in the Mother Goose rhymes. For example, in one task, subjects are asked to think of all the possible things Mother Hubbard could have done when she found her cupboard bare.

In another series which we call the *Ask-and-Guess Test*, subjects are shown a picture such as one of Tom, the Piper's son, stealing a pig and being chased by someone. First, the subject is asked to think of all of the questions he can about what is happening, questions which cannot be answered by looking at the picture. Then he is asked to think of all of the possible things which could have caused the action and finally to list all of the possible consequences, both immediate and long-range. These tasks seem to yield good results both with children and adults.

Efforts are also being made to develop nonverbal tests of creative thinking. One such task confronts the subject with a page of 42 circles or squares and requires him to sketch as many objects as he can which have a circle or square as the main element in the design. The number of extra details in Buck's H-T-P Test and the number of unusual details also give promise of providing useful measures.

Responses obtained from some of these tasks can be scored in a variety of ways to yield measures of various creative thinking abilities. For example, four apparently meaningful indices have been developed from responses to the toy improvement task. An *ideational fluency* score is obtained by counting the number of relevant responses given, regardless of their quality. Second, a *spontaneous flexibility* score is obtained by counting the number of different approaches used in modifying the toy, such as: adding something; combining with something else; giving sensory appeal such as odor, light, sound, motion, etc.; changing color; changing material; making larger or smaller; changing position; etc. Third, an *inventivlevel* score is based on a modification of the criteria used by the U. S. Patent Office in determining whether or not an invention has sufficient inventive level to be patented. Fourth, a *constructiveness* score provides a measure of the extent to which the subject provided a constructive solution rather than just point out defects.

The tasks and concepts just described are only a few of those which we have invented and experimented with. Many new ideas need testing. Most of the tasks for children in the fourth grade and below require individual administration. It is doubtful that satisfactory tests of a multiple-choice type can be developed; thus, detailed scoring manuals must be developed for evaluating each task. Most of the tasks which have been used in batteries of tests have been administered under rather brief time limits. There is need for experimentation with tasks which can be completed over longer periods of time. The abilities involved in doing creative thinking are complex and there are dangers in using any single index to represent an individual's creative potential. Present instruments, however, are satisfactory enough to permit research. Shortly it should be possible also to provide for use by school psychologists and counselors standardized batteries of tests of creative thinking which should be as useful and as easy to administer and evaluate as such individually administered intelligence tests as the Wechsler Intelligence Scale for Children and the Stanford-Binet.

Creative Thinking and School Learning

Thus far, the clearest picture of the school learning of the highly creative child has been obtained by attempting to differentiate the highly creative as identified by our tests from the highly intelligent as identified by traditional tests of IQ. Members of the highly creative group ranked in the upper 20 per cent in their classes on the creativity measure but not in the upper 20 per cent on traditional measures of IQ. Members of the highly intelligent group ranked in the upper 20 per cent on measures of IQ but not on creativity. Those in a third group ranked in the upper 20 per cent on both measures. Regardless of the measure of IQ used (Stanford-Binet, Wechsler Intelligence Scale for Children, California Test of Mental Maturity, and Otis Quick-Scoring) about 70 per cent of the top 20 per cent on creativity would have been excluded from gifted groups selected only on the basis of IQ.

Prior to our studies, Getzels and Jackson had conducted a

similar study with high school students at the University of Chicago. They found a mean difference of 23 IQ points between these two groups but no difference in the mean achievement of the two groups as measured by standardized achievement tests. We had adequate achievement data in only one of the schools studied. Subjects in this school had been administered the Wechsler Intelligence Scale for Children, the Gates Reading Tests, and in grades three through six the Iowa general educational development battery consisting of reading skills, study-work skills, English skills, and arithmetic skills. Although there was a mean difference of 25.6 IQ points between the highly intelligent and the highly creative groups, there was no statistically significant difference on any of the achievement measures. In fact, not even the direction is consistent from measure to measure.

When the rankings of teachers on a variety of characteristics were compared, it was found that the highly creative are considered less desirable as pupils, less well known by the teachers, less ambitious, and less studious and hardworking. These findings would seem to make traditional concepts of over- and underachievement questionable, if not meaningless. Traditionally, the highly creative group would be regarded as overachieving or the high IQ group as under achieving. Teachers in this school, however, ranked the highly intelligent pupils as more ambitious and hardworking or studious than the highly creative. In other words, the highly creative pupils achieve as well as do the highly intelligent pupils, without appearing to strive as hard. My guess is that these highly creative children are learning while they appear to be "playing around," possibly through manipulative and/or exploratory activities which the teacher tries to prevent.

Additional evidence concerning the role of creative thinking in school learning is obtained when we partial out the effects of IQ statistically. When this is done, the relationships between the measures of creativity and all of the measures of achievement are statistically significant. Partial correlations run as high as .48 with the Iowa Reading Skills Tests.

It may be that somewhat different results will be obtained in some schools. In fact, we have just obtained achievement data from the fourth and fifth grades of a school in a small town and preliminary results are somewhat at variance with those found in the study above. Our first hypothesis is that in one school children are taught in such a way that creative thinking is rewarded and the creative thinking abilities thus become important means of acquiring basic skills and that this is not done in the other schools. More complete data are now being obtained to try to answer some of the puzzling questions surrounding these phenomena.

Illustrative of the complexity of this problem are the results from an exploratory study of the achievement of the 70 participants in the 1959 Minnesota Summer Guidance Institute. Using the Miller Analogies and the Ohio State Psychological Examination as measures of "intelligence" and a battery of tasks devised by the author as a measure of creativity, highly intelligent and highly creative groups were differentiated as already described. As in the earlier studies, 70 per cent of the most creative (upper 20 per cent) were not included in the upper 20 per cent on the Miller and Ohio State Psychological. Although achievement of the highly "intelligent" group on a comprehensive test on counseling and guidance was higher than that of the highly creative group, the creatives tended to make greater gains than their more "intelligent" colleagues as measured by pre- and post-tests. The achievement tests, however, drew almost entirely upon the memory, cognitive, and convergent thinking abilities of the student, and the Institute sample was in general less talented intellectually than the elementary and secondary samples thus far studied.

Special Blocks to Creativity

Thus far, promising leads have been obtained concerning a number of factors which appear to block the development of creative thinking abilities. Several of these will be discussed briefly.

Premature Attempts to Eliminate Fantasy

Many teachers and parents regard fantasies as something unhealthy and to be eliminated. Fantasies such as imaginative role playing, telling fantastic stories, making unusual drawings, and the like should be considered as normal aspects of a child's thinking. Certainly we want a sound type of creativity, but it is essential that this type of fantasy be kept alive until the child's intellectual development is such that he can engage in sound creative thinking. We have seen many indications in our testing of first and second grade children that many with apparently impoverished imaginations seemed to have been subjected to concerted efforts to eliminate fantasy from their thinking too early.

Restrictions on Manipulativeness and Curiosity

Another impediment to the development of creative thinking is the restriction placed on the child's manipulativeness and curiosity. Apparently the young child has an almost irresistible tendency of manipulation and exploration of objects and this seems to be the basis of curiosity and much inventiveness. Our studies show a significant relationship between degree of manipulation and quality and quantity of inventive responses. Boys are more manipulative than girls and become increasingly more manipulative from first through third grade but girls do not change significantly. To develop creative thinking, even to permit children to learn effectively, it appears important to permit and encourage them to manipulate, to play around with, objects and ideas, to the extent possible within the limits of safety.

Overemphasis on Sex Roles

Cultural emphasis on sex roles is the source of many conflicts for the highly creative individual and interferes with his school learning and with the full development of creative thinking abilities. The high degree of sensitivity involved in creative thinking has a distinctly *feminine* character in our society; the independence and autonomy required has a distinctly *masculine* character. Thus, the highly creative boy is likely to appear more effeminate than his male peers and the highly creative girl is likely to appear more masculine than hers.

Several of these problems of sex-role identification are highlighted in our studies of creativity in the early school years. In the first grade, many of the boys refused to try to think of ways of improving the nurse's kit because it was "something girls played with." Some restructured the situation, changing it to a doctor's kit and then proposing changes. First-grade boys gave more responses than girls for improving the fire truck while girls gave more for improving the nurse's kit. Thereafter, boys became increasingly superior to girls regardless of the sex association of the toy, at least through the fourth grade. This, too, seems to be the function of stronger social sanctions against girls than boys for manipulative and exploratory activities at this stage of development.

In a standardized group situation involving scientific toys such as rockets, magnets, flying saucers, topsy-turvey tops, and the like, the reluctance of girls to play around with the toys and try to explain their operation was clearly apparent

at every grade level from the second through sixth. Many of
the girls stated emphatically that this was "something for
boys" and beyond the comprehension of girls. At almost
every grade-level, the boys demonstrated and explained at
least twice as many ideas and principles as the girls.

Overemphasis on Prevention

Individual administration of problems involving the invention of alternative solutions to frustrating situations has
shown that the imagination of many children is inhibited by
emphasis on prevention. Many third-grade subjects were so
obsessed with the thought that Mother Hubbard should have
prevented her predicament that they were reluctant to consider possible solutions to her problem. This may be related
to the criticism of some observers that American education,
both civilian and military, prepares only for victory or success and not for coping with possible frustration or failure—
we try to prevent everything.

Induction of Fear and Timidity

In testing first-grade children, we have been unable to
evoke maximum performance from some subjects because
of their fear and timidity. This same kind of behavior was
apparent in the administration of a creativity test to schizo-
phrenics approaching their release from the hospital. We
can only speculate that this reluctance to risk a response has
been induced by too severe restrictions on curiosity, manipulativeness, imaginative play, and unusual ideas.

Emphasis on Verbal Skills

The school's overemphasis on verbal skills and insufficient
emphasis on problem-solving also interferes with the highly
creative child's learning and the development of his creative

thinking abilities. Among highly creative individuals, verbal abilities will frequently be below some of their other abilities. Since pupils are usually graded on the basis of what they can put on paper, many highly creative children probably do not receive credit for what they really learn.

Personality Adjustment of the Highly Creative Child

A large share of the highly creative child's adjustment problems appear to be centered in his psychological isolation and estrangement from his peers and teachers. Peer groups exercise rather severe pressures against their most creative members. In no group thus far studied have we failed to find relatively clear evidence of the operation of these pressures, though they are far more severe in some classes than in others.

When we select the most creative members of each sex in each classroom and match them for sex and IQ with other children in the same classroom, three characteristics stand out as differentiating the highly creative children from the less creative ones. First, there is a tendency for them to gain a reputation for having wild or silly ideas. Their teachers and peers agree on this. Second, their work is characterized by ideas "off the beaten track." This comes out as a differentiating characteristic in their drawings both when we use the number of unique details and when we use the number of nonessential details. This helps explain the difficulty teachers and peers have in evaluating their ideas and perhaps why they do not show up better than they do on traditional intelligence tests. Their ideas simply do not conform to the standardized dimensions, the behavioral norms, on which responses are judged. Third, they are characterized by humor and playfulness. All of these characteristics help explain both the estrangement and the creativity.

The results of an experimental study also help us to understand this problem. We formed groups of five children and in each we placed one of the most creative children in the class, as identified by our tests. We then placed each group in a situation requiring creative thinking and involving competition among groups. The focus of observation during this hour-long activity was upon the techniques used by the groups to control the most creative member and the behavior of the most creative member in coping with these pressures. Much of the behavior observed suggests that the highly creative individual is responsible for many of his own woes.

In the second grade, the most highly creative individuals were generally quite unpleasant, showing little consideration for the group, little or no goal orientation, little or no identification with the group, and little or no heed to the leadership attempts of their less creative peers. In the third grade, the most creative subjects tended to work independently and were ignored for the most part. This tendency persisted into the fourth grade where the most creative members assumed little responsibility for leadership and were given little credit in final ratings for the important contributions which they actually made to the group's success. The highly creative in the fifth grade manifested more leadership attempts than in the fourth grade but brought upon themselves open criticism and attack for "being too scientific," "being too greedy," and the like. These tendencies became more pronounced in the sixth-grade groups.

As we have surveyed these and many other similar kinds of evidence, it has seemed to us that the school's job is one of helping the highly creative child to learn to be less obnoxious without sacrificing his creativity. Stein[9] has offered a set of interesting suggestions concerning the social role of the creative industrial researcher. If we translate Stein's principles to apply to the school child, our objective in helping

[9] M. I. Stein. A transactional approach to creativity. In C. W. Taylor and F. Barron (Eds.), Scientific creativity: Its recognition and development. New York: John Wiley, 1963. (Ch. 18.)

the highly creative youngster would run something like the following: Help the highly creative child to maintain his assertiveness without being hostile and aggressive. He must be aware of his superiors, peers, and subordinates as persons. He may work alone but he must not be isolated, withdrawn, or uncommunicative. He must "know his place" without being timid, submissive, or acquiescent and must "speak his mind" without being domineering. As he tries to gain a point, he can be subtle but not cunning or manipulative. In all relationships, he must be sincere, honest, purposeful and diplomatic. In the intellectual area, he must learn to be broad without spreading himself too thin, deep without being "bookish" or "too scientific," and "sharp" without being overcritical.

The above model obviously asks much of the child, but at least it provides a model which the highly creative child apparently needs to achieve and should challenge the teacher, counselor, and administrator.

In another group of creativity studies, subjects were chosen on the basis of outstanding adult achievement. This approach uses essentially a criterion of eminence, as was done by Galton. A major difference, however, is that the present research employs testing and interviewing techniques with living persons, rather than analyzing published records on eminent men of the past. These investigations are also differentiated by a primary focus on the emotional, motivational, and attitudinal traits of their subjects. Some represent an application of clinical procedures to the study of creativity. Others rely chiefly on standardized psychometric instruments. The former is illustrated by Anne Roe's studies of small groups of eminent American scientists, principally biologists and physicists.[10]

A more purely psychometric approach is represented by the re-

[10] Anne Roe. A psychological study of eminent biologists. *Psychol. Monogr.*, 1951, **65**, No. 14; A psychological study of physical scientists. *Genet. Psychol. Monogr.*, 1951, **43**, 121–235.

search of Raymond B. Cattell and his associates,[11] in which highly productive research workers in physics, biology, and psychology were examined with the 16 P. F. Test, a self-report inventory yielding scores in sixteen personality traits identified through factor analysis. Cattell also applied the 16 P. F. Test items to published biographical material in an attempt to quantify the personality descriptions of eminent men of the past. This procedure is similar to that followed by Cox and Terman to estimate the childhood IQ's of past geniuses.

Both clinical and psychometric techniques were utilized in the comprehensive project described by MacKinnon in the following paper. In this research, data were gathered through an intensive study of each individual, extending over several days and employing a wide variety of assessment procedures. In comparison with other similar studies, this project was also characterized by a more thorough-going effort to identify individuals who had made truly creative contributions. The criterion was thus specifically defined in terms of creativity, rather than in terms of the more heterogeneous concept of eminence. Another desirable feature is the use of control groups of less eminent persons in the same fields. On the other hand, a limitation of the experimental design stems from the lack of cross-validation. When two groups (such as a highly creative and a less creative group) are compared in a very large number of items, a few significant differences will emerge by chance alone. Insofar as some characteristics consistently differentiated creative persons studied in different fields, however, this finding would constitute independent verification of genuine differences not attributable to chance.

[11] R. B. Cattell. The personality and motivation of the researcher from measurements of contemporaries and from biography. In C. W. Taylor and F. Barron (Eds.), *Scientific creativity: Its recognition and development.* New York: John Wiley, 1963. (Ch. 9.)

Donald Wallace MacKinnon

The Nature and Nurture of Creative Talent*

Whatever light I shall be able to shed on the nature and nurture of creative talent comes in the main from findings of researches carried on during the last six years in the Institute of Personality Assessment and Research on the Berkeley campus of the University of California, and supported in large part by the Carnegie Corporation of New York.

In undertaking such a study one of our first tasks was to decide what we would consider creativity to be. This was necessary, first, because creativity has been so variously described and defined, and second, because only when we had come to agreement as to how we would conceive creativity would we be in a position to know what kinds of persons we would want to study.

We came easily to agreement that true creativeness fulfills at least three conditions. It involves a response or an idea that is novel or at the very least statistically infrequent. But novelty or originality of thought or action, while a necessary aspect of creativity, is not sufficient. If a response is to lay claim to being a part of the creative process, it must to some extent be adaptive to, or of, reality. It must serve to solve a problem, fit a situation, or accomplish some recognizable goal. And, thirdly, true creativeness involves a sustaining of

* D. W. MacKinnon. The nature and nurture of creative talent. *Amer. Psychologist*, 1962, **17**, 484–495. (Pp. 484–493.) Reprinted by permission of the author and the American Psychological Association.

the original insight, an evaluation and elaboration of it, a developing of it to the full.

Creativity, from this point of view, is a process extended in time and characterized by originality, adaptiveness, and realization. It may be brief, as in a musical improvisation, or it may involve a considerable span of years as was required for Darwin's creation of the theory of evolution.

The acceptance of such a conception of creativity had two important consequences for our researches. It meant that we would not seek to study creativity while it was still potential but only after it had been realized and had found expression in clearly identifiable creative products—buildings designed by architects, mathematical proofs developed by mathematicians, and the published writings of poets and novelists. Our conception of creativity forced us further to reject as indicators or criteria of creativeness the performance of individuals on so-called tests of creativity. While tests of this sort, that require that the subject think, for example, of unusual uses for common objects and the consequences of unusual events, may indeed measure the infrequency or originality of a subject's ideas in response to specific test items, they fail to reveal the extent to which the subject faced with real life problems is likely to come up with solutions that are novel and adaptive and which he will be motivated to apply in all of their ramifications. . . .

The fields which we finally sampled were those of creative writing, architecture, mathematics, industrial research, physical science, and engineering. . . .

In reporting the findings of our researches, I draw most heavily upon data obtained from our study of architects. . . . It is in architects, of all our samples, that we can expect to find what is most generally characteristic of creative persons. Architecture, as a field of creative endeavor, requires that the successful practitioner be both artist and scientist— artist in that his designs must fulfill the demands of "Delight," and scientist in that they must meet the demands of "Firmnesse" and "Commodity," to use the words of Sir Henry Wotton. But surely, one can hardly think that the requirements of effective architecture are limited to these three demands. The successful and effective architect must, with the skill of a juggler, combine, reconcile, and exercise the diverse skills of businessman, lawyer, artist, engineer, and advertising man, as well as those of author and journalist, psychiatrist, educator, and psychologist. In what other profession can one expect better to observe the multifarious expressions of creativity? . . .

In our study of architects we began by asking a panel of experts—five professors of architecture, each working independently—to nominate the 40 most creative architects in the United States. All told they supplied us with 86 names instead of the 40 they would have mentioned had there been perfect agreement among them. While 13 of the 86 architects were nominated by all five panel members, and 9 nominated by four, 11 by three, and 13 by two, 40 were individual nominations each proposed by a single panel member.

The agreement among experts is not perfect, yet far greater than one might have expected. Later we asked 11 editors of the major American architectural journals, *Architectural Forum, Architectural Record,* the *Journal of the American Institute of Architects,* and *Progressive Architecture,* to rate the creativity of the 64 of the nominated architects whom we invited to participate in the study. Still later we asked the 40 nominated creative architects who actually accepted our invitation to be studied to rate the creativity of the invited 64 architects, themselves included. Since the editors' ratings of the creativity of the architects correlated +.88 with the architects' own ratings, it is clear that under certain conditions and for certain groups it is possible to obtain remarkable agreement about the relative creativeness of individual members of a profession and thus meet the first requirement for an effective study of creative persons.

A second requirement for the successful establishment of the traits of creative individuals is their willingness to make themselves available for study. . . .

The invitation to this group, as to all the creative groups which we have studied, was to come to Berkeley for a weekend of intensive study in the Institute of Personality Assessment and Research. There, in groups of ten, they have been studied by the variety of means which constitute the assessment method—by problem-solving experiments; by tests designed to discover what a person does not know or is unable or unwilling to reveal about himself; by tests and questionnaires that permit a person to manifest various aspects of his personality and to express his attitudes, interests, and values; by searching interviews that cover the life history and reveal the present structure of the person; and by specially contrived social situations of a stressful character which call for the subject's best behavior in a socially defined role.

The response of creative persons to the invitation to reveal themselves under such trying circumstances has varied considerably. At the one extreme there have been those who replied in anger at what they perceived to be the audacity of psychologists in presuming to study so ineffable and mysterious a thing as the creative process and so sensitive a being as a creative person. At the other extreme were those who replied courteously and warmheartedly, welcoming the invitation to be studied, and manifesting even an eagerness to contribute to a better understanding of the creative person and the creative process.

Here we were face to face with a problem that plagues us in all our researches: Are those who are willing to be assessed different in important ways from those who refuse? With respect to psychological traits and characteristics we can never know. But with respect to differences in creativeness, if any, between the 40 who accepted and the 24 who declined our invitation, we know that the two groups are indistinguishable. When the nominating panel's ratings of creativity were converted to standard scores and the means for the 24 versus the 40 were compared, they were found to be identical. When the editors' ratings were similarly converted to standard scores, the mean for the nonassessed group was slightly higher (51.9) than for the assessed sample (48.7), but the difference is not statistically significant.

Certainly we cannot claim to have assessed the 40 most creative architects in the country, or the most creative of any of the groups we have studied; but it is clear that we have studied a highly creative group of architects indistinguishable in their creativity from the group of 24 who declined to be studied, and so with the other groups too.

A third requirement for the successful determination of the traits of highly creative persons in any field of endeavor is that the profession be widely sampled beyond those nominated as most creative, for the distinguishing characteristics of the restricted sample might well have nothing to do with their creativeness. Instead they might be traits characterizing all members of the profession whether creative or not, distinguishing the professional group as a whole but in no sense limited or peculiar to its highly creative members. In the case of the architects, to use them once again as an example, two additional samples were recruited for study, both of which matched the highly creative sample (whom I shall now call Architects I) with respect to age and geographic location of practice. The first supplementary sample (Architects II) had had at least two years of work experience and association with one of the originally nominated creative architects. The second additional sample (Architects III) was composed of architects who had never worked with any of the nominated creatives.

By selecting three samples in this manner, we hoped to tap a range of talent sufficiently wide to be fairly representative of the profession as a whole; and we appear to have succeeded. The mean rating of creativity for each of the three groups—the ratings having been made on a 7-point

scale by six groups of architects and experts on architecture
—was for Architects I, 5.46; for Architects II, 4.25; and for
Architects III, 3.54, the differences in mean ratings between
each group being statistically highly significant.

So much for method and research design. I turn now to a
discussion of the nature of creative talent as it has been revealed to us in our researches.

Persons who are highly creative are inclined to have a good
opinion of themselves, as evidenced by the large number of
favorable adjectives which they use in self-description and
by the relatively high scores they earn on a scale which measures basic acceptance of the self. Indeed, there is here a
paradox, for in addition to their favorable self-perceptions
the very basic self-acceptance of the more creative persons
often permits them to speak more frankly and thus more
critically and in unusual ways about themselves. It is clear,
too, that the self-images of the more creative differ from the
self-images of the less creative. For example, Architects I, in
contrast to Architects II and III, more often describe themselves as inventive, determined, independent, individualistic,
enthusiastic, and industrious. In striking contrast Architects
II and III more often than Architects I describe themselves
as responsible, sincere, reliable, dependable, clear thinking, tolerant, and understanding. In short, where creative
architects more often stress their inventiveness, independence, and individuality, their enthusiasm, determination, and
industry, less creative members of the profession are impressed by their virtue and good character and by their
rationality and sympathetic concern for others. . . .

As for the relation between intelligence and creativity,
save for the mathematicians where there is a low positive
correlation between intelligence and the level of creativeness,
we have found within our creative samples essentially zero
relationship between the two variables, and this is not due to
a narrow restriction in range of intelligence. Among creative
architects who have a mean score of 113 on the Terman

Concept Mastery Test, individual scores range widely from 39 to 179, yet scores on this measure of intelligence correlate —.08 with rated creativity. Over the whole range of intelligence and creativity there is, of course, a positive relationship between the two variables. No feebleminded subjects have shown up in any of our creative groups. It is clear, however, that above a certain required minimum level of intelligence which varies from field to field and in some instances may be surprisingly low, being more intelligent does not guarantee a corresponding increase in creativeness. It just is not true that the more intelligent person is necessarily the more creative one.

In view of the often asserted close association of genius with insanity it is also of some interest to inquire into the psychological health of our creative subjects. To this end we can look at their profiles on the Minnesota Multiphasic Personality Inventory (MMPI), a test originally developed to measure tendencies toward the major psychiatric disturbances that man is heir to: depression, hysteria, paranoia, schizophrenia, and the like. On the eight scales which measure the strength of these dispositions in the person, our creative subjects earn scores which, on the average, are some 5 to 10 points above the general population's average score of 50. It must be noted, however, that elevated scores of this degree on these scales do not have the same meaning for the personality functioning of persons who, like our subjects, are getting along well in their personal lives and professional careers, that they have for hospitalized patients. The manner in which creative subjects describe themselves on this test as well as in the life history psychiatric interview is less suggestive of psychopathology than it is of good intellect, complexity and richness of personality, general lack of defensiveness, and candor in self-description—in other words, an openness to experience and especially to experience of one's inner life. It must also be noted, however, that in the self-reports and in the MMPI profiles of many of our creative subjects, one can find rather clear evidence of psychopathology, but also evidence of adequate control mechanisms, as the success with which they live their productive and creative lives testifies.

However, the most striking aspect of the MMPI profiles of all our male creative groups is an extremely high peak on the *Mf* (femininity) scale. This tendency for creative males to score relatively high on femininity is also demonstrated on the Fe (femininity) scale of the California Psychological Inventory (CPI) and on the masculinity-femininity scale of the Strong Vocational Interest Blank. Scores on the latter scale (where high score indicates more masculinity) correlate —.49 with rated creativity.

The evidence is clear: The more creative a person is the more he reveals an openness to his own feelings and emotions, a sensitive intellect and understanding self-awareness, and wide-ranging interests including many which in the American culture are thought of as feminine. In the realm of sexual identification and interests, our creative subjects appear to give more expression to the feminine side of their nature than do less creative persons. . . .

The perceptiveness of the creative and his openness to richness and complexity of experience is strikingly revealed on the Barron–Welsh Art Scale of the Welsh Figure Preference Test, which presents to the subject a set of 62 abstract line drawings which range from simple and symmetrical figures to complex and asymmetrical ones. In the original study[12] which standardized this scale, some 80 painters from New York, San Francisco, New Orleans, Chicago, and Minneapolis showed a marked preference for the complex and asymmetrical, or, as they often referred to them, the vital and dynamic figures. A contrasting sample of nonartists

[12] F. Barron and G. S. Welsh. Artistic perception as a possible factor in personality style: Its measurement by a figure preference test. *J. Psychol.*, 1952, **33**, 199–203.

revealed a marked preference for the simple and symmetrical drawings.

All creative groups we have studied have shown a clear preference for the complex and asymmetrical, and in general the more creative a person is the stronger is this preference. Similarly, in our several samples, scores on an Institute scale which measures the preference for perceptual complexity are significantly correlated with creativity. In the sample of architects the correlation is $+.48$.

Presented with a large selection of one-inch squares of varicolored posterboard and asked to construct within a 30-minute period a pleasing, completely filled-in $8'' \times 10''$ mosaic, some subjects select the fewest colors possible (one used only one color, all white) while others seek to make order out of the largest possible number, using all of the 22 available colors. And, again citing results from the architects, there is a significant though low positive correlation of $+.38$ between the number of colors a subject chooses and his creativity as rated by the experts.

If one considers for a moment the meaning of these prefences on the art scale, on the mosaic test, and on the scale that measures preference for perceptual complexity, it is clear that creative persons are especially disposed to admit complexity and even disorder into their perceptions without being made anxious by the resulting chaos. It is not so much that they like disorder per se, but that they prefer the richness of the disordered to the stark barrenness of the simple. They appear to be challenged by disordered multiplicity which arouses in them a strong need which in them is serviced by a superior capacity to achieve the most difficult and far-reaching ordering of the richness they are willing to experience. . . .

On the Allport–Vernon–Lindzey Study of Values . . . all of our creative groups have as their highest values the theoretical and the esthetic. For creative research scientists the theoretical value is the highest, closely followed by the esthetic. For creative architects the highest value is the esthetic, with the theoretical value almost as high. For creative mathematicians, the two values are both high and approximately equally strong. . . .

A summary description of the creative person—especially of the creative architect—as he reveals himself in his profile on the California Psychological Inventory reads as follows:

He is dominant; possessed of those qualities and attributes which underlie and lead to the achievement of social status; poised, spontaneous, and self-confident in personal and social interaction; not of an especially sociable or participative temperament; intelligent, outspoken, sharp-witted, demanding, aggressive, and self-centered; persuasive and verbally fluent, self-confident and self-assured; and relatively uninhibited in expressing his worries and complaints.

He is relatively free from conventional restraints and inhibitions, not preoccupied with the impression which he makes on others and thus perhaps capable of great independence and autonomy, and relatively ready to recognize and admit self-views that are unusual and unconventional.

He is strongly motivated to achieve in situations in which independence in thought and action are called for. But, unlike his less creative colleagues, he is less inclined to strive for achievement in settings where conforming behavior is expected or required. In efficiency and steadiness of intellectual effort, however, he does not differ from his fellow workers.

Finally, he is definitely more psychologically minded, more flexible, and possessed of more femininity of interests than architects in general. . . .

We administered a word association test to our subjects and found the unusualness of mental associations one of the best predictors of creativity, and especially so when associations given by no more than 1% to 10% of the population, using the Minnesota norms,[13] are weighted more heavily than those given by less than 1% of the population. Among architects, for example, this weighted score is for Architects

[13] W. A. Russell and J. J. Jenkins. The complete Minnesota norms for responses to 100 words from the Kent-Rosanoff Word Association Test. Tech. Rep. No. 11, 1954, University of Minnesota Contract N8 onr-66216, Office of Naval Research.

I, 204; Architects II, 128; and Architects III, 114; while for the total sample this measure of unusualness of mental associations correlates +.50 with rated creativity. . . .

Our problem is complicated by the fact that though our creative subjects have told us about their experiences at home, in school, and in college, and about the forces and persons and situations which, as they see it, nurtured their creativeness, these are, after all, self-reports subject to the misperceptions and self-deceptions of all self-reports. . . .

In reporting upon events and situations in the life histories of our subjects which appear to have fostered their creative potential and independent spirit, I shall again restrict myself to architects. One finds in their histories a number of circumstances which, in the early years, could well have provided an opportunity as well as the necessity for developing the secure sense of personal autonomy and zestful commitment to their profession which so markedly characterize them.

What appears most often to have characterized the parents of these future creative architects was an extraordinary respect for the child and confidence in his ability to do what was appropriate. Thus they did not hesitate to grant him rather unusual freedom in exploring his universe and in making decisions for himself—and this early as well as late. The expectation of the parent that the child would act independently but reasonably and responsibly appears to have contributed immensely to the latter's sense of personal autonomy which was to develop to such a marked degree.

The obverse side of this was that there was often a lack of intense closeness with one or both of the parents. Most often this appeared in relation to the father rather than to the mother, but often it characterized the relationship with both parents. There were not strong emotional ties of either a positive or a negative sort between parent and child, but neither was there the type of relationship that fosters overdependency nor the type that results in severe rejection. Thus, if there was a certain distance in the relationship between child and parent, it had a liberating effect so far as the child was concerned. If he lacked something of the emotional closeness which some children experience with their parents, he was also spared that type of psychological exploitation that is so frequently seen in the life histories of clinical patients. . . .

The families of the more creative architects tended to move more frequently, whether within a single community, or from community to community, or even from country to country. This, combined with the fact that the more creative architects as youngsters were given very much more freedom to roam and to explore widely, provided for them an enrichment of experience both cultural and personal which their less creative peers did not have.

But the frequent moving appears also to have resulted frequently in some estrangement of the family from its immediate neighborhood. And it is of interest that in almost every case in which the architect reported that his family differed in its behavior and values from those in the neighborhood, the family was different in showing greater cultural, artistic, and intellectual interests and pursuits.

To what extent this sort of cultural dislocation contributed to the frequently reported experiences of aloneness, shyness, isolation, and solitariness during childhood and adolescence, with little or no dating during adolescence, or to what extent these experiences stemmed from a natural introversion of interests and unusual sensitivity, we cannot say. They were doubtless mutually reinforcing factors in stimulating the young architect's awareness of his own inner life and his growing interest in his artistic skills and his ideational, imaginal, and symbolic processes.

Almost without exception, the creative architects manifested very early considerable interest and skill in drawing and painting. And also, with almost no exception, one or both of the parents were of artistic temperament and considerable skill. Often it was the mother who in the architect's early years fostered his artistic potentialities by her example as well as by her instruction. It is especially interesting to note, however, that while the visual and artistic abilities and interests of the child were encouraged and rewarded, these interests and abilities were, by and large, allowed to develop at their own speed, and this pace varied considerably among the architects. There was not an anxious concern on the part of the parents about the skills and abilities of the child. What is perhaps most significant was the wide-spread definite lack of strong pressures from the parents toward a particular career. And this was true both for pressures away from architecture as well as for pressures toward architecture by parents who were themselves architects.

Like Torrance, MacKinnon concludes his paper with a consideration of educational practices that may interfere with the development of creativity. In common with many psychologists who have investigated the creative process, MacKinnon urges the separation of the productive from the evaluative phase in the development of new ideas.

The danger for one's creative potential is not the judging or evaluating of one's experience but that one prejudges, thus excluding from perception large areas of experience. The danger in all parental instruction, as in all academic instruction, is that new ideas and new possibilities of action are criticized too soon and too often. Training in criticism is obviously important and so widely recognized that I need not plead its case. Rather I would urge that, if we wish to nurture creative potential, an equal emphasis be placed on perceptiveness, discussing with our students as well as with our children, at least upon occasion, the most fantastic of ideas and possibilities. It is the duty of parents to communicate and of professors to profess what they judge to be true, but it is no less their duty by example to encourage in their children and in their students an openness to all ideas and especially to those which most challenge and threaten their own judgments.

12

Concluding Remarks

While contributing to the advancement of knowledge about individual differences, the authors whose works have been cited in this book were not invariably correct in their interpretations. As can be seen from subsequent developments, not all their conclusions have withstood the test of time. False starts have been included among the selections because they are an integral part of the development of science. It is hoped that their inclusion will help the reader to realize that research is truly an adventure. The investigator who demands complete advance security will never push back the frontiers of the unknown. Thus the selections reproduced in this book may themselves serve to illustrate some of the findings of current creativity research cited in Chapter 11.

Nor are all false starts and erroneous conclusions limited to the early stages of a science. The expansion of knowledge only multiplies the loci where the investigator may be misled. This condition makes for lively controversy at all stages of scientific progress. But it should not deter the investigator from pursuing his research and presenting his interpretations. The history of differential psychology has been particularly productive of controversy. Through the conflict of divergent views, a fuller understanding of the nature and origins of individual differences has gradually been hammered out. And the process goes on and on.

Research on the nature of intelligence (Chs. 3–4) is providing categories for describing the individual's intellectual functioning. Alternative systems of classification—varying in the number and kind of categories, traits, or factors—may fit the data equally well. The choice depends in part on the use to be made of the categories and in part on the heuristic value of the system. Factor analysis is not a device for discovering basic, immutable units of behavior but a technique for introducing order into a mass of otherwise unmanageable facts.

One of the most controversial topics in all psychology is that of heredity and environment (Chs. 5–7). Concerned with the very origins of individual differences in behavior, views on this topic have run the gamut from extreme hereditarianism to extreme environmentalism. Psychologists are now coming to recognize that traditional questions about this problem were often so formulated as to be unanswerable and meaningless. Granting the interaction of hereditary and environmental factors in all behavior, they are now concentrating more and more on the specific mechanisms whereby hereditary and environmental factors influence behavioral development. The growing realization that the course of intellectual development is not rigidly fixed has led to a sharp upsurge of research on extreme intellectual deviates, including mental defectives at one end of the scale and creative geniuses at the other (Chs. 9–11). The emphasis has shifted from the identification of ability to its cultivation. Current interest in the psychological effects of cultural deprivation has provided both renewed impetus for investigating the origins of individual differences and new settings in which to test hypotheses about them (Chs. 8–9).

Throughout differential psychology, tests have served as a major tool for gathering data (Ch. 2). In fact, the early tests of Galton, Cattell, and Binet opened the way for a science of individual differences. In this area, too, we can recognize a shift in emphasis with time. Psychological testing has itself begun to reflect the influence of recent findings regarding the nature of intelligence, the role of heredity and environment, and other topics of differential psychology. Whereas the original purpose of testing was primarily classification, tests are being used increasingly to help in understanding the person. The misuse of tests to attach labels to individuals and place them in rigid categories is, fortunately, declining. Rather, tests are employed to identify each person's present strengths and weaknesses —to estimate how far he has developed the prerequisite intellectual skills for mastering specific tasks. In addition, the individual's experiential background is investigated in the effort to understand the sources of his particular pattern of talents and defects.

The theme of individual differences runs through all of modern psychology. As this book has demonstrated, the roots of differential psychology can be traced to many diverse psychological specialties —from statistics to animal learning. Conversely, differential psychology can contribute to psychology as a whole. The fundamental aim of differential psychology is no different from that of all psychology, namely, the understanding of behavior. Differential psychology approaches this problem through a comparative analysis of behavior under varying environmental and biological conditions. By relating observed behavioral differences to other concomitant circumstances, it should prove possible to tease out the relative contribution of different factors to behavioral development. If we can discover why one person reacts differently from another, we should know what makes people react as they do.

Name Index

(Pages of selections are shown in boldface type. Persons cited as subjects, as in Galton's and Terman's investigations of eminent men, are not listed in the index.)

Alexander, F., 160
Anastasi, A., 1, 75, 119, 170, **170–186**, 208, 237
Anderson, H. H., 268
Arlitt, A. H., 188, 189, **189–192**
Asch, S., 78

Barker, R. G., 175, 176
Barron, F., 237, 267, 268, 279, 281, 289
Bayley, N., 252
Beach, F. A., 165, 167, 182
Bessel, F. W., 2
Binet, A., 7, 8, 29, **30–34**, 34, **35–40**, 41, **41–44**, 66, 249, 250, 297
Bingham, W. V., 212
Birch, H. G., 162, 167
Boring, E. G., 1
Brigham, C. C., 188
Bruner, F. G., 10
Bryan, A. I., 75, 78
Buck, J. N., 271
Burks, B. S., 129, 130
Burt, C., 65, **66–69**, 72, 83, **83–87**, 258

Cattell, J. McK., 6, 9, 10, 23, **24–25**, 26, **26–29**, 29, 255, 297
Cattell, R. B., 210, 216, 217, 268, 281
Chein, I., 82

Child, I. L., 183
Chow, K. L., 166, 167
Christal, R. E., 95
Clark, M. P., 79
Cox, C. C., 254, 255, 263, 281

Darwin, C., 3, 4, 283
Dennis, W., 161
Dobzhansky, T., 173
Drews, E., 268

Ebbinghaus, H., 7
Erlenmeyer-Kimling, L., **155–158**

Farrand, L., 9, **26–29**
Fechner, G. T., 3
Ferrari, G. C., 7
Finch, F. H., 209
Foley, J. P., Jr., 176
Freeman, F. N., 130

Galton, F., 4, 5, 6, 12, **13–22**, 23, 24, **25**, 29, 66, 107, 108, 118, 119, 238, 239, **239–248**, 249, 280, 297
Gantt, W. H., 161
Garrett, H. E., 72, **73–83**, 83, 85
Gates, A. I., 182
Getzels, J. W., 265, 268, 272
Ghiselin, B., 267
Golann, S. E., 237
Gonick, M. R., 175

Gordon, H., 194
Guicciardi, G., 7
Guilford, J. P., 71, 87, **87–105,** 264, 265, 266, 267, 269

Haldane, J. B. S., 164
Harrell, R. F., 182
Hebb, D. O., 159, **160–169,** 169
Helmholtz, H. L. F. v., 3
Henri, V., 7, 8
Hirsch, J., 147, **148–154,** 154, **155–158**
Hobhouse, L. T., 160
Holt, E. B., 160
Holzinger, K. J., 130
Husén, T., 217, **218–225**

Jackson, P. W., 265, 268, 272
Jastrow, J., 6
Jaynes, J., 182
Jenkins, J. J., 291

Kallmann, F. J., 160
Kelley, T. L., 57, 80
Kelly, R. L., 10
Kay, C. B., 194, **195–201,** 202
Keys, N., 259
Kinnebrook, D., 1, 2
Kirk, S. A., 226, **226–236**
Kite, E. S., 30, 35, 41
Knobloch, H., 181
Köhler, W., 160, 161
Kraepelin, E., 7
Krechevsky, I., 147

Lange-Eichbaum, W., 263
Lashley, K. S., 160
Leahy, A. M., 130, 131, **132–136**
Lehman, H. C., 258
Leibnitz, G. W., 160
Lentz, T. F., 210
Liddell, H. S., 161
Lilienfeld, A. M., 181
Locke, J., 160
Lorenz, K., 167
Lorge, I., 212, 217
Lowenfeld, V., 267

MacKinnon, D. W., 267, 281, **282–295**
McNemar, Q., 220
Maller, J. B., 210
Maskelyne, N., 1, 2
Masserman, J. H., 161
Mendel, G., 4, 137
Merrill, M. A., 24
Milner, E. A., 183, 184
Mitchell, B. C., 130
Mooney, R. L., 268
Myerson, L., 175

Nissen, H. W., 166, 167
Norsworthy, N., 10

Oden, M. H., 248, 252, 259, 261
Oehrn, A., 7
Osborn, A. F., 268
Owens, W. A., Jr., 217

Parnes, S. J., 268
Pasamanick, B., 181
Pavlov, I. P., 161
Pearson, K., 5, 20, 22, 107, 108, **108–118,** 120, 159
Pepinsky, H. B., 268
Pepinsky, P. N., 268
Perl, R., 78
Pressey, S. L., 259

Quetelet, L. A. J., 241

Reichard, S., 79
Riesen, A. H., 166
Riess, B. F., 167
Roe, A., 280
Russell, W. A., 291

Schiller, B., 74, 78
Schneck, M. R., 75
Scott, R. B., 183
Searle, L. V., 147
Sears, R. M., 248
Semmes, J., 166, 167
Senden, M. v., 166
Sheldon, W. H., 175

Sherman, M., 194, **195–201**, 202
Simon, Th., 7, 29, **30–34,** 34, **35–40,** 41, **41–44**
Skeels, II. M., 130
Skodak, M., 130
Spearman, C., 10, 11, 45, 46, **46–50,** 51, **51–56,** 56, 57, 58, 61, 62, 65, 85, 120
Stein, M. I., 268, 279
Stern, W., 9
Stevens, S. S., 167
Sunne, D., 190

Taylor, C. W., 237, 267, 268, 279, 281
Terman, L. M., 7, 24, 190, 248, **249–263,** 281
Thompson, H. B., 10
Thomson, G. H., 258
Thorndike, E. L., 75, 76, 119, 120, **120–129,** 159, 160
Thorndike, R. L., 265
Thorpe, W. H., 167
Thurstone, L. L., 57, **58–64,** 65, 71, 76, 77, 79, 80, 87, 92, 102, 258

Thurstone, T. G., 76, 79
Tinbergen, N., 168
Torrance, E. P., 265, 266, **266–280,** 294
Tryon, R. C., 138, **138–147,** 147, **148–154,** 154
Tuddenham, R. D., 209, **210–217,** 217

Vernon, P. E., 69, **69–72,** 258

Wallis, W. D., 135
Watson, J. B., 160
Weber, E. H., 3
Welsh, G. S., 289
Wheeler, L. R., 202, **203–208,** 208
Whiting, J. W. M., 183
Williams, J. R., 183
Woodworth, R. S., 10
Woodyard, E., 182
Wotton, H., 284
Wright, B. A., 175
Wundt, W., 2, 3, 5, 6

Yerkes, R. M., 8, 213, 215